D0147216

FEMINISM
and the
BIBLE

FEMINISM
and the
BIBLE

An Introduction
to Feminism
For Christians

Dr. Jack Cottrell

COLLEGE PRESS PUBLISHING COMPANY
Joplin, Missouri

Copyright © 1992
College Press Publishing Company

Printed and Bound in the
United States of America
All Rights Reserved

Library of Congress Catalog Card Number: 92-70126
International Standard Book Number: 0-89900-413-X

TABLE OF CONTENTS

PREFACE

"Just what is 'feminism' anyway?"

Feminism is without question one of the most important sociological movements of modern times. Just about everyone knows about its presence and its influence. But exactly what is it? Who are these "feminists"? What do they believe? What do they want? What are their goals? How are they going about achieving these goals? How shall we evaluate their beliefs and goals in the light of the Bible? This book is an attempt to answer these kinds of questions.

A. Types of Feminism

One thing we learn very quickly when we begin to study feminism is that all feminists are not alike. Beyond a certain small core of beliefs and goals, their world views and methods diverge considerably. In this book we shall distin-

11

guish four major types of feminists and shall try to explain the basic beliefs and goals of each.

This is not, however, a comprehensive, in-depth study of every aspect of the categories of feminism. We have a specific focus, namely, the relation of feminism to the Bible and to Biblical teaching. Indeed, in a real sense the very things that separate the kinds of feminism as distinct categories are their varying approaches to spirituality in general, and their views of the Bible in particular. Thus our main purpose in this study is to present a survey of each of the four major types of feminism as it relates to the nature, authority, interpretation, and teaching of the Bible. We shall ask how feminists view or use the Bible, and we shall also ask how the Bible views them. Thus I have called this book, *Feminism and the Bible: An Introduction to Feminism for Christians*.

The four types of feminism are secular, goddess, liberal Christian, and Biblical. They may be briefly described as follows:

(1) *Secular feminists* are those who have abandoned all religious beliefs as having any positive relation to feminist philosophy. Their concerns are wholly secular, not spiritual. At best they ignore the Bible; at worst they regard it as an enemy. These are the feminists most people think of when they think of the original "women's libbers."

(2) *Goddess feminists* are similar in many ways to the secular feminists, but they want to place their lives and their work as feminists within a spiritual framework. But they have deliberately rejected traditional mainstream religions, especially those of the Judeo-Christian tradition, as being inherently anti-feminist. Thus they have sought their spiritual connections in other types of religion, particularly those that involve pagan goddess worship. Their feminist philosophy is couched in the symbols and terminology of the goddess.

(3) *Liberal Christian feminists,* most of whom have some kind of Christian background, agree with the goddess femi-

nists that they must work within some kind of spiritual framework. They also agree that the Judeo-Christian tradition must be viewed negatively by feminists. But unlike goddess feminism, the liberal Christian feminists are not willing to abandon this tradition altogether. Though they do not accept the Bible as divinely inspired and fully authoritative, they see some positive value in using it and in remaining within the church. They generally see a real liberating message imbedded within the core of the Bible and seek to elaborate upon it. Their goal is to liberate the Bible from its patriarchal captivity.

(4) *Biblical feminists* agree with liberal Christian feminists that they must remain within the church and relate their feminism to the Bible. But unlike any of the other forms of feminism, Biblical feminists accept the full and final authority of the Bible as the divinely-inspired Word of God. They also believe that the Bible when rightly interpreted teaches the feminist philosophy of egalitarianism. Their main task as feminists is to show how the Bible can and must be so interpreted as to advocate egalitarianism.

B. How To Read This Book

This book contains eight chapters. Chapter 1 deals with the first wave of feminism in the nineteenth and early twentieth centuries. Chapter 2 is an overview of the origins and character of modern secular feminism, which began feminism's second wave. Then follow two chapters each on goddess feminism and liberal Christian feminism. The last two chapters discuss Biblical feminism.

Since (quite frankly) much of the material in the middle chapters is somewhat heavy or technical, it may be better for the average person not to try to read this book straight through. I recommend instead that the reader begin with chapters 1 and 2, then skip to chapters 7 and 8. The material in chapters 3-6 may then be read according to individual interests.

C. Definitions of Terms

Throughout this study several terms will appear quite often; thus it will be useful to define and distinguish them here at the outset.

(1) *Egalitarianism.* This term expresses the basic philosophy of feminism. It comes from the French term for "equality," and could just as well be written *equalitarianism.* It is the belief in the fundamental equality of the sexes. Except for biology men and women should be regarded as having equality in every way: equal worth; equal value of their work (and therefore equal pay); equal opportunity to pursue whatever vocational or economic goal they desire; equal access to all social, political, and religious roles. All role distinctions based on gender, especially relationships of authority and submission, must be abolished.

(2) *Hierarchicalism.* This is the basic philosophy of most non-feminists. It is the belief that there are inherent differences between the sexes that go beyond anatomy. These differences are such that, either by chance or by God's design, it is natural or intended for men to be "in charge" and for women to follow, at least in certain crucial roles. Thus role distinctions must be maintained, including relationships of authority and submission.

(3) *Feminism.* This is a sociological movement whose basic goal is to promote the egalitarian philosophy. It is more than just the belief in egalitarianism; it is belief plus action. Egalitarians can exist in considerable numbers, but they are not "feminists" until they begin to fight for their belief through deliberate political or social action.

(4) *Androcentrism.* This is a term used by feminists to describe what they believe is a perverted philosophy of the sexes. It is used as a pejorative term with negative and condemnatory overtones. It literally means "man-centered" or "male-centered." It refers to the idea that men are central, superior, and dominant as compared with women, and

that society should reflect this difference. The adjective "androcentric" can be used to describe a book, a philosophy, or a religion. For example, feminists would say that hierarchicalism is an androcentric philosophy.

(5) *Patriarchalism*. This term literally refers to "the rule of the fathers." It is another pejorative term used by feminists to describe the actual state of affairs in a religion, church, or society wherever egalitarianism is absent and androcentrism is the reigning philosophy. A patriarchal religion or society is one which is controlled by men for the sake of men, and in which men of power dominate everything and everyone else, including women. From the feminist perspective this is the ultimate obscenity.

D. Background

The table of contents gives a sufficient overview of the contents of this book, so there is no need to summarize them here. A few words about the background of the author and of the origin of the book may be useful, though.

I am writing from the perspective of a seminary professor who has dealt with this subject in the classroom in various ways for almost two decades. I teach and write from the perspective of a conservative, Evangelical Christian, as one who accepts the full and final authority of the Bible as the divinely-inspired Word of God. Also, I teach and write as one who interprets the Bible hierarchically.

By no means must this book be considered as just another diatribe against feminism, however. Indeed, it is for the most part descriptive and comparative. It is an attempt to understand the various feminist movements and their beliefs. This does not mean that evaluation is absent, of course; but this is not the primary thrust of this work. Only in the final chapter is any sustained critique offered, and this is directed against the alleged Biblical basis of egalitarianism.

It may be appropriate to explain how this particular

book came about. It is not the book I started out to write. My intention was to write an entire book devoted to an evaluation of Biblical feminism and its interpretation of the Bible. After deciding that a brief introduction to the various types of feminism would be useful for such a book, I began to put together what I intended to be a fifteen- or twenty-page survey. This is it. Now I am ready to get back to the main project.

One final note: all Scripture quotations are from the New American Standard Bible unless stated otherwise.

1 THE FIRST WAVE OF FEMINISM

Late twentieth century feminism, dating from the early 1960s, is not the first such feminist movement. The "first wave" of feminism in the United States began in the late 1840s and lasted until 1920. It was part of a worldwide crusade for women's rights, in which the United States was considered to be the leader.[1] This chapter is a brief survey of this first wave, with special attention being given to how the Bible fared in the hands of determined feminists.

I. THE ISSUES

The rights for which women were fighting in the nineteenth century may seem rather peculiar to modern minds, because they are now taken for granted as belonging to men and women alike and can easily be assumed to have been always enjoyed by both sexes. This is a false assumption, however. In the early 1800s many basic rights were legally denied to women. The main reason why this is not still the case is that in the 1840s a number of women decided to fight for the overturning of all laws discriminating against females.

What were the issues which aroused these women of the first wave? One of the most basic was the right to vote, or suffrage. Though this was not the primary focus in the beginning,[2] it was always an important part of the women's movement and soon became its focal point, remaining such until the vote was won once and for all in 1920. This is why many think of this first wave of feminism as the "woman suffrage movement," though this was not the only issue at stake.

The original feminists did not regard the right to vote as an end in itself or as a mere symbol of their emancipation. It was seen as the necessary means to the greater end of more wide-sweeping changes in the legal system and the moral climate in general. As these women saw it, males are innately flawed and cannot be trusted to bring about the necessary changes by themselves. As Richard Evans says, "The argument had long been present in feminist propaganda that women's moral behaviour was superior to men's." At first the feminists simply issued demands that men change their behavior and bring themselves up to the women's standards. They soon concluded, though, that men are just not constitutionally able to match women's innately superior morality. "The suffrage was demanded so that women could help curb immorality and disorder not by education and moral suasion but by legal enforcement and government coercion."[3]

More specifically, women needed the right to vote so that they could have a voice in shaping the laws that would guarantee women's rights in other areas. Chief among these were matters of economic rights, which were the issues most emphasized at the beginning of the movement. These included the right for all women to own property, then denied to married women; the right to enter various trades and professions then closed to women in general (such as medicine and law); and the right to collect and control their own earnings, also a problem for married women at the time.[4] Such rights are taken for granted now. One of the earliest documents of feminism's first wave is the Seneca Falls declaration on women's rights, drawn up in 1848. In a section called "Declaration of Sentiments" it sums up women's complaints against the male-dominated system of the day, thus providing a compendium of the issues at stake. These include the following: women are not allowed to vote, leaving them without voice and representation. Married women are slaves to their husbands and must transfer all their economic and property rights to their husbands. Divorce laws favor men and discriminate against women. Women are excluded from many professions and from the most profitable employments. Women are denied college education. In most cases women are forbidden to participate in church leadership and ministry. Moral expectations for women are more strict than those for men (i.e., the "double standard"). Men take it upon themselves to tell women what is "proper" for them. Through unjust laws regarding the above, women are degraded, disfranchised, oppressed, and robbed of their self-respect.[5]

It is perhaps no coincidence that the first wave of feminism arose at about the same time as the anti-slavery movement began, and that many women as well as men were both feminists and abolitionists. They regarded women as existing in a kind of slavery and in need of emancipation no less than the black slaves laboring on southern plantations at the time.

II. THE LEADERS

While some men gave support to the feminist movement, the primary leaders were women themselves. The most prominent names are Elizabeth Cady Stanton, Susan B. Anthony, Lucretia Mott, and Lucy Stone. Others include Paulina Wright Davis, Ernestine Rose, Abigail Kelley Foster, Martha Wright, Mary Ann McClintock, the Quaker sisters Angelina and Sarah Grimke, and Anna Howard Shaw. Also included is Frances Willard, who founded the Woman's Christian Temperance Union in 1874 and joined hands with the suffrage movement.

Here we are particularly interested in Elizabeth Cady Stanton (1815-1902), because of her views concerning the Bible and its relation to the feminist movement. Stanton was brought up in a strict Presbyterian household (the Old Scotch Presbyterian Church). Her father, Daniel Cady, was a U.S. Congressman and a New York Supreme Court justice. In 1840 she married Henry B. Stanton, a lawyer and abolitionist, and became the mother of seven children.

While attending a school for girls in Troy, New York, Stanton was "seriously influenced" by the preaching of Charles G. Finney. She describes herself as "one of the first victims" during Finney's six-week revival meeting in Troy.[6] This connection with Finney and the "Second Great Awakening" may have had some influence on Stanton, because Finney and the revivalist movement in general encouraged social reform, including involvement in the abolitionist and women's rights movements.[7] Several of the women's conventions were held in Finney's Tabernacle.[8]

Stanton was first motivated to participate in the temperance and abolitionist movements, but her passion soon became women's rights. In her early years she personally experienced discrimination. She wanted to study Greek, but no formal opportunities for such study were open to women. Only by special arrangement was she permitted to enroll in the Johnstown Academy, normally open only to boys. Since no colleges were open to women, she attended Emma Willard's school for girls, Troy Female Seminary, graduating in 1832. She studied law by reading her father's lawbooks, learning how U.S. laws discriminated against women; but she could not become a lawyer because women were not admitted to the bar.[9]

Thus Stanton had ample motivation to devote her considerable talents to the cause of women's rights. She became an acknowledged leader in the feminist movement from its very beginning. One of her colleagues called her "the greatest liberator of our time."[10] Her prominence and influence in the movement made her views concerning the Bible and the church (to be considered below) all the more significant.

III. THE BEGINNINGS OF THE MOVEMENT

The feminist movement of the nineteenth century was effectively launched in 1848 when Stanton, Lucretia Mott, and others issued the call for a women's convention. It was held in the Wesleyan Methodist Chapel in Seneca Falls, New York, on July 19-20, 1848, with about 300 in attendance.[11] The centerpiece for the convention was the "Declaration on Women's Rights," drawn up by Stanton[12] and signed by 68 women and 32 men.[13]

The Declaration had two parts, a "Declaration of Sentiments" and a list of resolutions. The former section begins as a parody of the Declaration of Independence and amends it thus: "We hold these truths to be self-evident: that all men and women are created equal." It has a negative tone, being mostly a listing of the ways in which the "unjust laws" of the day deprived women of their rights. (These were summarized above.) The listing is given to prove this thesis: "The history of mankind is a history of repeated injuries and usurpations on the part of man toward woman, having in direct object the establishment of an absolute tyranny over her." The second section, the resolutions, is a statement of affirmations and goals to be sought, e.g., woman's highest obligation is to seek her own happiness; woman is man's equal; laws discriminating against women are against nature; woman's moral superiority entitles her to speak and teach in all religious assemblies; all double standards must be abolished; limitations on women are due to a "perverted application of the Scriptures"; women must be allowed to vote; and the male monopoly of the pulpit and other professions must be overthrown. In both sections the declaration of equality is based upon the order of nature as intended by the great Creator.[14]

Just two weeks later a second convention was held in Rochester, New York, during which the movement began to be more formally organized. The third meeting was in 1850 at Worcester, Massachusetts. It was the first to claim to be a *national* women's rights convention, having delegates from nine states. Except for 1857, conventions were held each year up to 1860. The 1852 convention in Syracuse was significant in that it was the first in which Stanton and Susan B. Anthony joined forces. They remained a team for nearly fifty years, with Anthony managing the business affairs and Stanton doing most of the writing.

IV. ORGANIZATIONS

According to Evans, no organization devoted exclusively to women's rights was formed in the early years of the movement. Since their interests paralleled those of the abolitionist movement, women activists cast their lot with groups such as the Anti-Slavery Equal Rights Association. The impetus to organize exclusively as feminists came in the years following the Civil War. Since the women had so ardently supported the anti-slavery cause, they expected the abolitionists to rally to *their* cause as soon as the war was over. When such support was deliberately withheld, Stanton, Anthony and others formally withdrew from the Anti-Slavery Association and founded the Woman Suffrage Association in 1868.[15]

A crisis came in 1869 when the organization divided into moderate and radical factions. The latter was led by Stanton and Anthony and took the name of National Woman Suffrage Association. Stanton was its first president.[16] It fought for women's rights in general and sought an amendment to the U.S. Constitution guaranteeing women the right to vote. The moderate faction was led by Lucy Stone; it formed the American Woman Suffrage Association. Its tactics were less bold and more indirect; it concentrated on the suffrage issue; and it favored fighting for changes on the state constitutional level. Also, it did not harbor the hostility toward the Bible and Christianity that was characteristic of Stanton and her group.[17]

The two groups reunited in 1890 as the National American Woman Suffrage Association. At first Stanton's group dominated the new organization; she was its first president. She retired in 1892 and was succeeded by Anthony, who retired in 1900. The newer members tended to be more moderate, and ultimately "Stanton was obliged to withdraw from the movement because of her anti-clericalism." Continued infighting slowed the progress of the movement and kept it from being very effective up until World War I.[18]

V. THE BIBLE AS WOMAN'S ENEMY

One significant element of the first wave of feminism, especially within the radical group, is its opinion of the importance of the Bible in reference to the question of women's rights. The view was widespread, though by no means universal, that the Bible is the chief obstacle to women's equality and the major hindrance to the cause of women's rights.

Stanton herself accepted the view that "the Bible, with its fables, allegories and endless contradictions, has been the great block in the way of civilization."[19] She mockingly affirms that "from the inauguration of the movement for woman's emancipation the Bible has been used to hold her in the 'divinely ordained sphere,' prescribed in the Old and New Testaments."[20] "The wonder is that women . . . make a fetich [sic] of the very book which is responsible for their civil and social degradation."[21] As Barbara Welter says, Stanton believed that the Bible "more than any other influences, perpetuated woman's bondage."[22]

Stanton was not the only feminist who held this view of the Bible. Clara B. Neyman declared, "The Bible has been of service in some respects; but the time has come for us to point out the evil of many of its teachings."[23] Whatever advances have been made in women's rights have been made "in spite of Bible influence," said Josephine Henry.[24] In the words of another of Stanton's cohorts, the Bible "always has been, and is at present, one of the greatest obstacles in the way of the emancipation and the advancement of the sex." She added that "this book has been of more injury to [woman] than has any other which has ever been written in the history of the world."[25]

This same judgment is made of Christianity in general. As Henry declared, "No institution in modern civilization is so tyrannical and so unjust to woman as is the Christian Church."[26] Stanton avowed that "all the religions on the face of the earth" – including Christianity – degrade women; "and so long as woman accepts the position that they assign her, her emancipation is impossible."[27] Welter notes that in 1884 Stanton wrote an article called "What Has Christianity Done for Women?" Welter sums up her answer as "nothing much and nothing good."[28] Citing the account of the widow's mite in Mark 12:41-44, Stanton criticizes the church for promoting self-sacrifice instead of self-development on the part of women. "But when women learn the higher duty of self-development, they will not so readily expend all their forces in serving others. . . . 'Self-development is a higher duty than self-sacrifice,' should be woman's motto henceforward."[29]

This kind of judgment was made because of what was

seen as a very degrading view of women in both the Old and New Testaments, especially the idea that the Creation and/or the Fall requires women to be in subjection to men. In view of this perception of the Bible as a hindrance to the women's movement, most feminists felt that some kind of response had to be made to it. This response took three basic forms, which we may call the moderate, the liberal, and the radical.

The moderate view did not consider the problem to be the Bible itself, but rather the acceptance of perverted and sexist *interpretations* of the Bible. The Bible as originally intended by its divine author and as rightly interpreted by man is not hostile to women. This view was expressed in the 1848 Seneca Falls Declaration, which spoke against "a perverted application of the Scriptures."[30] This seems also to have been the view of Lucy Stone, the leader of the moderate split in 1869.[31] Later on many who took this view were adherents of metaphysical or "New Thought" religions (such as Mary Baker Eddy's "Christian Science"), which believed that the Bible must be interpreted symbolically or mystically. These agreed that the Bible is harmful to women if taken literally, but when understood according to its inner or mystical meaning it affirms the equality of women with men.[32]

The liberal view accepted the naturalistic view of the Bible that had been developing since the end of the eighteenth century and had been given impetus by the application of the theory of evolution to the development of culture in general and religion in particular. It viewed the Bible as a purely human book which records the history of one of the world's many religious traditions, and which has no special divine authority and no more relevance for today than scores of other such books. As such the Bible "has lost its hold on the human mind" and should just be ignored.[33]

The radical view agreed with the liberal understanding of the *nature* of the Bible as a purely human book with no divine authority, but it did not agree that it could simply be ignored. Why not? Because the Bible is still being distributed in mass quantities, and the majority of people still believe that it is God's inspired Word and thus are still using it as a divinely given mandate to keep women in subjection. Thus some positive action with regard to the Bible must be taken. Whether it is just a matter of wrong interpretation or a false view of its nature, either way the influence of the Bible must be neutralized. This was Stanton's view. "No matter how some people protested its wisdom and beauty and others protested its irrelevance, Mrs. Stanton was determined to attack it as 'religious superstitions' which, more than any other influences, perpetuated woman's bondage."[34] As Stanton said, "So long as tens of thousands of Bibles are printed every year, and circulated over the whole habitable globe, and the masses in all English-speaking nations revere it as the word of God, it is vain to belittle its influence."[35] Something must be done, and Stanton considered herself to be just the person to do it.

VI. THE WOMAN'S BIBLE

Despite the conservative influences of her early life, Elizabeth Cady Stanton ultimately came under the influence of the more liberal minds and forces of the nineteenth century. Her view of the Bible was shaped by liberal interpreters such as Bishop Colenso, by Unitarian thinkers who had even gone beyond Unitarianism, and by the atheist Robert Ingersoll.[36]

As a result of these influences, Stanton became very liberal in her view of the nature of the Bible. She denied that it is in any way inspired by God or that it is the Word of God. "I do not believe that any man ever saw or talked with God, I do not believe that God inspired the Mosaic code, or told the historians what they say he did about

woman."[37] She asks, "Does any one at this stage of civilization think the Bible was written by the finger of God, that
the Old and New Testaments emanated from the highest
divine thought in the universe? Do they think that all the
men who wrote the different books were specially
inspired?"[38] Not according to Stanton. She declared it to be
of human origin the same as any other book. "It is full of
contradictions, absurdities and impossibilities, and bears
the strongest evidence in every line of its human origin."[39]
"We have made a fetich [sic] of the Bible long enough. The
time has come to read it as we do all other books, accepting
the good and rejecting the evil it teaches."[40]

In Stanton's view, part of the evil taught by the Bible is
its view of women. The problem is not just incorrect interpretations of the Bible, but the Bible itself. She declared
that "the Bible treats women as of a different class, inferior to man or in subjection to him"; "the Bible degrades
the Mothers of the Race."[41] As bad as the Old Testament is,
the New Testament is no better. "In fact, her inferior position is more clearly and emphatically set forth by the Apostles than by the Prophets and the Patriarchs."[42] According
to Welter, Stanton "fully shared" the belief expressed in the
following quotation from Robert Ingersoll: "As long as
woman regards the Bible as the charter of her rights, she
will be the slave of man. The Bible was not written by a
woman. Within its lids there is nothing but humiliation
and shame for her."[43]

According to Stanton she and her fellow feminists had
no alternative but to take the radical stance and attempt
to counteract the influence of the Bible. She proposed to
neutralize it by producing a woman-authored "woman's
Bible" that would show the world what the Bible is really
like.

A. The Project

Stanton says that in 1889 she first "proposed to a committee of women to issue a Woman's Bible, that we might have women's commentaries on women's position in the Old and New Testaments."[44] She herself would coordinate the project. The end result was a work produced in two volumes, issued in 1895 and 1898, with the simple title, *The Woman's Bible*. In the first volume twenty-three women are named as members of the "Revising Committee," while in the second volume twenty-five are named. The latter list includes eighteen of those in the former list, with five "foreign members" being included among the new names.[45] The only noteworthy names in the lists are those of Stanton and Mrs. Robert Ingersoll.

More important than the committee members as such are the names of those who actually wrote the commentaries and essays which make up the content of *The Woman's Bible*. In the first volume, which covers only the Pentateuch, only eight writers are listed. In the second volume, which covers Joshua to Revelation, nine authors are indicated, including five of those who participated in the first volume. Again, with the exception of Stanton, the names of the authors would not be recognized outside a very small circle.

The second volume also includes an appendix in which are printed the letters and further comments of nineteen women, including some of the committee members and commentators.

The writers whose work appears in *The Woman's Bible* include those who took a moderate view of the Bible as well as those who took the liberal view. In fact, most of the participants were in the moderate category. Their view was well expressed by Phebe Hanaford, who said that because of the advances in knowledge and the higher education of women, "many interpretations of the Bible are felt to be obsolete," hence the new "Women's Commentary" was deemed necessary. But, she declared, we need not doubt that the Scriptures, rightly interpreted, teach the equality of the sexes.[46]

As already noted, some who held this view did so by virtue of their "New Thought" or metaphysical approach to the Bible. This was true of some of the writers in *The Woman's Bible*, notably Clara B. Colby and Ursula Gestefeld. For example, the latter contrasts the exterior meaning of the Pentateuch with its inner or esoteric meaning, affirming that "the obvious inconsistencies and absurdities" on the outward level "may or may not be true as history without affecting the truth of the book itself which lies in its meaning."[47]

A few of the participants took the more liberal view represented by Stanton herself, including Ellen B. Dietrick and Josephine K. Henry. According to Welter, "Of all the members of the Committee, Henry was the only one to back up Stanton's bald statements that both the Old and the New Testaments were insulting and degrading to women."[48] This does not mean that the tone of *The Woman's Bible* favors the moderate view, however. Stanton remained its coordinator, its editor, and the chief author of its contents. She herself wrote about two-thirds of its material; all the other authors combined produced the other one-third. "It was, as Mrs. Stanton herself called it, very much her 'child.'"[49]

While Stanton allowed the moderate members of the project to express their ideas and to present the "correct" interpretations of various Bible passages as they saw them, she herself in no uncertain terms repudiated the moderate approach in general. She especially decried a retreat to "esoteric" meanings and insisted that "in plain English" the Bible itself is simply degrading to women. No mystical symbolism can enable one to "twist out of the Old or New Testaments a message of justice, liberty or equality from God to the women of the nineteenth century."[50]

Thus the purpose of Stanton's project was very clear. Once the true nature of the Bible's teaching concerning women is known, no one can use the Bible any longer to keep women in a position of subjection and servitude.

B. *The Contents*

In describing the nature of *The Woman's Bible,* Stanton often uses the term *revision* or something similar. The committee is called the "Revising Committee."[51] The object, she says, is "to revise" the texts referring to women. This is misleading, however, since this term usually refers to a new *translation*; and *The Woman's Bible* is actually a commentary rather than a translation. But it is not a commentary on the whole Bible. The object is to comment on "only those texts and chapters directly referring to women, and those also in which women are made prominent by exclusion." This involves only about one-tenth of the total text, says Stanton.[52] The method is to print selections from the text of the King James Version, with the interspersing of whatever commentary is deemed appropriate. The choice of texts is often arbitrary, since a number of texts dealing with women are omitted. Curiously, there is no commentary on Galatians 3:28.

The Bible is seen to be a mixture of good teaching and bad teaching. Sometimes the comments call attention to a Biblical teaching that presents women in a positive light. For example, Genesis 1:26-28 is said to teach "a simultaneous creation of both sexes, in the image of God." This concept of a simultaneous creation of male and female is seen as important for countering the idea of male supremacy based on the male's priority in creation.[53] The status of the prophetess Huldah is seen as being presented in a very favorable light in 2 Kings 22:11-20.[54] The example and recorded words of Jesus are seen as a positive model and guide for all acceptable teaching and interpretation.[55] As one commentator said, "Jesus is not recorded as having uttered any . . . claim that woman should be subject to man, or that in teaching she would be a usurper. The dominion of woman over man or of man over woman makes no part of the sayings of the Nazarene."[56] Though it receives no formal commentary, Galatians 3:28 is always spoken of with approval.[57] Welter remarks that this "was practically the only quotation from Saint Paul which Mrs. Stanton did not disapprove of."[58]

Although a few parts of the Bible draw a grudging endorsement even from Stanton, most of the passages dealing with women are seen as unredeemably evil. "Parts of the Bible are so true, so grand, so beautiful, that it is a pity it should have been bound in the same volume with sentiments and descriptions so gross and immoral," says Stanton.[59] The Pentateuch as a whole really takes a beating at the hands of the feminist commentators. "It is most demoralizing reading," says Stanton, "giving all alike the lowest possible idea of womanhood."[60] "How thankful we must be that we are no longer obliged to believe, as a matter of fact, . . . each separate statement contained in the Pentateuch," says Hanaford.[61] The New Testament as a whole is also pictured in a very negative light, especially the epistles attributed to Paul. "As for the passages now found in the New Testament epistles of Paul, concerning women's non-equality with men and duty of subjection," says Ellen Dietrick, "there is no room to doubt that they are bare-faced forgeries, interpolated by unscrupulous bishops" in an effort "to reduce women to silent submission."[62]

The rest of this section on the contents of *The Woman's Bible* will focus on a few examples of the way the texts are interpreted in the commentary. The first example is Genesis 1-3. We have already commented on some of the favorable elements extracted from Genesis 1:26-28, especially the idea of the simultaneous creation of male and female. Also, the plural reference in 1:26 ("Let us make man"), combined with the reference to the image of God as male and female in 1:27, is seen as implying a "feminine element in the Godhead." Thus, "instead of three male personages, as generally represented, a Heavenly Father, Mother, and Son would seem more rational."[63]

Genesis 2, on the other hand, receives a quite different

treatment. The idea that Genesis 1 and Genesis 2 are "two contradictory accounts" of creation is accepted. The first account dignifies woman and makes her "equal in power and glory with man. The second makes her a mere afterthought." Why is it added? "It is evident that some wily writer, seeing the perfect equality of man and woman in the first chapter, felt it important for the dignity and dominion of man to effect woman's subordination in some way."[64]

What about Genesis 3? The main point of the commentary is to interpret what is said about Eve in a way exactly opposite of the traditional view, which relates the submission of women in part to Eve's priority in the Fall (see 1 Timothy 2:14). Instead of a villain, Eve is portrayed as a strong and courageous heroine. "As our chief interest is in woman's part in the drama, we are equally pleased with her attitude, whether as a myth in an allegory, or as the heroine of an historical occurrence." Stanton says that "the unprejudiced reader must be impressed with the courage, the dignity, and the lofty ambition of the woman. . . . Compared with Adam she appears to great advantage through the entire drama." The tempter sensed her high character and did not try to tempt her with worldly pleasures but appealed to her "intense thirst for knowledge" which Adam could not satisfy.[65] It is obvious that "the conduct of Eve from the beginning to the end is so superior to that of Adam." Throughout the temptation Adam was standing beside Eve ("her husband with her," 3:6), but he maintained a cowardly silence. His behavior then was contemptuous, and his subsequent conduct "was to the last degree dastardly." The superiority of the woman is obvious.[66]

A second example is Stanton's speculations on the reference to Huldah in 2 Kings 22:11-20. "The greatest character among the women thus far mentioned is Huldah the prophetess, residing in the college in Jerusalem," she says. Huldah was a statesman [sic] as well as an expert in Jewish jurisprudence, able both to advise the common people and to teach kings, while her husband was the humble keeper of the robes. "While Huldah was pondering great questions of State and Ecclesiastical Law, her husband was probably arranging the royal buttons and buckles." Stanton stresses the King James Version's rendering in verse 14, that Huldah "dwelt in Jerusalem in the college." Now, says Stanton, "this is the first mention of a woman in a college. She was doubtless a professor of jurisprudence, or of the languages."[67] (Stanton does not pursue the fact that "college" is a mistranslation of the term *mishneh* in 2 Kings 22:14. The NASB translates it "second quarter," the NIV as "second district.")

A third example is the rehabilitation of Jezebel. Like Eve, poor Jezebel has simply been misunderstood, especially by the Jewish historian that reports on the events of her life in 1 Kings 21:1-15. The historian is "evidently biassed against Jezebel by his theological prejudices," since she is from a rival religion. Even though the historian obviously hates her, the facts he records "prove that, notwithstanding her unfortunate and childish conception of theology, Jezebel was a brave, fearless, generous woman, so wholly devoted to her own husband that even wrong seemed justifiable to her, if she could thereby make him happy." And certainly her conduct overall is no more "satanic" than the savage deeds attributed to her antagonist, Elijah.[68]

A fourth example is the speculation concerning Priscilla, given in the comments on Romans 16:1ff. She is unequivocally spoken of as "the Apostle Priscilla," who "in co-operation with her husband, the Apostle Aquila, performed the important task of founding the Church of Rome." Paul himself was in fact only a second-rate apostle "who gladly shared the 'Apostolic dignity' with all the good women he could rally to his assistance." Thus Paul "virtually pronounces Priscilla a fellow-Apostle and fellow-Bishop." The same is true of Phebe, who is called a minister (diakonos), which "may be legitimately interpreted either presbyter, bishop, or Apostle." Thus it is clear that in Paul's mind there was an "equality of male and female Apostles."[69]

A fifth and last example is 1 Timothy 2:9-14. It is interesting that some of the more obvious New Testament passages about women receive little or no comment. We have mentioned that Galatians 3:28 is not included at all. First Corinthians 14:34-35 and Ephesians 5:22ff. receive one paragraph each. First Timothy 2:9-14 does warrant several pages of comment, however. But Stanton herself offers only four paragraphs, three of which deal with verses 9-10 and none with verses 11-14. Lucinda Chandler has a longer essay in which she describes Paul's prohibition of women teaching men (verse 12) as a "tyrannical edict." In this statement Paul is obviously not inspired but is "biassed by prejudice."[70] Much of her essay is devoted to repudiating the reference in verse 14 to Eve's part in the Fall. "The doctrine of woman the origin of sin, and her subjection in consequence, planted in the early Christian Church by Paul, has been a poisonous stream in Church and in State."[71]

From these examples it is obvious that the question of the factuality of the Fall as such, and the factuality and meaning of Eve's primacy in the Fall, is of pivotal significance regarding the whole issue of feminism. These early feminists could not allow the Biblical affirmations and their traditional understanding to go unchallenged, for their whole cause is threatened thereby. The centrality of this subject and the feminists' contempt for the whole Biblical system related thereto are seen in this final statement in *The Woman's Bible* by Stanton:

> The real difficulty in woman's case is that the whole foundation of the Christian religion rests on her temptation and man's fall, hence the necessity of a Redeemer and a plan of salvation. As the chief cause of this dire calamity, woman's degradation and subordination were made a necessity. If, however, we

accept the Darwinian theory, that the race has been a
gradual growth from the lower to a higher form of
life, and that the story of the fall is a myth, we can
exonerate the snake, emancipate the woman, and
reconstruct a more rational religion for the nineteenth century, and thus escape all the perplexities of
the Jewish mythology as of no more importance than
those of the Greek, Persian and Egyptian.[72]

C. The Results

Not all feminists were in favor of *The Woman's Bible*
project. Many felt that it was a mistake. Some of these
simply did not share Stanton's radically liberal view of the
Bible. These included two younger women who later took
over the presidency of the organization for the first two
decades of the twentieth century, Carrie Chapman Catt
and Anna Howard Shaw. They had a much more positive
view of the Bible than Stanton, and felt that the project
was a waste of time that could have been used working for
the vote. Even some who may have accepted Stanton's
view of the Bible were opposed to the project on practical
grounds, e.g., that it would be a source of division at a time
when unity was crucial for the movement.[73]

Though it did not cause division, it certainly caused controversy within the movement. The controversy came to a
head at the 1896 convention of the National American
Woman Suffrage Association, when the following resolution was presented for a vote: "That this Association is
non-sectarian, being composed of persons of all shades of
religious opinion, and that it has no official connection
with the so-called 'Woman's Bible,' or any theological publication." A long and earnest debate ensued, during which
Susan B. Anthony came to the defense of her long-time
friend and associate, and spoke out against the adoption of
the resolution. She said that it would be an act of censor-

ship and a vote of censure against Stanton herself. "I shall be pained beyond expression if the delegates here are so narrow and illiberal as to adopt this resolution," she said. Nevertheless it was adopted, 53 to 41.[74]

Did the publication of *The Woman's Bible* have any influence on the outcome of the first wave of feminist activity? Not really. Thereafter Stanton's own influence was diminished, and (as already noted) she was obliged to withdraw from the movement because of her "anti-clericalism," or opposition to the clergy and things religious.[75]

The real significance of *The Woman's Bible* has to do with feminism's "second wave," the one which began in the 1960s. It seems that most feminists today (except the conservatives or evangelicals) see Stanton and her work as a source of inspiration. *The Woman's Bible* has become a kind of model for how to handle the Bible in the context of feminism. Secular feminists are emboldened to follow its example of attacking the Bible head-on, fearlessly and irreverently. Liberal Christian feminists are inspired by its efforts to reinterpret the Bible rather loosely in view of "women's experience." Some of the actual interpretations of Scripture which appeared in *The Woman's Bible* are still repeated today (sometimes even in evangelical texts).

But more important than the content of the book is its symbolical value for today. Elizabeth Cady Stanton is seen as a true feminist heroine, and her *Woman's Bible* is taken as an encouragement to pursue the cause of women's liberation no matter what obstacles have to be overcome. It is viewed as a paradigmatic act of defiance against outmoded patriarchal religious beliefs that oppose women's progress. It is regarded as a symbol of women's emancipation from centuries of servitude imposed either by the Bible itself or by biased male interpretation of the Bible. Thus it is not uncommon to see occasional references both to Stanton and to *The Woman's Bible* in current feminist literature.

To evangelical or Bible-believing Christians, especially those who take a traditional approach to gender roles, *The*

Woman's Bible is seen in a very different light. Its coarse
and irreverent treatment of the Bible and the God of the
Bible is seen as a logical result of theological liberalism; it
is what one can expect when the full authority of Scripture
is abandoned. Its caricature of Biblical truth and its speculative, imaginative interpretation are seen as typical of
feminist bias and willingness to sacrifice objectivity in the
service of the cause. It is not regarded as mounting any
substantial challenge to Biblical truth, especially truth
about gender roles. But it is something to be aware of,
simply because of the role it still plays among feminists
today.

VII. CONCLUSION

The first wave of feminism ended on a successful note in
1920 with the ratification of the nineteenth amendment to
the U.S. Constitution, which recognized the right of women
to vote. This right had already been won on the state level
in nearly a score of states, beginning with Wyoming in
1890. An amendment on the federal level, called the
"Anthony Amendment," had been proffered since 1878 but
was defeated by both the House and the Senate up through
World War I. The active role of women in the war effort
turned the tide in their favor, and the renewed influence of
the National American Woman Suffrage Alliance (with
over two million members in 1917) made a difference. The
amendment was passed by the House in January 1918 and
by the Senate in June 1919. In August 1920 Tennessee
became the thirty-sixth state to ratify it, making it a part
of the Constitution.[76]
Once the vote was won, the original feminist movement
fragmented and lost momentum.[77]

Endnotes

1. See Richard J. Evans, *The Feminists: Women's Emancipation Movements in Europe, America and Australasia 1840-1920*, revised ed. (New York: Barnes and Noble, 1979), pp. 44ff. Its rapid progress "gave American feminism the reputation of being the most successful in the world in the late nineteenth century" (p. 58).

2. Ibid., p. 47.

3. Ibid., p. 233.

4. Ibid., pp. 46-47.

5. Seneca Falls Declaration, in Judith Hole and Ellen Levine, *Rebirth of Feminism* (New York: Quadrangle Books, 1971), pp. 432-433.

6. Nancy A. Hardesty, *Women Called To Witness: Evangelical Feminism in the 19th Century* (Nashville: Abingdon, 1984), pp. 43-44, 60.

7. Evans, *The Feminists*, p. 45.

8. Hardesty, *Women Called To Witness*, p. 126.

9. "Stanton, Elizabeth Cady," *The Encyclopedia Americana*, International Edition (Danbury, CT: Grolier, 1983), 25:592.

10. Josephine K. Henry, in an untitled appendix to *The Woman's Bible*, Part II (New York: European Publishing Company, 1898), p. 208.

11. Hardesty, *Women Called To Witness*, p. 125.

12. "Stanton, Elizabeth," *Encyclopaedia Britannica*, 15th ed. (1975), Micropaedia IX:525.

13. Esther W. Hymer, "Woman Suffrage," *The Encyclopedia Americana*, International Edition (Danbury, CT: Grolier, 1983), 29:103.

14. Seneca Falls Declaration, in Hole and Levine, pp. 431-435.

15. Hardesty, *Women Called To Witness*, p. 127. See Evans, *The Feminists*, pp. 47-49.

16. "Stanton, Elizabeth Cady," *Encyclopedia Americana* (1983), 25:592.

17. Evans, *The Feminists*, pp. 49-50. See Hardesty, *Women Called To Witness*, p. 127.

18. Evans, *The Feminists*, pp. 54-55.

19. Stanton, in *The Woman's Bible*, II:9.

20. Stanton, in *The Woman's Bible*, Part I (New York: European Publishing Company, 1895), p. 7.

21. Ibid., II:12.

22. Barbara Welter, "Something Remains to Dare: Introduction to *The Woman's Bible*," in the reprint of *The Woman's Bible* under the title *The Original Feminist Attack on the Bible*, 2 vols. in 1 (New York: Arno Press, 1974), p. xxxiv.

23. Clara B. Neyman, in *The Woman's Bible*, II:17.
24. Henry, in *The Woman's Bible*, II:206.
25. "E.M.," in *The Woman's Bible*, II:201, 203.
26. Henry, in *The Woman's Bible*, II:205.
27. Stanton, in *The Woman's Bible*, I:12.
28. Welter, "Something Remains to Dare," p. xxiii.
29. Stanton, in *The Woman's Bible*, II:131.
30. Seneca Falls Declaration, in Hole and Levine, p. 434.
31. Welter, "Something Remains To Dare," p. xvi.
32. Ibid., pp. x-xi.
33. See Stanton's remarks in *The Woman's Bible*, I:11.
34. Welter, "Something Remains To Dare," p. xxxiv.
35. Stanton, in *The Woman's Bible*, I:11.
36. Welter, "Something Remains To Dare," pp. vii-ix.
37. Stanton, in *The Woman's Bible*, I:12.
38. Ibid., I:61.
39. Ibid., II:213.
40. Ibid., II:8.
41. Ibid., II:7-8.
42. Ibid., II:113.
43. Welter, "Something Remains To Dare," p. ix.
44. Stanton, in *The Woman's Bible*, I:9.
45. *The Woman's Bible*, I:3; II:5.
46. Phebe Hanaford, in *The Woman's Bible*, I:139, 142.
47. Ursula Gestefeld, in *The Woman's Bible*, I:143, 147. See also II:186-187.
48. Welter, "Something Remains To Dare," p. xxx.
49. Ibid., p. xix.
50. Stanton, in *The Woman's Bible*, II:214. See I:7-8.
51. Ibid., I:5.
52. Ibid.
53. Ibid., I:14-15, 21.
54. Ibid., II:81-82.
55. Ibid., II:143.
56. Lucinda B. Chandler, in *The Woman's Bible*, II:164-165.
57. Ibid., II:163; Ellen B. Dietrick, in *The Woman's Bible*, II:136.
58. Welter, "Something Remains to Dare," p. xxiii.
59. Stanton, in *The Woman's Bible*, I:61.
60. Ibid., I:66.
61. Phebe Hanaford, in *The Woman's Bible*, I:121.
62. Ellen B. Dietrick, in *The Woman's Bible*, II:150.

63. Stanton, in *The Woman's Bible*, I:14-15.

64. Ibid., I:20-21. See similar comments by Ellen B. Dietrick, I:16-18. Her opinion, she says, "is that the second story was manipulated by some Jew, in an endeavor to give 'heavenly authority' for requiring a woman to obey the man she married" (p. 18).

65. Stanton, in *The Woman's Bible*, I:24-25.

66. Lillie D. Blake, in *The Woman's Bible*, I:26-27.

67. Stanton, in *The Woman's Bible*, II:81-82.

68. Ellen B. Dietrick, in *The Woman's Bible*, II:74-75.

69. Ibid., II:153-154.

70. Lucinda B. Chandler, in *The Woman's Bible*, II:162-163.

71. Ibid., II:163.

72. Stanton, in *The Woman's Bible*, II:214. The second sentence in this paragraph, that "as the chief cause" of the Fall "woman's degradation and subordination were made a necessity," does not reflect the Biblical teaching on this subject.

73. Welter, "Something Remains To Dare," p. xviii.

74. *The Woman's Bible*, II:215-217. This report on the resolution and a transcript of Anthony's remarks are the last item in the volume.

75. Evans, *The Feminists*, p. 54.

76. Hymer, "Woman Suffrage," p. 104; Evans, *The Feminists*, p. 225.

77. Evans, *The Feminists*, p. 233.

2 SECULAR FEMINISM: THE MODERN WAVE

The so-called "second wave" of feminism[1] began in the early 1960s and continues strong into the 1990s. Over these three decades the movement has crystallised into four distinct types. The first we may call *secular feminism*, because unlike the other three it has neither spiritual roots nor spiritual concerns. The second is called *goddess feminism*, the third *liberal Christian feminism*, and the fourth *evangelical Christian feminism* or *Biblical feminism*. Each of these will now be discussed in this order.

This chapter is devoted to an explanation and evaluation of secular feminism, which in many ways is the most direct successor of feminism's first wave and a consistent child of the *Woman's Bible* project. Though many of the women in the first wave had strong religious convictions, their main goals were secular in nature, e.g., economic and property rights, elimination of job discrimination, and the

41

right to vote. A person did not have to be motivated by religious faith in order to work for these goals. These are the same kind of goals sought by secular feminists of the second wave, who are mostly women without any religious convictions whatsoever and who may often be described as profane and vulgar. These are women who have inherited the spirit of Elizabeth Cady Stanton in that they regard the Bible as uninspired, uninspiring, and irrelevant for today. Like Stanton they regard its teaching, especially about women, to be oppressive and worthy only of repudiation. In many ways their goals are the exact opposite of Biblical teaching.

Richard Evans has concluded that the second wave of feminism differs in two significant ways from the first wave, in that its intellectual roots lie in two theories which the original feminists rejected, namely, socialism and sexual freedom. "It is the combination of socialism — though in a multitude of forms, some of them barely recognisable — and sexual liberation, that distinguishes the ideology, the beliefs and the aims of the present-day Women's Liberation movement from those of the feminists of the nineteenth century." Thus in spite of superficial resemblances, the ideas of the new feminists are really very different from those of their predecessors.[2]

One thing the two waves of feminism definitely have in common is the idea that society is patriarchal, i.e., structured so that men have power over women, who have a secondary and subservient roll. The goal of secular feminism is to set women free from the bondage of male domination in the context of a secular world view with secular motives, secular goals, and secular means of reaching these goals.

This chapter is intended to be an introduction to the origins and character of secular feminism, and an evaluation of its goals in the light of Biblical faith. (Hereafter, unless stated otherwise, the terms *feminism* and *women's liberation* will be used to refer to the second wave.)

I. ARCHITECTS OF THE MOVEMENT

There are certain women whose names are almost synonymous with the women's liberation movement because it was their work that established the movement and gave it its direction and shape during its first decade. These architects of the movement were certainly inspired by the nineteenth century pioneer feminists, and they learned from some who wrote "between the times," such as Simone de Beauvoir. Some say the second wave began in 1953 with the English translation of de Beauvoir's book, *The Second Sex.*[3] Cohen says this book "contained the seeds of nearly every protest ever expressed by women's liberation."[4] It was not the real beginning of the movement, however, since it was not accompanied by the overt political action and protests that were necessary to gain media attention and draw popular support to the cause. The literary and political achievements that accomplished this were the work of such women as Betty Friedan, Kate Millett, Germaine Greer, and Gloria Steinem.

A. Betty Friedan

Betty Friedan is thought of as an ambitious, intelligent woman who could have pursued a career as a psychologist, but who gave it up at the request of a prospective husband that she did not marry after all.[5] Eventually (in 1947) she married Carl Friedan and became a housewife and a mother. She also came to be called the "Mother Superior to Women's Lib."[6]

Friedan is credited with launching the women's liberation movement with the publication of her "ground-breaking polemic,"[7] *The Feminine Mystique,* in 1963.[8] Ronald and Beverly Allen call this book "the catalyst for the modern women's movement" and describe its importance thus:

43

... It is difficult to overestimate the influence of this book on the direction of society in America over the last two decades. What Darwin's, *The Origin of the Species* is to evolutionary biology, and Wellhausen's, *Prolegomena to the History of Israel* is to recent biblical criticism, *The Feminine Mystique* is to women's liberation. This book was the spark that ignited the blaze of a modern movement of staggering proportions.[9]

What is the point of Friedan's book? In general, it deals with "the psychic disaster caused by the repression of educated women."[10] It is an expose of what is called "'the disease with no name,' the malaise of the suburban housewife."[11] Friedan analyzes what she thought to be the feeling of many women, that culture had created a "feminine mystique," i.e., the concept of an ideal femininity as the loving, doting housewife whose interests are limited to house, spouse, and children. The problem is that women, especially the more talented ones (such as herself), are not satisfied with this culturally-imposed role. They feel trapped by this "unwanted domesticity," which smothers their own true identities.[12] They see themselves as "isolated, unstimulated, sexually deprived, trapped by babies, frittering away their talents in boredom and drudgery, ... victims of male oppression in an exploitative capitalist culture."[13]

Some housewives were insulted by Friedan's book, which they took to be a put-down both of a noble career and of themselves for choosing it. Others such as Jim and Andrea Fordham challenged the accuracy of Friedan's analysis of women's plight, calling it a "drastically distorted version of reality." While it may have been a realistic description of her own dissatisfaction with the housewife's lot, the "feminine mystique" as a general cultural fact, they say, was "simply a fabrication," a contrived idea invented by Friedan and shored up by a misreading or misrepresentation of data.[14]

Whether this is the case or not, there is no question that many women identified with Friedan; and "her description caught on widely, particularly among intellectuals in American universities."[15] Thus the women's liberation movement was born.

Betty Friedan's other main contribution to the launching of feminism was the founding of the National Organization for Women (NOW), on June 29, 1966. She was one of its chief organizers and its first president.[16] She was also the one who initiated the Women's March for Equality in August 1970 and the National Women's Political Caucus in March 1971, which will be mentioned below.

Though Friedan was not as radical as many of the early feminists and has since backed away from some of the extremes espoused by the movement,[17] she must be recognized as one of its primary sources.

B. Kate Millett

A second architect of secular feminism is Kate Millett, dubbed "the high priestess of the Women's Liberation movement" by Time magazine.[18] She has also been called the "Mao Tse-tung of Women's Liberation" and the "Karl Marx of the women's movement."[19] Living the life of a professional intellectual, Millett graduated from the University of Minnesota and also studied in Japan and at Oxford University, where she enjoyed a jet-set lifestyle and earned academic honors. Back in the U.S. she joined the "struggling artist" clan, living in a Bowery loft and lecturing at Barnard College.[20]

The work that made Millett a star in the movement was her book, Sexual Politics, published in 1970.[21] It landed her on the cover of Time magazine, which called it "the Bible" of women's liberation.[22] The book is a scholarly attack on the male power structure of patriarchy, the cultural mind-set that male supremacy is natural and normal. It sets forth the thesis that all male-female differences except anatomy are cultural in origin, not biological.

It is especially noteworthy that *Sexual Politics* is a celebration of the sexual revolution, a theme that took on added significance when Millett later in a public meeting was pressed into admitting that she is a lesbian. From that point on, women's liberation and homosexual liberation were linked arm in arm, and lesbianism became an aspect of the feminists' agenda.[23]

C. Germaine Greer

At about this same time another woman, Germaine Greer, was also emerging as an architect of secular feminism. An Australian by birth, in 1964 Greer moved to England with a scholarship to do doctoral work at Cambridge University. She was part of the original "beat generation," totally irreverent, an "absolute original" who led "a thoroughly bohemian existence." She was physically striking, a *femme fatale*, a six-foot "Amazon beauty."[24]

The book that established Greer as a feminist leader was called *The Female Eunuch*.[25] It appeared first in England in 1970 and was published in the U.S. in 1971. Like Friedan's and Millett's works, *The Female Eunuch* is an attack on what is regarded as a cultural construct that is repressive to women and is a denial of their true nature. The book assails the model of meek and drab femininity set forth by our male-dominated culture as ideal womanhood. Such a model, says Greer, castrates women and makes them female eunuchs. Over against this she describes her own concept of authentic womanness in terms of total sexual freedom. With a liberal use of four-letter vulgarisms her book glorifies the "lusty wench" (and lust itself) as the ideal and urges women to be more aggressive in sexual matters. In summary, it is "a glowing tribute to straightforward, spontaneous female sexuality" of the heterosexual variety.[26]

Greer herself was a living example of her own philosophy. In a totally uninhibited way she flaunted her sexuality; she preached sexual freedom and practiced what she preached. For example, prior to the writing of her book she attempted to create a pornographic magazine, for which she and all the other editors posed obscenely.[27] The magazine failed after one issue. (It must be remembered that all this was happening only at the threshold of the sexual revolution, when this sort of lifestyle was still considered scandalous.)

This, then, is one of the women who became a feminist heroine, and who by the publication of her book was "launched into the stratosphere of American feminism."[28]

D. Gloria Steinem

The fourth major architect of the women's movement is Gloria Steinem. The youthful Steinem, described as "a dream girl" who was "stunningly beautiful" as well as "modest, poised, [and] tactful," was also a standout in the academic world. She graduated from Smith College magna cum laude and was awarded a scholarship to study in India. She continued to be regarded as "the intellectuals' pinup," and was a Playboy Bunny for a brief time before her feminist consciousness began to awaken.[29]

When it did awaken, Steinem became involved in the women's movement with such enthusiasm and effectiveness that she soon was acknowledged as one of its leaders. She was on the cover of the August 16, 1971, issue of *Newsweek* as "the personification of women's liberation." In January 1972 *McCall's* named her "Woman of the Year."[30]

Steinem's major role in the movement began in late 1971 with the launching of *Ms.* magazine, of which she was the editor until 1987. The first issue was a forty-page insert in *New York* magazine for December 20, 1971; the first independent issue appeared in the spring of 1972.[31] Thus the gospel of feminism was made available in a convenient form on a monthly basis at newstands everywhere.

The following statement from the magazine (an appeal for subscribers) reflects how it sees itself in the context of the women's movement:

> What a difference a magazine can make. When *Ms.* was first launched . . . , it was a different world. We led the way, and we changed the world. . . .
> We began as the voice of a movement; we've become the voice of a compelling, pervading force. In the beginning, we spoke for a minority; now we speak for a vast majority. Our vision has been transformed, for the change we seek is, like a river flowing to the sea, unstoppable.
> *Ms.* stands squarely on the leading edge of change. . . .
> *Ms.* is the magazine of record for women. When the rest of the media wants to know how women feel about an issue, they ask *Ms.* We're right there in the forefront, reporting on the women and to the women in the forefront of change.[32]

Since this is a self-assessment, it may be guilty of a degree of over-statement, but there is no doubt that *Ms.*, under the editorship of Steinem, has had a significant influence for the cause of feminism.

E. Conclusion

Many other women have been active in the secular feminist movement, but these four – Friedan, Millett, Greer, and Steinem – stand out above the others. These are the four whose picures Marcia Cohen chose to put on the cover of her book, *The Sisterhood*, which is subtitled "The True Story of the Women Who Changed the World." Change it they did, but whether for good or for ill is something that can be decided only from a Biblical perspective, which will be considered below.

II. GROUPS AND ORGANIZATIONS

In its beginning the secular feminist movement gained momentum in several ways, including the formation of various groups and organizations. Some of these were formal and some informal, but all were designed for the sole purpose of promoting the feminist agenda.

A. Consciousness Raising Groups

In the early years some of the most effective groups were the small informal meetings known as consciousness raising groups. Sometimes they went by other names, such as rap groups, affinity groups, collectives, support groups, or cells. In these gatherings women of all ages discussed with intimacy and openness the burning issues and questions relating to women's liberation, such as the following: "What did you do as a little girl that was different from what little boys did? Why? Was your brother given privileges you were not? What was your first sexual experience like? Have you ever felt that men have pressured you into sexual relationships? Can you be aggressive? Do you believe in monogamy? Is love a trap for women? How are the sex roles divided in your house? Why did you marry in the first place? Is there another way for two people to love each other and live together? Have you had close relationships with women? Were they satisfying? What is the role of religion in oppressing women? What work would you most like to do, and what has stopped you?"[33]

As Cohen says, "Such groups soon would pollinate the country, from small university towns in Iowa to larger cities like Seattle, from fishing villages in Maine to prairie towns in Nebraska. In small pockets across the land, women would hear about those 'consciousness-raising' sessions" and join together to discuss such questions as the above.[34] Those who participated were supposed to be enlightened concerning their oppressed condition and their need for liberation, partly by their own guided introspection and partly by the testimonies of their "sisters."

B. The National Organization for Women

The movement's most effective formal organization by far is the National Organization for Women, or NOW. Some of the earliest feminists, including Betty Friedan, came to the conclusion that they needed a civil rights organization for women similar to the NAACP. Friedan was prevailed upon to start it. On June 28-29, 1966, she met with a group of women in Washington, D.C., and NOW was formed. At the time of its incorporation it had 300 charter members, and Friedan became its first president.[35]

With the founding of NOW, says *Time,* "Women's Liberation formally began."[36] NOW was "the first militant feminist group in the twentieth century to combat sex discrimination in all spheres of life."[37] It gave the movement an effective tool for organized political activism, a means of channeling women's pent-up frustration and energy into action, a way of putting pressure on individuals, companies, and government agencies. Its first official political action, in late 1966, was to petition the Equal Employment Opportunity Commission to ban separate male/female want ads. Other such projects followed. Also, at its second annual convention on November 18, 1967, it adopted a controversial Bill of Rights for women (written by Friedan) which set forth the basic goals of the movement. (This will be discussed in the next section.)

In its first few years NOW was plagued by internal dissension. Some members thought it went too far on such subjects as abortion, and others accused it of not being radical enough. Some in the latter category broke away and started their own organizations; but none has been as enduring and effective as NOW, which has continued to be in the forefront of feminism's fight for economic rights, for lesbian and gay "rights," for abortion "rights," and for an Equal Rights Amendment.

C. Smaller Radical Groups

In the late 1960s several smaller and usually more radical organizations sprang up within the movement, mostly in the larger metropolitan areas. In 1967 Shulamith Firestone and Pam Allen formed Radical Women, later called New York Radical Women. Hole and Levine call this "an important 'seed bed' group" of the women's movement; "individual members and later breakaway groups were among the first to formulate much of the theory and analysis generally accepted by the movement today." It is credited with originating consciousness raising groups.[38]

The New York Radical Women soon spawned two other groups, WITCH and the Redstockings. The first coven of WITCH, the "Women's International Terrorist Conspiracy from Hell," appeared on Halloween in 1968. They took this name because they claimed that witches were the original opponents of women's oppression. Their first action was to put a hex on the New York Stock Exchange, the citadel of capitalism. Other autonomous covens soon sprang up across the country. While keeping the WITCH acronym, they changed their name to match their actions, e.g., Women Incensed at Telephone Company Harassment, or Women Infuriated at Taking Care of Hoodlums.[39]

In early 1969 another radical group led by Shulamith Firestone and Ellen Willis left the New York Radical Women and started the Redstockings. They took over the consciousness raising technique as one of their main projects and were influential in its becoming a widespread tool of the movement.[40]

A radical faction within the NOW organization, led by Ti-Grace Atkinson and Flo Kennedy, felt that NOW was not egalitarian enough and was not moving swiftly enough. On October 17, 1968, they split away and formed "The October 17 Movement," later changing their name to The Feminists. In September 1969 they picketed a New York marriage license bureau to protest marriage as a "slavery-like practice." They were known for being "vociferously anti-male." Their definition of *radical feminism* as the annihilation of sex roles became widely accepted in the movement. Hole and Levine say they had an influence that was far greater than their numbers.[41] Another group formed in 1968 was the Women's Equity Action League, or WEAL. Its purpose was to fight sex discrimination in three areas: employment, *de facto* tax inequities, and especially education. It used class action suits to bring about changes through existing laws and executive orders.[42]

Other such groups formed at about the same time included the New York Radical Feminists,[43] the Radicalesbians, the Women's Radical Action Project (WRAP), and the Society for Cutting Up Men (SCUM). This last one was mostly the action of one man-hating woman, Valeria Solanis, who wrote "The SCUM Manifesto." It called for the killing of all men who are not in the Men's Auxiliary of SCUM. Solanis proceeded to practice what she preached by shooting and wounding an acquaintance, Andy Warhol.[44]

III. THE GOALS OF SECULAR FEMINISM

Without question, secular feminism has been one of the most focused, vocal, and forceful advocacy movements of our time. From its very beginning its adherents have had well-defined goals and have worked tirelessly to achieve them. Exactly what are these goals?

A. The Women's Bill of Rights

A good summary of the initial objectives of the women's movement can be seen in the NOW Bill of Rights, adopted at their 1967 meeting. This Bill of Rights demanded the following: (1) an Equal Rights Amendment to the U.S. Constitution; (2) the enforcement of laws banning sex discrimination in employment; (3) maternity leave rights in employment and in social security benefits, with pregnancy being considered as a "temporary disability"; (4) tax deductions for home and child care expenses for working parents; (5) public child care centers; (6) equal and unsegregated education; (7) equal job training opportunities and allowances for women in poverty; and (8) the right of women to control their reproductive lives, i.e., the legalization of abortion.[45]

A few years later, in 1975, the Women's Action Alliance released a similar document with a different title, the "U.S. National Women's Agenda." Claiming to represent "the women of the United States of America," it demanded from government and the private sector firm policies and programs concerning the following:

(1) Elimination of sex-role, racial and cultural stereotyping at every level of the educational system, and in educational materials.

(2) Incorporation of women's issues into all areas of educational curricula.

(3) Development of programs that counter prevailing myths and stereotypes regarding women workers and that recognize the ability of women and men alike to set goals and to achieve success in work.

(4) Ending stereotyped portrayals of women and girls in all media and encouraging efforts to portray them in positive and realistic roles.

(5) Implementation of the legal right of women to control their own reproductive systems.

(6) Inclusion of realistic curricula on health and human sexuality throughout the educational process.

(7) Protection of the right to privacy of relationships between consenting adults.

(8) Extensions of all civil rights legislation to prohibit discrimination based on affectional or sexual preference.[46]

Jim and Andrea Fordham have summed up this agenda thus: "Stripped of feminist jargon and code words, these eight items comprise the key objectives of the unisex agenda — abolition of sex roles, devaluation of the traditional marriage and family, legitimization of homosexuality, 'free' universal day care of children, abortion on demand, and feminist indoctrination in the schools."[47]

B. Moderate Versus Radical

As *Time* magazine has said, "The goals of the movement range from the modest, sensible amelioration of the female condition to extreme and revolutionary visions."[48] The Bill of Rights and the Women's Agenda summarized above include what are actually some of the more modest or moderate objectives of secular feminism. The more moderate goals have to do with specific concrete changes in laws and policies affecting women; some of them would seem reasonable to all fair-minded people. These include the demands for equal access to clubs, restaurants, organizations, public office, and professions; equal educational and employment opportunities; and equal pay for equal work.

However, those who think that this is the essence of secular feminism can only be called naive. It has many goals, not necessarily shared by all feminists, that are quite radical in nature. Thus the distinction is usually made between moderate and radical feminism,[49] or in other terms liberal and radical feminism.[50] Sometimes the distinction is not obvious until one begins to read the literature of feminism itself. This was the case with Christina Sommers, Associate Professor of Philosophy at Clark University. Once she began to read the works of feminists, she saw that her "understanding of feminism was far too simplistic. The old and honorable goal of equality of opportunity had been superseded. Someone like me who still thought in terms of simple equity was, if not a dinosaur, at the very least mired in the most primitive state of 'feminist consciousness.' "[51] Sommers now distinguishes between moderate "equity feminists" and radical "gender feminists."[52]

Feminism's radical agenda requires not just a number of

specific changes within the present framework of things, but a "drastic revision of society in general."[53] It involves not just a change in programs, but a change in ideology or mindset, a change in the way people think about the relation between the sexes and every cultural expression of that relationship. It involves not just equality, but also such things as power and autonomy and freedom and independence. Women must be seen not only as equal with men, but as independent of men and as possessing complete power and autonomy over their own lives. Cohen cites a statement from Millett: "Women's autonomy is what women's liberation is all about."[54]

This radical feminist goal requires an all-out assault on the most basic of traditional relationships, i.e., those involving marriage, parenthood, and the family. Women must learn to live without marriage; they must learn to get along without men in every way. They must learn to express their sexual natures through lesbian relationships. If they prefer men, they should be free to enter whatever kind of sexual relationships with them that they choose. If pregnancy occurs they must be completely free to have an abortion if they so desire. (Some even call for biological and genetic researchers to try to develop some way for men to have babies.[55]) If a child is born, free universal day care or communal parenting must be available so that one is not tied down by a child. As feminist writer Gabrielle Burton says, women's liberation is seeking the most radical revolution of all, because "it is challenging the nuclear family structure, monogamy, sexual expressions, child-rearing practices, the economy, and our ways of thinking."[56]

In discussing feminism and the college curriculum Christina Sommers cites some contemporary examples of this radical thinking. She refers to Alison Jaggar, who teaches women's studies at the University of Cincinnati.

. . . She claims that the family is "a cornerstone of oppression" that "enforces heterosexuality" and

"imposes the prevailing masculine and feminine character structures on the next generation." Lauding the
day when the miracle of science will allow us to alter
basic human functions like insemination, lactation
and gestation, she says, "one woman could inseminate another . . . men and nonparturitive women
could lactate . . . fertilized ova could be transferred
into women's or even men's bodies."[57]

Sommers remarks that "gender feminist literature is
replete with proposals for abolishing marriage and the
family in favor of various forms of androgeny or bisexuality." She cites a male feminist, Richard Wasserstrom, who
argues that all differences between the sexes are arbitrary
and irrelevant. In a truly just society, he says, "you would
no more notice the sex of a person with whom you were
romantically involved than you would notice eye color. He
recommends bisexuality as the ideal romantic relationship
because heterosexuality or even homosexuality is a reflection of prejudice and bigotry."[58]

The sum of it is that radical feminists are demanding
autonomous control over all aspects of sexuality, with the
right to make all the rules and to break them at will. Thus
it is no accident that lesbianism and abortion are seen as
sacred rights for all women. The right to abortion is not
just a matter of pragmatic selfishness; it goes to the very
heart of feminist ideology. As one feminist says, "The abortion controversy is not only about life; it's about control
over women's sexuality and power."[59] The same is true of
lesbianism, to which secular feminism has been firmly
committed ever since Kate Millett "came out of the closet"
in 1970. As a feminist leaflet of that day said, what is at
stake in defending lesbianism is not just a few women's
sexual pleasure but rather "the freedom *of all women* to
openly state values that fundamentally challenge the basic
structure of patriarchy."[60] NOW has admitted that twenty
percent of its members are lesbians, but some former mem-

bers say this number should be considerably higher.

Of course it is possible for a person in his or her own mind to support only the moderate goals of women's liberation and to repudiate the radical agenda. The difficulty comes when one opts to become an active participant or supporter of the movement as such. Jim and Andrea Fordham contend that on a practical level the two agendas cannot be separated, and that the movement itself is more identified with and committed to the radical ideals than the moderate. Some may try to suggest "that feminism is just about 'equal pay for equal work,' but if you read the literature of lib you will never again accept that idea." They note that most people support equal pay and equal opportunity. "But a feminist, it seems, is something else. Whether she admits it or prefers to hide the fact, a feminist is someone who is encouraging a restructuring of society through obliteration of the sex roles."[61]

The bottom line is that the basic goals of feminism are radically ideological. The more moderate goals are simply concrete examples of how this radical philosophy comes to expression in a few areas.

C. A Gender-Free Society

The ultimate goal of secular feminism can be summed up in a single concept, namely, a gender-free or unisex society. As Mary Daly says, "Radical feminists are fundamentally agreed in the advocacy of total elimination of sex roles." They are "concerned with overturning the sex role system."[62] Gilder claims that they want to live by a "remorseless egalitarian code" and try to "twist their lives and bodies into the unisex mold."[63] Phyllis Schlafly has discerned this fact about feminists: "Based on their dogma that there is no real difference between men and women (except their sex organs), they demand that males and females have identical treatment always." A primary goal of women's liberation is to prohibit anyone's making any difference or separation between the sexes anytime.[64] Examples of how this is put into practice are prohibiting father-son and mother-daughter banquets and making sure that school books do not portray women doing housework any more often than men.[65]

"War has been declared," says Sommers, "not on inequality but upon gender."[66] The Fordhams call it "the sex-role revolution," and warn that "most people just are not aware of the deep-down radical nature of this movement."[67] They cite an early authoritative feminist work that states clearly that "each major branch of the women's movement . . . is working toward the elimination of the sex-role system." Also, "Whatever the tactics employed and language used, the goal for feminists is a sexual revolution . . . to eliminate sexism in all its manifestations."[68] They sum up their point in this unequivocal paragraph:

> Here is the crux of the feminist belief – the central ingredient that ties together all major feminist initiatives; it is the total faith that if somehow we could do away with the male and female social roles, then, and only then, would we have human equality, sharing, caring and universal happiness among persons all over the world. Whatever their short-term objectives or pragmatic rhetoric of the moment, the one essential of the hardcore feminists who propel the women's liberation movement is the absolute necessity of doing away with sex roles.[69]

IV. MEANS AND METHODS

The secular feminists have to be counted as among the most determined crusaders the world has ever known. To say the least, they have not been timid in their quest to achieve their goals. They have been willing to use almost any means or method available. Often they have turned to existing legal channels, putting pressure on the courts, legislators, and government agencies. On the other hand they have often resorted to more bizarre types of activism. In general there seems to be a tacit commitment to the philosophy that the ends justify the means.

The formation of the National Organization for Women gave the feminists what has probably been their single most effective tool for influencing change. Through its organizational power it has been able to focus the energies of thousands of women into specific projects while at the same time commanding the attention of the media. As mentioned, its first official action was to petition the Equal Employment Opportunity Commission (EEOC) to ban separate male/female want ads. When the EEOC was slow in responding, NOW organized a picketing action against its regional offices and filed suit against it to force it to comply with its own rules. The Commission finally acted in 1968.[70]

From its beginning NOW has also been involved in more direct types of action. For example, in February 1969 it organized an invasion of an exclusive men-only dining room in a New York City hotel, much to the management's chagrin and the media's delight.[71] Over the years it has sponsored many other such protests as well as rallies and marches of various kinds, especially in support of the ERA crusade in the late 1970s and early 1980s.

In July 1971 another activist group was formed, the National Women's Political Caucus. Its purpose was to bring the influence of the women's movement to bear upon the political process, especially "to seek out and promote candidates of either sex, preferably women, who will work to eliminate 'sexism, racism, violence and poverty.' "[72] With the support of U.S. Representatives Bella Abzug and Shirley Chisholm, it encouraged more women to seek elective office. It also sought to influence the platforms and processes of the national party conventions. An early planning note by Betty Friedan (its instigator), written on the back of a blank check, reads thus:

In 1972 we will go into the national conventions of
both major parties with bargaining power to support
women candidates, working with other under-repre-
sented groups. We will work in primaries and elec-
tions across party lines and outside existing parties,
drawing in women who have lost faith in the elective
process, to elect women candidates committed to our
goal.[73]

In its early years secular feminism relied as much on
unorthodox methods as conventional means to draw attention to itself. In its first decade, several well-planned
protests placed the women's movement in the national
spotlight. One was the Miss America protest of September
7, 1968, which was planned by Robin Morgan, the creator
of WITCH. The purpose was to condemn the pageant's
alleged male chauvinist exploitation of women as sex
objects. Activities during the day included a "Freedom
Trash Can" ceremony, during which items such as dish-
cloths, girdles, false eyelashes, copies of *Playboy*, and bras
were symbolically tossed into the can. (This is probably the
origin of the "bra-burning" myth that many people associate with women's liberation.) Several feminists were able
to get into the pageant hall itself, where they disrupted the
coronation ceremony with a noisy demonstration – all on
national TV.[74]

Another demonstration with more tangible results
occurred in 1970, when a group of women led by Susan
Brownmiller staged a sit-in in the New York offices of the
Ladies' Home Journal. The purpose was to force this influential women's magazine – which up to this time had been
an apostle of the accursed "feminine mystique" – to begin
to promote the agenda of the feminist movement, with the
thought that other such magazines would follow suit. On
March 18, with a photographer in tow, a group of three or
four score women, some carrying posters labeled *Women's
Liberation Journal,* barged into the office of the editor-in-

chief. In a thoroughly raucous and threatening manner they occupied all the empty spaces in the office while Brownmiller read and reread a list of demands. These demands included the replacement of all male editors with women, the elimination of all ads that degrade women, a change in the general content of the magazine to show that there is a viable alternative to marriage and family, and one issue to be edited entirely by members of the women's movement themselves. After the editor-in-chief agreed to publish a feminist supplement, the siege ended. The eight-page supplement, entitled "The New Feminism," appeared in the August issue.[75] Thus began what Jim and Andrea Fordham call "the long campaign to persuade the mass media to adopt feminist views on sex roles and homosexuality."[76]

In the same year Betty Friedan organized still another media-blessed demonstration, a nationwide 24-hour "women's strike for equality," highlighted by the "Women's March for Equality" in downtown New York City. This took place on August 26, 1970, to commemorate the fiftieth anniversary of women's suffrage. All the elite of the movement and thousands of their supporters took over Fifth Avenue that day. Their three central demands were equal opportunity in employment and education, free abortion on demand, and 24-hour child care centers. This and other coordinated activities drew nationwide attention to their cause and led many doubters to take women's liberation more seriously.[77]

One other event that illustrates the feminists' considerable ability to promote themselves and garner support is the First National Women's Conference, held in Houston on November 18-21, 1977. This meeting was funded by five million dollars in tax money and was attended by 12,000-15,000 women. Though it claimed to represent all the women of America, its organizers made sure that most of the delegates and all of the major speakers and official actions furthered the feminist agenda. (The California spokeswoman reported that ninety-five of their ninety-six delegates were lesbians; only one of the forty-some women on the planning commission was pro-life.) Twenty-six resolutions were passed, including those supporting ERA, abortion, free 24-hour child care centers, and full legal rights for homosexuals and lesbians. Most of those who attended considered the conference to be "the heady, climactic celebration of the women's movement."[78] Whether or not this conference really represented American women in general was seriously disputed by the 15,000 who attended the Pro-Life, Pro-Family Coalition counter-rally being held simultaneously in another part of Houston.[79]

V. THE SUCCESS OF THE WOMEN'S MOVEMENT

Without doubt the women's liberation movement has been one of the most successful movements in history in reference to achieving its stated goals. In the 1990s in the West the status of women in particular and the conventional wisdom concerning sex roles in general are worlds apart from the pre-feminist 1950s. "You've come a long way, baby," is not just an advertising slogan. As one conferee remarked to a reporter at the National Women's Conference in Houston, "Whether or not you're for the women's movement, it has changed your life."[80] In Michael Levin's opinion, "No doctrine is more influential in shaping institutional and public life than feminism." This is evidenced not just by the historical landmarks and statistical changes noted below, but also by the changes in the way many people think, e.g., the ready acceptance of a "quota mentality" and of feminist censorship of school-books (and even hymnbooks and the Bible).[81]

When one considers especially the more moderate goals as set forth early in the movement, it is obvious that most of them have been met. The determined tactics have worked, for the most part. The condensed chronologies of feminist events and achievements in Cohen's book and in the book by Hole and Levine make this clear.[82] An Equal Pay Act was passed in the same year Friedan's *Feminine Mystique* was published (1963). In 1964 Congress passed a Civil Rights Act expressly prohibiting sex discrimination in employment. In 1967 the EEOC began to hold hearings on sex discrimination, and in 1968 it issued guidelines forbidding male/female want ads. In 1969 President Nixon established a Task Force on Women's Rights and Responsibilities to make recommendations on legislation. In 1970 New York, Alaska, and Hawaii liberalized their abortion laws; and the U.S. Department of Labor and the United Auto Workers came out in support of the ERA. In 1972 the Equal Employment Opportunity Act was passed, prohibiting sex discrimination. In 1973 the Supreme Court legalized abortion. In 1974 the Equal Credit Opportunity Act prohibited credit discrimination based on sex or marital status, and a record number of women (18) were elected to the House of Representatives. In 1975 *Time* magazine's Man of the Year was twelve women.

In 1960 34.8% of women were in the work force, compared with 57.8% in 1989. In 1960 the number of female lawyers and judges was 7,500; in 1989 it was 180,000. The number of female doctors has climbed from 15,672 to 108,200, and female engineers from 7,404 to 174,000. The number of women in elective office has more than tripled since 1975. In the 1950s women made up only 20% of college undergraduates, compared with 54% in 1989.[83]

It is true that the women's liberation movement cannot claim to be the only cause of these changes, but it is no doubt responsible for them in a large measure.

Perhaps the only major defeat of the women's movement thus far has been its failure to get an Equal Rights Amendment added to the U.S. Constitution. Despite feminists' heroic efforts and a blatantly illegal extension by Congress,[84] even the extended deadline passed without its ratification. But this defeat is more symbolic than practical since, as Gilder notes and as the above data indicate, the movement is gaining its ends piecemeal, and "feminists are winning quietly by legal and legislative action what they cannot win by referenda."[85]

It is true that the women's movement has a much lower profile today than during its first decade, and this has led some to observe that it is passé. Five years ago Dinesh D'Souza declared, "While women in America are doing better than ever before, the women's movement is in decay and despair." The evidence given includes comments from certain leading feminists themselves. E.g., Friedan speaks of feminism's "profound paralysis," and Brownmiller admits that "the steam has run out of feminism."[86] The *New York Times* labeled the mid-1980s "post-feminist."[87] A 1989 *Time* cover story asks, "Is the feminist movement – one of the great social revolutions of contemporary history – truly dead? Or is it merely stalled and in need of a little consciousness raising?"[88]

It is true that the more radical aspects of the movement have not been widely accepted and are presently at bay. For example, the lesbian issue seems to be on a back burner just now, and ERAmania seems to have died down. The early stars of the movement have backtracked a bit from some of their early extremes.[89] Some are speaking of a second phase in which the nuclear family remains central and women learn to balance their new freedom with traditional roles.[90]

This does not mean, however, that feminism is no longer a cultural force. In fact, it is just the opposite. The reason why the women's movement may seem passé is that there is not as much open warfare as in the late 1960s and early 1970s. The feminists claim that the reason there is so little open warfare is that the war is over and they have won it. "Its triumphs . . . have rendered it obsolete." As Harvard professor Carol Gilligan says, "Saying the women's movement is dead is like saying the cold war is dead. No. No. It's over. It's won."[91] The things for which the earlier feminists fought are taken for granted by today's women; "a vast majority revels in the breakthroughs made during the past quarter-century."[92] As Levin observes, "Should feminism seem passé, this is almost certainly because it has attained presuppositional status." Its tenets are "too commonplace to warrant explicit statement."[93] As Gilder puts it,

> ... Though rejecting feminist politics and lesbian posturing, American culture has absorbed the underlying ideology like a sponge. The principal tenets of sexual liberation or sexual liberalism – the obsolescence of masculinity and femininity, of sex roles, and of heterosexual monogamy as the moral norm – have diffused through the system and become part of America's conventional wisdom. . . .[94]

This is not to say that feminists are satisfied and complacent; they still feel they have more work to do. *Time* magazine speaks of "enormous battles ahead" over such issues as the wage gap, divorce and poverty, and the "second shift." This last item is a reference to the fact that many of the women who have found "liberation" through a career outside the home still wind up having all the traditional roles at home as well.[95] Compared with what has already been accomplished, however, facing these problems is a bit like mopping-up exercises.

VI. SECULAR FEMINISM AND BIBLICAL FAITH

Our task now is to evaluate secular feminism in the light of traditional Biblical faith. This task should not be overly difficult, since the contrast between secular feminism and Biblical teaching is almost absolute. An important word here is *almost*, since not every aspect of the women's movement is objectionable. Some of its more moderate goals, such as equality in employment, pay, and education, are certainly fair and just by any standard. The problem lies in the more radical aspects of feminism, including both its basic theory and many of the practical applications thereof.

The fact that we are dealing here with *secular* feminism in itself points to the basic contrast between it and the Bible. In the Biblical world view God and the supernatural are real, and the natural world of which human beings are a part is the creation of God and interacts with the supernatural. The norms by which we live originate in God; he reveals them to us in the Bible, which is our final and absolute authority. The secular world view, as seen in the very meaning of the word, says that this natural world is the totality of being. It is all that exists; there is no God and there is no supernatural realm as such. Everything in the world originates solely from within it, including the Bible and all moral "norms." All norms are relative, and the final judge in all cases is the individual himself or herself.

The women's liberation movement, or secular feminism, is almost altogether the product of women who reject the divine origin and absolute authority of the Bible, and usually the very existence of God as such. It is well known that Betty Friedan was a signer of *Humanist Manifesto II*, a document unequivocally affirming a secular, atheistic world view. Friedan is quoted as saying, "Feminism is an essential stage of humanism. We must keep evolving."[96] Gloria Steinem has declared, "By the year 2000 we will, I hope, raise our children to believe in human potential, not God."[97]

Thus we are not surprised at secular feminism's emphasis on *autonomy*, which is its underlying motif. Autonomy means that there is no power higher than the self, that the self makes its own rules. The voices of secular feminism cry out, "We women have begun to own our own souls." "Claim yourself as your own." "Pursue your own good in your own way." "Answer only to yourself." Concerning this spirit of autonomy Nancy Cross rightly remarks, "Autonomy and individuation, owning our own souls, is foreign, alien, to the 'not I who live, but Christ' heart of the Christian faith."[98] Every woman and every man is a slave to God unconditionally by creation, and potentially and voluntarily by redemption. Autonomy is a myth, and seeking it is the root of all other sins.

Also contrary to Biblical teaching is the basic tenet of feminism, the ideological presupposition that underlies its general goal of a gender-free society. This basic tenet is the idea that there is no ontological distinction between men and women besides anatomy, and that even this distinction is an evolutionary accident and should be erased if possible. In the minds of radical feminists one should pay as little attention to the difference between male and female as to the difference between the black and white races. However, this idea is not only contrary to Scripture but to the conclusions of science as well. This point has been explained admirably from the latter perspective by Michael Levin in *Feminism and Freedom*. From the Biblical perspective, we need go no further than Genesis 1:27, which says that when God made humankind, he made them "male and female." The distinction is not accidental but deliberate, and it goes much deeper than anatomy. It is at the foundation of the continuing role distinctions which God has ordained regarding men and women (1 Timothy 2:12-13). The wife is the "weaker vessel, since she is a woman" (1 Peter 3:7).

The rejection of any absolute distinction between males and females is the basis of radical feminism's attack on the normative nature of marriage and the nuclear family, and its rabid advocacy of total sexual freedom, lesbianism, and abortion – all of which stands in direct opposition to the Bible.

Our attention is quickly drawn to the anti-marriage, anti-family stance of the more radical feminists. When the group known as The Feminists picketed a New York marriage bureau to protest the institution of marriage, it distributed a leaflet asking whether the wife knows "that you are your husband's prisoner." It called marriage a "slavery-like practice" and declared, "We can't destroy the inequities between men and women until we destroy marriage."[99] The feminist Marlene Dixon wrote, "The institution of marriage is the chief vehicle for the perpetuation of the oppression of women."[100] Ti-Grace Atkinson also agreed that marriage is a form of slavery and declared that any real change in the status of women would require the overthrow of marriage and the family. "People would be tied together by love, not legal contraptions. Children would be raised communally; it's just not honest to talk about freedom for women unless you get the child-rearing off their backs."[101] In his summary of Juliet Mitchell's book, *Woman's Estate*, Timothy Foote says that she "regards the family both as the greatest implement of women's oppression and the last bulwark of capitalism."[102] Other feminists have called the nuclear family "that cradle of evil"[103] and "a cornerstone of oppression."[104] Shulamith Firestone's book *The Dialectic of Sex* gives the following solution to the repression of women and children, according to Foote's summary:

> . . . The answer is a society in which marriage and the family will be abolished, along with all involuntary education. Children, if conceived at all, will be incubated outside the body of the mother. Polarized sex roles will disappear in favor of polymorphous perversity practiced in new social units called "households," loosely linked, nonauthoritarian collections of people, including small children, who contract to live together for periods of seven to ten years, but are free to do exactly what they want.[105]

Cohen calls Firestone's book a "deadly serious, driving, impatient assault on the 'tyranny' of the biological family. . . . 'Pregnancy,' Firestone wrote, 'is barbaric.' "[106]

Some may think that such sentiments represent only the earlier and more radical of the secular feminists and that they are not characteristic of feminism today. George Gilder took account of this possibility between the time when he wrote *Sexual Suicide* (1973) and its revision, *Men and Marriage* (1986). His conclusion is that "although some observers believe that feminism and sexual liberalism no longer threaten family values, little in fact has changed." Contemporary feminists, he says, must be honest "in facing the inevitable anti-family consequences of their beliefs."[107]

As the flip side of its attack on marriage and the family, secular feminism remains firmly committed to abortion and lesbian rights. The 1989 *Time* cover article on the status of the women's movement included a small chart showing various shifts of emphasis between the early days of feminism and now. Then it was ERA; now it is ABC (Act for Better Child Care). Then it was "having it all"; now it is "doing it all." Then it was the "fast track"; now it is the "mommy track," and so on. The only "buzz word" that has remained constant is – abortion rights. Then it was abortion rights; now it is STILL abortion rights.[108] Likewise, although taking a lower profile now on lesbianism, this is still an integral part of secular feminism's basic platform.

Since no one really denies that the Bible is the leading advocate of the traditional view of marriage and the family, we need not go into detail concerning the anti-Biblical nature of radical feminism's views on these subjects. As soon as they are quoted, they stand out as the very antithesis of the Bible.

Thus we are not surprised when we hear secular feminists attack the Bible itself, along with the church, in terms reminiscent of Elizabeth Cady Stanton. This is what Annie Gaylor does in a recent article in *The Humanist*. Appealing twice to Stanton, she chides those who try to appeal to the Bible to support their feminist beliefs. She points out how they take Galatians 3:28 out of context, and try to read more feminism into the life of Jesus than is there. The real motto of Christianity, she says, ought to be the words of Jesus in John 2:4, "Woman, what have I to do with thee?" Feminists must forget "the mythical Jesus" and the Bible and the church. "Two thousand years of disastrous patriarchal rule under the shadow of the cross ought to be enough to turn women toward the feminist 'salvation' of *this* world."[109] As Ti-Grace Atkinson said in a lecture at Catholic University in Washington, D.C., in 1971, "The struggle between the liberation of women and the Catholic Church is a struggle to the death. So be it!"[110]

We must agree that the struggle between the liberation of women *as secular feminists understand* it and Biblical teaching rightly understood IS "a struggle to the death." But Bible-believing Christians must believe that in the end the Bible will prevail.

VII. SECULAR OPPONENTS OF SECULAR FEMINISM

Not all opponents of secular feminism base their opposition on Biblical teaching. Some of its more effective critics have appealed simply to reason and to science, calling for honest scholarship in the use of the data. One early female critic of the women's movement was Midge Decter, an editor for *Harper's* magazine. She presented a very anti-feminist interpretation of woman's lot in *The New Chastity and Other Arguments Against Women's Liberation.*[111] Jim and Andrea Fordham (a journalist and a sociologist, respectively) questioned the objectivity of the scholarship, the accuracy of the data, and the soundness of the basic premises of feminism in *The Assault on the Sexes.* George Gilder wrote *Sexual Suicide* and its revision, *Men and Marriage,* to affirm that "the differences between the sexes are the single most important fact of human society," contrary to the unisex goals of feminism.[112] He explores the biological basis of these differences while defending his basic premise that monogamous marriage is essential to civilization. Michael Levin's recent book, *Feminism and Freedom,* is one of the most important critiques of feminism from the secular perspective. Levin has served as professor of philosophy at City College of New York and for the Graduate Center of the City University of New York. He contends that feminism is biologially unsound, irrational, and antidemocratic.

We must remember that some of the more moderate feminists themselves, though they be secular to the core, still decry the extremists' attacks on marriage and the family as such. In some cases this is even a matter of some radicals "having second thoughts" and wondering if they have not gone too far.[113]

VIII. CONCLUSION

This chapter has been an attempt to give a brief explanation and evaluation of secular feminism, the women's liberation movement of the latter twentieth century. Some Bible-believers may think that they have no need to explore the nature of this movement, especially since its beliefs and goals are so diametrically opposed to Christianity.

But that is just the point. For the most part, it *is* diametrically opposed to Biblical teaching about sexuality, sex roles, marriage, and the family. That in itself would not be significant if we were dealing here with only a small uninfluential ripple in the broad stream of history. But the fact is that the feminist movement has enjoyed an almost unprecedented success in influencing modern western culture to mold itself around the feminist views on these crucial subjects. And in these areas where its radical views oppose Scriptural truth, every victory for secular feminism is a defeat for the cause of God and truth. Bible-believers cannot let this antibiblical tide roll on without attempting to understand and oppose it as an enemy.

This is not simply ivory-tower academics. Just minutes before I sat down to write this conclusion, I read the letters to the editor in our local newspaper. One letter, laced with angry feminist rhetoric, was a defense of abortion rights. In a decidedly anti-male spirit it attacked "patriarchy," demeaned the Bible, and condemned all those who "stomp us [women] down with your repressive laws." The point is that secular feminism is still a force to be dealt with. To this letter-writer and others like her, we must prepare ourselves to speak the truth in love, and be ready to make a defense and give an account for the hope that is within us.

Endnotes

1. Marcia Cohen, *The Sisterhood: The True Story of the Women Who Changed the World* (New York: Simon and Schuster, 1988), pp. 24, 154. Cohen refers to an article by Martha Weinman Lear called "The Second Feminist Wave," in *The New York Times Magazine* for March 10, 1968. Cohen's book is a breezy history of the rise of the women's movement, giving a behind-the-scenes look at many of the major events. A more scholarly volume covering the early years is Judith Hole and Ellen Levine, *Rebirth of Feminism* (New York: Quadrangle Books, 1971).

2. Richard J. Evans, *The Feminists: Women's Emancipation Movements in Europe, America and Australasia 1840-1920,* revised ed. (New York: Barnes and Noble, 1979), pp. 242-245.

3. Simone de Beauvoir, *The Second Sex,* tr. H.M. Parshley (New York: Alfred A. Knopf, 1953). It was originally published in French in 1949.

4. Cohen, *The Sisterhood,* p. 168.

5. Ibid., pp. 62-64.

6. Ibid., p. 309.

7. Ibid., p. 15, and text for illustration no. 16, after p. 128.

8. Betty Friedan, *The Feminine Mystique* (New York; Norton, 1963).

9. Ronald and Beverly Allen, *Liberated Traditionalism: Men and Women in Balance* (Portland: Multnomah Press, 1985), p. 33.

10. Cohen, *The Sisterhood*, text for illustration no. 16, after p. 128.

11. Michael Levin, *Feminism and Freedom* (New Brunswick, NJ: Transaction Books, 1987), p. 7.

12. "The New Feminists: Revolt Against 'Sexism,'" *Time* (Nov. 21, 1969), p. 54; "Where She Is and Where She's Going," *Time* (March 20, 1972), p. 27.

13. George Gilder, *Men and Marriage* (Gretna, LA: Pelican Publishing Company, 1986), p. 167.

14. Jim and Andrea Fordham, *The Assault on the Sexes* (New Rochelle, NY: Arlington House, 1977), pp. 121-131.

15. Gilder, *Men and Marriage*, p. 167.

16. Cohen, *The Sisterhood*, pp. 133-139.

17. See her book, *The Second Stage* (New York: Summit, 1981). As early as 1972 she was attacking Gloria Steinem for the latter's "female chauvinism" (Cohen, *The Sisterhood*, pp. 349-50).

18. "Women's Lib: A Second Look," *Time* (Dec. 14, 1970), p. 50.

19. Cohen, *The Sisterhood*, pp. 236-237.

20. Ibid., pp. 143-144.

21. Kate Millett, *Sexual Politics* (Garden City, NY: Doubleday, 1970).

22. *Time*, August 31, 1970; and Dec. 14, 1970, p. 50.

23. See Cohen, *The Sisterhood*, pp. 239-251.

24. Ibid., pp. 117-118, 255-256.

25. Germaine Greer, *The Female Eunuch* (New York: McGraw-Hill, 1971).

26. Cohen, *The Sisterhood*, pp. 128, 255-258.

27. Ibid., pp. 124-125.

28. Ibid., p. 258.

29. Ibid., pp. 103-104, 113-114.

30. Ibid., pp. 322-323.

31. Ibid., pp. 326ff., 395.

32. "We've Changed So Much," *Ms.* (June 1984), pp. 86-87.

33. On the origin and nature of these groups, see Hole and Levine, *Rebirth of Feminism*, pp. 125-126, 131-139. For these and other questions, see ibid., pp. 138-139; Fordham, *The Assault on the Sexes*, pp. 110-111; Cohen, *The Sisterhood*, pp. 175-176.

34. Cohen, *The Sisterhood*, p. 176.

35. Ibid., pp. 130-137.

36. "Women's Liberation Revisited," *Time* (March 20, 1972), p. 29.

37. Hole and Levine, *Rebirth of Feminism*, pp. 81-82.

38. Ibid., pp. 115-119, 137, 406.

39. Ibid., pp. 126-130; Cohen, *The Sisterhood*, pp. 167-168;

Margot Adler, *Drawing Down the Moon: Witches, Druids, Goddess-Worshippers, and Other Pagans in America Today,* revised ed. (Boston: Beacon Press, 1986), p. 179.

40. Hole and Levine, *Rebirth of Feminism,* pp. 136-142, 410.

41. Ibid., pp. 90, 142-147; Cohen, *The Sisterhood,* pp. 165-166, 392.

42. Cohen, *The Sisterhood,* pp. 392-394; Hole and Levine, *Rebirth of Feminism,* pp. 95-98, 409.

43. Hole and Levine, *Rebirth of Feminism,* pp. 152-157.

44. Cohen, *The Sisterhood,* pp. 157-158. Hole and Levine (p. 91) spell her name "Solanas."

45. The text is printed in full in Hole and Levine, *Rebirth of Feminism,* pp. 441-442.

46. Fordham, *The Assault on the Sexes,* pp. 53-54.

47. Ibid., p. 54.

48. *Time* (March 20, 1972), p. 29.

49. Levin, *Feminism and Freedom,* p. 3.

50. Cohen, *The Sisterhood,* p. 369.

51. Christiana Hoff Sommers, "Feminism and the College Curriculum," *Imprimis* (June 1990), 19:1.

52. Ibid., p. 2.

53. *Time* (March 20, 1972), p. 30.

54. Cohen, *The Sisterhood,* p. 251.

55. In her book *Women and Madness* Phyllis Chesler says that science must find a way "to either release women from biological reproduction – or to allow men to experience the process also" (Garden City, NY: Doubleday, 1972; p. 299).

56. Cited in Fordham, *The Assault on the Sexes,* p. 32.

57. Sommers, "Feminism and the College Curriculum," p. 2.

58. Ibid.

59. Sister Madonna Kolbenschlag, in an address at the "Women in the Church" conference in Washington, D.C., October 10, 1986, as reported by Donna Steichen, "The Goddess Goes to Washington," *Fidelity* (December 1986), 6:41.

60. Cited in Cohen, *The Sisterhood,* p. 249.

61. Fordham, *The Assault on the Sexes,* pp. 117-118.

62. Mary Daly, *Beyond God the Father: Toward a Philosophy of Women's Liberation,* new paperback ed. (Boston: Beacon Press, 1985), pp. 124-125.

63. Gilder, *Men and Marriage,* p. xi.

64. Phyllis Schlafly, "What Is Women's Liberation All About?", *The Lookout* (August 23, 1981), p. 2.

65. Ibid., pp. 2, 4.

66. Sommers, "Feminism and the College Curriculum," p. 2.

67. Fordham, *The Assault on the Sexes*, p. 98.

68. Hole and Levine, *Rebirth of Feminism,* cited in ibid., pp. 100-101.

69. Fordham, *The Assault on the Sexes,* p. 253.

70. Cohen, *The Sisterhood,* pp. 391-392.

71. Ibid., pp. 13-22.

72. Ruth Brine, "Women's Lib: Beyond Sexual Politics," *Time* (July 26, 1971), p. 36.

73. Cohen, *The Sisterhood,* in illustration no. 56, after p. 128.

74. Ibid., pp. 149-153.

75. Ibid., pp. 184-196.

76. Fordham, *The Assault on the Sexes,* p. 44.

77. Cohen, *The Sisterhood,* pp. 273-287; Hole and Levine, *Rebirth of Feminism,* pp. 92-93. 420.

78. Ibid., pp. 362-363. See also "International Woman's Year, Houston: Behind the Scenes," *Cincinnati Right to Life Bulletin* (December 1977), pp. 2-3.

79. Ruthanne Garlock, "Feminist Power: The Battle of Houston," *Christianity Today* (December 30, 1977), pp. 38-40.

80. Ibid., p. 40.

81. Levin, *Feminism and Freedom,* pp. 8-9.

82. Cohen, *The Sisterhood,* pp. 389-398; Hole and Levine, *Rebirth of Feminism,* pp. 401-427.

83. Scott Brown et al., "Onward, Women!", *Time* (December 4, 1989), p. 82.

84. See Gilder, *Men and Marriage,* pp. 102-103, for a summary of the powers mobilized behind the effort to pass the ERA.

85. Ibid., p. 153.

86. Dinesh D'Souza, "The New Feminist Revolt: This Time It's Against Feminism," *Policy Review* (Winter 1986), p. 46.

87. Cohen, *The Sisterhood,* p. 377.

88. *Time* (December 4, 1989), p. 81.

89. Gilder, *Men and Marriage,* p. viii.

90. *Time* (December 4, 1989), p. 86. An example is Betty Friedan's book, *The Second Stage.*

91. *Time* (December 4, 1989), p. 82.

92. Ibid., pp. 81-82.

93. Levin, *Feminism and Freedom,* pp. 10-11.

94. Gilder, *Men and Marriage,* p. viii-ix.

95. *Time* (December 4, 1989), pp. 85-86. See Arlie Hochschild, *The Second Shift* (New York; Viking, 1989); and the review, "The Myth of Male Housework," *Time* (August 7, 1989), p. 62.

96. Betty Friedan, Kansas City *Times,* April 6, 1981, as cited in "Do These Women Speak for You?", a pamphlet prepared by Concerned Women for America; 370 L'Enfant Promenade, SW, Suite 800; Washington, D.C. 20024.

97. Gloria Steinem, in *Saturday Review of Education,* as cited in the pamphlet, "Do These Women Speak for You?"

98. Nancy M. Cross, "What's Christian About Christian Feminism?", *Fidelity* (December 1985), 5:10.

99. Hole and Levine, *Rebirth of Feminism,* pp. 144-145.

100. Cited in Fordham, *The Assault on the Sexes,* p. 114.

101. Cited in Fordham, *The Assault on the Sexes,* p. 102; see Cohen, *The Sisterhood,* p. 155.

102. Timothy Foote, "Lib and Let Lib," *Time* (March 20, 1972), p. 100.

103. From a review of *Sappho Was a Right-on Woman* in the *New York Times Book Review* (February 25, 1973), pp. 30-40, cited in George F. Gilder, *Sexual Suicide* (New York: Quadrangle, 1973), p. 3.

104. Alison Jaggar, cited in Sommers, "Feminism and the College Curriculum," p. 2.

105. Foote, "Lib and Let Lib," *Time* (March 20, 1972), p. 100.

106. Cohen, *The Sisterhood,* p. 259.

107. Gilder, *Men and Marriage,* p. x.

108. *Time* (December 4, 1989), p. 89.

109. Annie Laurie Gaylor, "Feminist 'Salvation,'" *The Humanist* (July/August 1988), 48:33-34.

110. Cohen, *The Sisterhood,* p. 202.

111. Midge Decter, *The New Chastity and Other Arguments Against Women's Liberation* (New York; Coward, McCann & Geoghegan, 1972). See the review by Melvin Maddocks, "Unraised Consciousness," *Time* (October 16, 1972), p. 88.

112. Gilder, *Men and Marriage,* p. vii.

113. See again the article by Dinesh D'Souza, "The New Feminist Revolt."

3 GODDESS FEMINISM: WHAT IS IT?

SANTA CRUZ – Nearly 400 women picked different notes and held them, catching their breaths at
different times so the sound droned unabated for five
minutes. The eerie monotones from this congregation
of sorts reverberated against the angular outside
walls of the Theater of Performing Arts and filtered
through clumps of tall pines on the UC Santa Cruz
campus. The Hymnic call was to the Goddess. Later
in the day, encouraged by the beat of bongo drums,
spontaneous groups of circling women danced barebreasted in scenes suggestive of frolicking wood
nymphs.

. . . More than a successful university extension
course, however, the event was indicative of a bur-
geoning spiritual dimension to the women's liberation
movement in America.[1]

What is represented in this news article is a second version of modern feminism, known as *goddess feminism*. This aspect of the women's movement became noticeable about a decade after the beginning of secular feminism, and has continued to gain momentum ever since.

Secular feminism by definition is all politics and no spirituality. Its agenda and its methods are truly political, in the broad sense of using power in the public arena in order to influence policy. Being secular, however, its activities are divorced from any spiritual or religious framework.

Some women have not been satisfied with this approach to feminism. They agree with the politics of secular feminism; they wholeheartedly endorse its agenda and pursue its goals. But they feel that something is lacking; they feel the need for a spiritual connection or spiritual basis for themselves *as feminists*. They deny that politics and spirituality are incompatible, declaring that the division between them is an artificial creation of that ubiquitous villain, patriarchy. Instead, they "regard political struggles and spiritual development as interdependent, and feel that both are needed to create a society and culture that would be meaningful to them." Thus "portions of the feminist movement seem to be combining political and spiritual concerns as if they were two streams of a single river."[2]

A problem exists at this point, however. While they do not see any conflict between feminist politics and spirituality as such, many of these women do believe that feminism is incompatible with the formal traditional religions of the world today. They regard these religions, especially those based on the Bible (Judaism and Christianity), as the very foundation of patriarchal cultural patterns and thus one of the chief causes of women's oppression for millennia. Unlike some women from within these traditions, they do not believe it is possible to modify or adapt them to the feminist cause; thus they reject them all as hopelessly irretrievable. For the most part, they are particularly emphatic "in regarding the Biblical tradition as irredeemably sexist."[3]

Many draw this conclusion after having grown up in
some branch of Judaism or Christianity. An example is
Mary Daly. Early in her feminist career (in 1968) she wrote
The Church and the Second Sex as a liberal Roman
Catholic. By the time it was reprinted in 1975, however,
she had made the transition from "radical Catholic" to
"postchristian radical feminist."[4] In the first edition she
still entertained the hope that Christianity could be sal-
vaged and the church changed, but by 1975 she had concluded "that sexism was inherent in the symbol system of
Christianity itself and that a primary function of Christianity in Western culture has been to legitimize sexism."[5]
Christianity is so "totally patriarchal" and its theology so
phallocentric and mysogynist "that merely removing symp-
toms will not cure the disease."[6]

Another example is Naomi Goldenberg, whose book
Changing of the Gods is subtitled "Feminism and the End
of Traditional Religions." Some religious feminists, she
says, "are trying to save Judaism and Christianity by
reform of the sexist practices in their traditions," while
others advocate their complete abandonment. Goldenberg
concludes, "Although I admire the energy of the reformers,
I see them engaged in a hopeless effort. Analysis of their
work reveals the futility of any attempt to defend patriarchal creeds."[7] As a precedent for this pessimism Goldenberg cites Elizabeth Cady Stanton — "the first feminist
critic of biblical traditions" — and her *Woman's Bible.*[8]

If the Biblical or Judeo-Christian tradition is no longer
an option, with other traditional religions faring no better,
where can a feminist turn to find spiritual fulfilment?
Many are finding it in an old tradition that remained
underground until occultism became culturally respectable
in the 1960s, namely, the variety of neo-pagan religions
that worship "the Goddess," especially witchcraft. Thus we
have a branch of feminism seeking to "return to the Goddess." Neo-pagan spirituality as such is distinct from feminism, having existed long before the women's movement

79

began. And certainly not all neo-pagans are feminists or women. But so many feminists are finding a spiritual home there that neo-pagan Goddess worship is often referred to as "women's spirituality." They especially like the emphasis on a feminine deity, or Goddess, since they consider the word *God* to be inseparably linked with maleness and patriarchy.[9]

Some see feminism and Goddess religion as highly compatible, even "made for each other." Adler says it is a form of spirituality "that does not compromise political concerns." Many have made the transition because "the step from the CR group to the coven was not long." Adler cites this observation from Morgan McFarland, a feminist Witch:

> ... I have begun to see a resurgence of women returning to the Goddess, seeing themselves as Her daughters, finding Paganism on their own within a very feminist context. Feminism implies equality, self-identification, and individual strength for women. Paganism has been, for all practical purposes, anti-establishment spirituality. Feminists and Pagans are both coming from the same source without realizing it, and heading toward the same goal without realizing it, and the two are now beginning to interlace.[10]

The bottom line, then, is that Goddess feminism has the same basic goals as secular feminism, but seeks them from within a spiritual framework. The main point of this chapter is to explain the nature of that framework as it has been adapted for feminist purposes.

I. THE GODDESS

There are many forms of neo-paganism, but one thing they have in common is a veneration of female deity or deities. "No matter how diverse Neo-Pagans' ideas about

80

deities, almost all of them have some kind of 'Thou Art God/dess' concept."[11] Exactly what is meant by "the Goddess," and how have feminists appropriated this concept for themselves?

A. Reconstruction of History

The first thing that feminists do with Goddess religion is use it to reconstruct the history of the last several thousand years or more. The point is to represent Goddess worship as the original nearly-universal religion, one which produced a "kinder, gentler" world of peace and genuine progress. Unfortunately, about five thousand or so years ago, the Goddess was overwhelmed and replaced by male gods and patriarchal cultures that have glorified domination, destruction, and death. We have reached the point that unless we reject the latter and return to the Goddess, our civilization and our planet are doomed.

1. The Original Goddess Culture

There are two versions of the nature of the original Goddess culture. One is that there was a time when the Great Goddess was regarded as reigning supreme, a situation which must have had as a corollary a matriarchal culture in which women were regarded as superior to men. The other is that the original culture honored both gods and goddesses alike, with the corollary that neither men nor women were regarded as supreme but rather lived in a kind of partnership arrangement.

One of the first to work out the Great Goddess hypothesis was Merlin Stone in her book *When God Was A Woman*. Mainly through an analysis of archeological discoveries she concluded that "the Great Goddess – the Divine Ancestress – had been worshiped from the beginnings of the Neolithic periods of 7000 BC until the closing of the last Goddess temples, about AD 500." Some even extend Goddess worship back into the Upper Paleolithic Age of about

25,000 BC.[12] Thus "in the beginning, people prayed to the Creatress of Life, the Mistress of Heaven. At the very dawn of religion, God was a woman." In that age "the Goddess was omnipotent, and women acted as Her clergy, controlling the form and rites of religion."[13] This Divine Ancestress, Mother Goddess, Queen of Heaven, and Lady of the Universe "was revered as the supreme deity," as "Goddess – much as people today think of God."[14] This female deity was not simply a figure in a fertility cult but was venerated "as creator and lawmaker of the universe, prophetess, provider of human destinies, inventor, healer, hunter and valiant leader in battle."[15]

A more recent and more passionate defense of the Great Goddess idea is *The Great Cosmic Mother* by Monica Sjöö and Barbara Mor. The evidence confirms, they say, "that the first 'God' was female."[16] This first God – Mother Earth or the Great Mother – was "the truly original Creatrix."[17] This was the original monotheism. "The worship of one God, like everything else in religion, began with the worship of the Goddess."[18] This Goddess worship was the original religion, and it "dominated human thought and feeling for at least 300,000 years."[19]

The corollary to this original Goddess religion was a matriarchal society. It is assumed that the supremacy of a female Goddess would be either the cause or the effect of a society dominated by women. Sjöö and Mor say it was the effect: "The religious beliefs, the mysteries and rites developed by ancient women, grew organically out of women's supreme roles as cultural producers, mothers, and prime communicators with the spirit world."[20] One of the main points of their book is that women were the original creators of culture, not men. This includes the creation of religion: "The first religions on earth were designed *by women*, for women, and in celebration of femaleness."[21] Which is the cause and which is the effect is not crucial; the main point is the supposed existence of the matriarchy. "The central thesis of the matriarchy argument," says Adler, is "that there have been ages and places where women held a much greater share of power than they do now."[22]

A major problem with this hypothesis is that there is a lack of conclusive evidence as to whether such ancient matriarchies actually existed. The same is true of a universal Mother Goddess religion itself: "Mainstream scholarship – some of it by women – is continuing to deal strong blows to the idea of such a universal religion."[23] Riane Eisler agrees that the evidence simply does not support the existence of prehistorical matriarchies.[24]

This lack of evidence has led some feminists to formulate a second, more moderate version of the nature of the original Goddess culture. According to this view there was not a single dominant "Great Goddess" but a plurality of goddesses – and gods, each of whom received an equitable share of human reverence. Also, the culture that accompanied this multifaceted pantheon was neither altogether patriarchal nor totally matriarchal, but it was varied enough for women to have a share of the power. As Adler sums it up, "Many feminists . . . tend to drop the arguments for a universal stage of matriarchy and instead simply state that goddess worship was widespread in many ancient societies," and that there were "societies where women held greater power than they do now." There were "goddesses from a thousand cultures" and "many ancient cultures where women wielded power."[25]

A recent proponent of this view is Riane Eisler, in her book *The Chalice and the Blade.* She does not necessarily deny that there was an era of female monotheism with "a complex religion centering on the worship of a Mother Goddess as the source and regeneratrix of all forms of life." What she does deny is that this "primacy of the Goddess" implies the existence of a culture in which women dominated men.[26] Her view is that in the original Goddess era neither men nor women dominated, but rather they shared power in a partnership model. The culture was neither patriarchal nor matriarchal; it was not hierarchical in either sense but was egalitarian. It was "a partnership society in which neither half of humanity is ranked over the other and diversity is not equated with inferiority or superiority."[27] An important aspect of Eisler's view is that neither men nor women wielded the masculine type of power that seizes and dominates, symbolized by the blade of a sword. Rather, their normative ideal was feminine power, the power to nurture and to give, as symbolized by the chalice.[28]

2. The Emergence of Patriarchy

Goddess feminists may not agree on all the details about the nature of the original Goddess culture, but they do agree that it existed in one form or another. They also agree that the era in which the Goddess prevailed and women either dominated or shared power was supplanted almost universally by a patriarchal culture in which the male God is supreme and males dominate females in general. The belief in such a "Fall" is a key element in this form of feminism.

This concept of the eclipse of the Goddess and the emergence of patriarchy is described in different ways but always very negatively, as might be expected. For example, Charlene Spretnak laments the time when the Earth Goddess or Mother Earth was

> . . . diminished and eventually suppressed almost to extinction by the introduction of the sky-God concept. That notion was brought into Europe by the Indo-European invaders, nomadic cattlemen who first migrated from the Eurasian steppes into southeastern Europe in about 4500 B.C. Eventually they spread all across Europe, establishing a patriarchal chieftain system, adoration of the warrior, and their Thunderbolt God. The sky-God, in addition to being a judgmental, vindictive patriarch, was alienated and spatially distant from experiential Earth wisdom. . . .[29]

This same point is made in more detail in Merlin Stone's *When God Was A Woman*. She dates the invasion by the Indo-Europeans a bit later, but the result was the same. Eventually the invaders' storm god or male deity prevailed over the Goddess, whose religion was seriously suppressed in the second and first millennia B.C., especially by the Hebrews. The female religion did not just naturally fade away, but "was the victim of centuries of continual persecution and suppression by the advocates of the newer religions which held male deities as supreme."[30]

Drawing on the same kind of historical data, Eisler posits a time when the partnership model inspired by the Goddess gave way to the dominator model associated with males and male gods. Thus "the original partnership direction of Western culture veered off into a bloody five-thousand-year dominator detour."[31] As early as the fifth millennium B.C. the war-like invaders began to disrupt the peaceful Goddess worshipers of the Neolithic societies, eventually supplanting their culture with one dominated by males and male deities and a value system that emphasized the power of the blade.[32]

Thus according to this kind of reconstruction, patriarchal religions and male-dominated history are "relatively recent," as Sjöö and Mor put it. Whereas the original Goddess religion dominated human thought for at least 300,000 years, the reactionary "Father God religions," in which God is conceptualized as a complete male, have been around for only about three or four thousand years.[33] A common idea is that all modern Western religions, which exalt male deities rather than the Goddess, have thus been developed for the express purpose of celebrating and legitimizing male power.[34]

3. Return to the Goddess

What is happening now as a result of the women's spirituality movement is a "return to the Goddess." According to Goddess feminists this is what must continue to happen on a larger and larger scale if feminism is going to achieve its ultimate goals – and if the world is going to survive. The challenge is to "reverse the reversal," to return to a religious and social system in which feminine values prevail, in which the power of the Blade is banished and the power of the Chalice once again prevails.[35] Such a return must be accomplished by women.

> Women, designed by evolution as the links between spirit and flesh, are perhaps also designed by the cosmos to lead the human world back, now, to the great celebration of the reconciliation of flesh and spirit. Thus, at the very edge of death, we will return to the beginning. That is, at the end of the world, we will return to the Goddess, the Great Mother of All Life, as her magic children. . . .[36]

Some take this idea of a return to the Goddess quite literally, as will be evident in the section on witchcraft below. They call themselves neo-pagans, venerate a female deity, and regard women as the true spiritual leaders. On the assumption that the usurping patriarchy has spent the last several thousand years perverting and falsifying reality in favor of males, these feminists are eager to reclaim and reinterpret history ("herstory") and culture in terms of females, which will then be the true version.

This applies especially to the area of spirituality. Goddess feminists are working hard to revise ("reclaim") the various elements of their neo-pagan (occult) religion as being originally gynocentric (woman-centered). For example, Diane Stein has written a book on the Chinese divination method known as I Ching, entitled *The Kwan Yin Book of Changes.*[37] According to the publisher's advertisement, in this book Stein "reclaims power stolen from women six thousand years ago." The full text of the advertisement explains this point in detail:

This is the age of reclaiming. Women, and others, are taking back a past, long camouflaged and hidden by a patriarchy fearful of losing its power. Where the Goddess and the spirituality of women and, the female side of all our natures was hidden and suppressed, now blossoms a new awareness grown from very, very ancient seeds. The heritage stolen long ago is being reclaimed . . . .

The traditional Chinese I Ching is almost entirely male dominated. It reflects a court hierarchy, sexist at its very core. . . . Where the traditional bases earthly government on the emperor and his hierarchy, this new approach is a government ruled by the consensus of the women who comprise her.

Women's reclaiming these energies of the I Ching is a thousand years overdue. Coming from a civilization where the woman warrior is very much alive in legend, tradition and reality, the I Ching as we know it has been distorted by the patriarchy which even now dominates China. *The Kwan Yin Book of Changes* is a balancing of the injustices that domination represents. It is a new cornerstone in the rebuilding of the Temple of the Goddess.[38]

In other books this same kind of revision is applied to the Tarot deck and to astrology.[39]

Although some do take it literally, not all "Goddess feminists" seek a literal return or revival of the ancient female religion. They see the return as more symbolic than actual, and the main point of the reconstruction of history in terms of the Goddess is to shatter the claims of contemporary patriarchy and its grip on modern culture. As Merlin Stone explains, her hope is

. . . that a contemporary consciousness of the once-widespread veneration of the female deity as the wise Creatress of the Universe and all life and civilization may be used to cut through the many oppressive and falsely founded patriarchal images, stereotypes, cus-

87

toms and laws that were developed as direct reactions to Goddess worship by the leaders of the later male-worshiping religions. For . . . it was the ideological inventions of the advocates of the later male deities, imposed upon that ancient worship with the intention of destroying it and its customs, that are still, through their subsequent absorption into education, law, literature, economics, philosophy, psychology, media and general social attitudes, imposed upon even the most non-religious people of today.[40]

This Goddess-consciousness must ultimately involve "death for the great male gods" and the end of a patriarchal approach to authority.[41] In this sense the symbolical "return to the Goddess" helps to demote males from their false thrones and to thrust women back into the mainstream of culture.

B. The Nature of the Goddess

This leads us to the very important question of the *nature* of the Goddess to which these feminists are seeking to return. Exactly what is meant by the term *Goddess*?

When most Christians use the term *God*, they are referring to a personal being who has objective existence distinct from this world and from created beings in general. Even when they speak of pagan gods and goddesses, most Christians assume that these terms refer to distinct beings that are thought to exist by their devotees but in actuality do not exist at all. It would be a serious mistake, however, to think that this is what feminists mean when they speak of the Goddess.

In Goddess feminism the Goddess is *not* an actual, distinct, personal, objectively-existing female deity. This is true even for the most seriously spiritual and for those who seek to return to the Goddess in a literal sense. The Goddess simply does not exist "as a being or person." Such a deity would not be any improvement over patriarchy. "The idea of a single Goddess, conceived of as transcendent and apart, creates as many problems as the male 'God.' Trading 'Daddy' for 'Mommy' is not a liberation."[42] The feminist witch Starhawk acknowledges that the term Goddess makes many people uneasy because it "can be mistaken for the worship of an external being." Thus she explains, "Let us be clear that when I say *Goddess* I am not talking about a being somewhere outside of this world."[43] Mary Daly has declared that "God" is not a noun but a verb, indeed the Verb of Verbs; "God" is not a being but is Be-ing.[44] This was written in 1973; since at least 1978 Daly has been using the term *Goddess* instead of *God* because the latter cannot be separated from patriarchy.[45] Even so, she says, it is a mistake to reify the deity as if it were a separate being or "the supreme being." There is no reified "noun-goddess," only the "Verb-Goddess."[46]

This does not mean that the Goddess has no existence at all. It *does* exist, but *not as a separate being*. Rather, the Goddess is identified with all being (in a kind of pantheistic sense), or with the life-force or spirit that animates all being (in a kind of panentheistic sense). The deity is not a transcendent Being, but is immanent in all being. The Goddess is the world, the universe.[47] Using the terms God and Goddess interchangeably, Sjöö and Mor say,

God is the universe. We are all now living inside the body of God. There is nowhere to go to get there, we are already here. There is nowhere to go to get outside of God; there is just a forgetting of this truth. It is impossible not to be living, right now and always, within God's body. It is only possible to be aware, or unaware, of this fact.[48]

Usually the Goddess is identified with one major aspect of the universe, namely, the planet Earth. The first deity was Mother Earth or the Earth Mother.[49] This idea is emphasized in the very title of the book by Sjöö and Mor,

The Great Cosmic Mother: Rediscovering the Religion of the Earth. The earth is personified "as a conscious and spiritual being" and is given the name *Gaia.*[50]

Even more specifically, the Goddess is thought of as being identified in some way with women themselves. In a way this could simply be a logical conclusion from the major premise that the Goddess is the universe (minor premise: women are part of the universe; conclusion: women are part of the Goddess). But there is more to it than this. Goddess feminists seem to believe that the Goddess – universal spirit, earth power – is more authentically present in women or represented in women than anywhere else. The Goddess *is* – literally *is* – a woman's true self or inner self or inner experience. This is true both individually and collectively. The Goddess is not transcendent either to the universe or to the individual; the Goddess is *within.* "Recognizing the divine Goddess within is where real religion is at."[51]

This is a point of general agreement and seems to be at the very heart and core of Goddess feminism. Thus it must be clearly understood. Merlin Stone sums it up thus: "One very important aspect of reclaiming a feminine spirituality is that of the vision or concept one has of deity or the divine. Within nearly all expressions of contemporary women's spirituality is the idea of Goddess not as a woman sitting on a throne above the clouds, i.e., transcendent, apart from us, but as immanent, within ourselves."[52] "You are the Goddess," says Hallie Inglehart. The term is a kind of "archetype or metaphor for female energy."[53] In an article entitled "goddess with a small g," one feminist said it thus: "I do not believe in a Goddess. Not a Goddess who exists as a being or person. Yes, the goddess who is each of us, the one within. . . . There is no one called 'Goddess' to seek outside of ourselves or to enter into us. There is only in each our own center of unity energy which is connected to all."[54] Another said, "I am and you are the goddess, she is here right now. She's alive; she's reinvented; she's chang-

90

ing and growing with us."[55] A modern "golden text" for feminists is a line from the Broadway play *for colored girls who have considered suicide when the rainbow is enuf,* when a beautiful black woman cries out, "I found God in myself and I loved her fiercely." This, says Carol Christ, admirably represents women's "fierce new love of the divine in themselves."[56]

Still we must remember that this "Goddess within" cannot be separated from the divine presence that exists in all things; there is thus a kind of mystical bond between women and the earth or nature in general. Carol Christ says that the Goddess brings the two together: "she is woman and she is nature."[57] Merlin Stone says that more and more women are seeing the Goddess as existing in all manifestations of life, as "the flowing energy in the very processes of life and living." Thus the Goddess is "the actual organic process, the flow, the changes, transitions, and transformations that the person, tree, or river go through."[58] According to Starhawk, the immanent Goddess "lies coiled in the heart of every cell of every living thing" and "is the spark of every nerve and the life of every breath."[59]

C. The Significance of the Goddess for Feminism

As we have seen, there is some disagreement as to just how much hard evidence exists for an unambiguous era of the "Great Goddess" and matriarchy. But one thing Goddess feminists agree on is the importance of the idealized vision of such an era for the future, whether it existed in the past or not. As Adler says, "The idea of matriarchy has ramifications that go beyond the question of whether or not the matriarchy ever existed in reality." What matters is the "creative use of the idea of matriarchy as *vision* and *ideal.*" The spiritual feminists "do not feel their future is contingent on a hypothesized past."[60] The power is in the idea itself. History or myth, it's all the same.[61]

Why is the Goddess concept so significant for feminists? Here we will isolate two main reasons. First, it is crucial for the purposes of feminism as such; second, it is crucial for the hope of the planet in general.

Regarding feminism as such, we must remember that its main goal involves both the overthrow of patriarchy and its thesis of male supremacy, and also the elevation of women to a status of equality and independent power. One of the main hindrances to achieving this goal, feminists believe, is the influence of the traditional religions, especially their concept of God as male. As long as the deity is thought of in male terms, the goal of women's liberation will never be achieved. As Mary Daly succinctly puts it, "If God is male, then the male is God."[62] Also, "If God in 'his' heaven is a father ruling 'his' people, then it is in the 'nature' of things and according to divine plan and the order of the universe that society be male-dominated."[63]

As Carol Christ puts it, "In religions in which God is primarily imaged in language associated with the male gender, maleness is deified as the source of all legitimate power and authority."[64] She also points out that the way people conceptualize God has a tremendous psychological effect on them even if they are atheists. The symbolism of a male God is so strong that it creates moods and motivations that "keep women in a state of psychological dependence on men and male authority," while at the same time it legitimates the political and social authority of fathers and sons in the institutions of society. "Religious symbol systems focused around exclusively male images of divinity create the impression that female power can never be fully legitimate or wholly beneficent."[65]

But if the deity is thought of as female, as Goddess, then male superiority is not of the very essence of things, and the keystone of patriarchy crumbles. If the deity is female, then the status and the morale of women are automatically elevated. Women can feel good and positive about their femaleness.

The second reason why a female deity is so important for Goddess feminists is that they see it as the only hope for the future of the planet earth. This concept involves the recognition of important distinctions between males and females as such (a point on which all feminists do not agree). Some attributes are characterized as feminine and some as masculine. In the prehistorical Goddess era, the feminine traits prevailed. These are the traits represented by Eisler's chalice symbolism: the attributes of caring and giving and nurturing, passive attributes that lead to peace and to harmony with each other and with nature.[66] Such was the spirit of the Goddess era.

But when the Goddess was eclipsed by male gods, and when patriarchy took over some five or six thousand years ago, everything changed. Human history and the earth itself began to experience the effects of the masculine temperament, which is inclined to war and violence and domination and death. This introduction of the male god idea was the true Fall of the universe, the beginning of everything bad upon the earth. In a world ruled by a male God, such things as warfare, aggression, suffering, sadism, human degradation, economic exploitation, and sheer ugliness are inevitable.[67] A particularly destructive result of the religion of the male God was the idea of a transcendent deity, one separated from the earth, leading to an ontological dualism in which the creation and the human body are seen as evil, which in turn leads to all sorts of alienated relationships and to the very idea of sin itself, especially sexual sin.[68]

All this sounds rather extreme, but it is the conventional wisdom among Goddess feminists. In Eisler's terms, "the roots of our present global crises" go back to that time when the supremacy of the life-giving Chalice was replaced by the destructive power of the Blade. That was when "the original partnership direction of Western culture veered off into a bloody five-thousand-year dominator detour," of which "our mounting global problems are in large part the

logical consequences."[69] Unless a paradigm shift occurs
and male dominance comes to an end, things will only get
worse, because "under an androcratic system our worsening problems are in fact insoluble." A dominator (i.e., male)
future can only end in global nuclear war.[70] Daly agrees
that phallocratic domination has produced "material pollution that threatens to terminate all sentient life on this
planet," as well as "the mind/spirit/body pollution inflicted
through patriarchal myth and language." She agrees that
"the fate of the human species and of the planet is at
stake," and that the only solution is a Goddess-based feminism.[71] Thus there is a "desperate need to return to a
world centered on woman and the idea of a Goddess."[72]

In the minds of Goddess feminists, then, the relation
between feminism and Goddess spirituality is not just incidental and is not even one option among many. They see it
as the key to the success of the women's movement and to
the salvation of modern civilization.

II. GODDESS FEMINISM AND WITCHCRAFT

Several times in this chapter references have been made
to witchcraft and to feminists who are witches. The fact is
that most feminists who are attracted to Goddess spirituality identify themselves as witches. This is because
witchcraft as an ancient religion already had a feminine
cast about it long before the rise of feminism as a cultural
force. Many of its rituals and beliefs were already Goddess
oriented, and it has always been primarily though not
exclusively identified with women. Thus it is not surprising that it should become the religion of choice among Goddess feminists.

This connection is explored by Margot Adler in her book
Drawing Down the Moon, which is an excellent detailed
survey of witchcraft and the many other forms of neo-
paganism in the United States today. One long chapter
deals specifically with feminism. It is called "Women, Fem-

inism, and the Craft."[73] She says, "The presence of the feminist movement as a force that connects with Neo-Paganism and modern Witchcraft has had many ramifications. Links have been forged between these groups and new strains have been created."[74] Naomi Goldenberg in *Changing of the Gods* also has a good analysis of this connection. Her chapter is called "Feminist Witchcraft – The Goddess Is Alive!"[75]

How is it possible that so many modern women, many of them highly sophisticated, can be drawn to a form of religion as primitive and sinister as witchcraft? This question assumes an understanding of witchcraft that is regarded as passé in Western culture today. The traditional image of witches as old hags with warts on their noses, dressed in long black robes and pointed hats, stirring some vile concoction and muttering curses, is quite outdated. Modern witches see themselves as normal people with normal jobs and normal roles in the community; they regard their religion as different but not sinister. They believe themselves to be in unbroken continuity with the "old religion" (that is, older than Christianity) especially of ancient Europe and Great Britain. They believe in the existence of a natural and neutral power or energy or life-force ("the Goddess") that permeates the universe and that can be manipulated by those who understand it and are tuned in to it. Knowing how to manipulate this force, to "move energy," is the special skill or craft of witches. It is also called magic.[76]

The terms *witchcraft* and *wicca* (sometimes *wicce*) are used interchangeably, the former being considered as a derivative of the latter, which is an old English word. Speculation abounds as to their exact connotation. An old unabridged Random House dictionary gives this notation as the origin of "witch": "OE *wicce*. See *WICKED*." Under "wicked" it says, "ME *wikked*, equiv. to *wikke* bad." This of course is the very connotation modern witches vehemently reject. Many prefer to find the origin of the terms in the

English root "wit," which connotes knowledge or wisdom.
Thus they speak of witchcraft as wisecraft or the craft of
the wise, and a witch as a wise woman. The idea is that a
witch is one who has the right knowledge to manipulate
energy. Others trace the terms to the root word "wic" or
"weik," which means to bend or turn or twist. This also
would refer to the ability to bend or manipulate the life-
force immanent in the universe. Adler prefers the latter
view; thus "a Witch would be a woman (or man) skilled in
the craft of shaping, bending, and changing reality."[77]
Goldenberg agrees; witches are those who know "how to
bend the world to their will."[78]

But what particularly draws feminists to witchcraft is
its emphasis on the Goddess, and thus its connection with
women and matriarchy and with that ancient age when
goddesses and women were supreme. It is thus a ready-
made way of "returning to the Goddess." Starhawk sums it
up in this paragraph:

> The Old Religion – call it Witchcraft, Wicca, the Craft,
> or with a slightly broader definition, Paganism or
> Neo-Paganism – is both old and newly invented. Its
> roots go back to the pre-Judeo-Christian tribal reli-
> gions of the West, and it is akin in spirit, form, and
> practice to Native American and African religions. Its
> myths and symbols draw from the woman-valuing,
> matristic, Goddess-centered cultures that underlie
> the beginnings of civilization. It is not a religion with
> a dogma, a doctrine, or a sacred book; it is a religion
> of experience, of ritual, of practices that change con-
> sciousness and awaken power-from-within. Beneath
> all, it is a religion of connection with the Goddess,
> who is immanent in nature, in human beings, in rela-
> tionships. Because the Goddess is *here*, She is eter-
> nally inspirational. And so Witchcraft is eternally
> reinvented, changing, growing, alive.[79]

Thus it is no wonder that witchcraft is *the* religion of
many feminists. Even in the 1979 edition of her book,

Adler noted that feminist covens were springing up all over the United States. Witchcraft was being "adopted as 'the religion' of a large portion of the feminist spiritual community," most of whom were not interested in other forms of neo-paganism.[80] In the 1986 edition Adler added, "The women's spirituality movement is now so large and undefinable that it is like an ocean whose waves push against all shores. There are some who have estimated that Starhawk's book *The Spiral Dance* has *alone* created a thousand women's covens and spiritual groups."[81]

At first there was some tension between traditional wiccans and the feminists who wanted to be witches. Some of the former accused the feminists of just wanting to use witchcraft as a means of promoting their political ends and of not embracing it sincerely and totally. In 1979 Adler noted that "positive reactions to feminism are not prevalent in the Craft."[82] The feminists disagreed, however, claiming that the Goddess herself was simply using feminism to make the craft more inclusive and to broaden its influence. They pointed out that both movements shared the common sorrow of male oppression and persecution, as well as a common spirit of rebellion. Soon many of the traditional witches came to accept this point of view and began to welcome the feminists and their political agenda into their circle. By 1986 Adler could say, "The tensions between the feminist and traditional Craft are much less evident."[83]

Most feminists and most witches would now see their movements as a natural partnership, as "two streams flowing to form a single river," with "the Old Religion providing the psychic interaction and the women's movement the political context, both seeking to transform the society and provide a more open life for all."[84] The final chapter in Sjöö and Mor's fierce defense of Goddess feminism relates their endeavor to witchcraft, and the book ends with a traditional wiccan prayer.[85] Mary Daly avows that "real knowledge implies participation in the Craft/Wisdom of Witches

(Witchcraft)."[86] Goldenberg declares that "all covens support feminist ideology to some degree."[87]

Several of the most prominent Goddess feminists are considered to be leading witches. Perhaps the most influential is Miriam Simos, who uses the name Starhawk. She has been described as "a matriarch of feminist spirituality."[88] We have quoted here from her book, *Dreaming the Dark*. Also important is her handbook for witches, *The Spiral Dance*.[89] We noted Adler's comment above that the latter book has probably created a thousand women's covens. One feminist book catalogue describes it thus:

> Considered by some to be a Wiccan "bible," this is an initiation workbook into the ancient religion of the Great Goddess, offered by a well-known priestess of the Craft. Contains . . . the basics of Wicca and feminist pagan theory. Shows how the path of Goddess offers transformative power to heal the political/spiritual split within self and society.[90]

One other influential feminist witch that deserves to be mentioned here is Z Budapest. (The Z stands for Zsuzsanna.) While Starhawk might be called a feminist who is a witch, Budapest is a witch who is a feminist. She has been called "the mother of the modern Goddess movement."[91] A Hungarian refugee, she moved to California and in 1971 founded the Susan B. Anthony Coven Number One, of which she is the high priestess.[92] She is an earthy woman who lectures widely and has written several books on feminist witchcraft, including *The Holy Book of Women's Mysteries*,[93] which has been called a "feminist survival guide" in which "women's rights and women's rites combine in a celebration of the Goddess."[94]

III. THE APPEAL OF GODDESS FEMINISM

Starhawk and Budapest are only two of "literally hundreds of other women" (according to Adler) who are spreading the gospel of Goddess feminism. "Workshops, classes, and lectures on women's spirituality and the power of the ancient goddesses are everywhere, at adult education centers, at feminist bookstores, and new age institutes." The idea of the Goddess, she says, has entered the mainstream of American culture. "It is absolutely common for women to mention the Goddess in public and have the person next to them actually know what they are talking about." Goddess feminists are even "entering theological seminaries in large numbers, and they are writing new history and new thealogy."[95]

Since she published *When God Was a Woman* in 1975, says Merlin Stone, she has been astonished at the large volume of subsequent research and writing devoted to all aspects of the Goddess. "The reclaimed information has been incorporated into writings on ecology, healing, sociology, history, psychology, philosophy, theology, the visual arts, and general global concerns. The Goddess has also found her way into paintings, sculpture, films, poetry, novels, drama, dance, and song."[96]

One only has to examine a volume such as *The Womanspirit Sourcebook*, compiled by Patrice Wynne, to be personally impressed with the large amount of material available on this subject.[97] Its front cover describes its contents thus: "A catalog of books, periodicals, music, calendars & tarot cards, organizations, video & audio tapes, bookstores, interviews, meditations, art." Adler's book, *Drawing Down the Moon*, likewise has a lengthy section (pp. 475-551) of resources relating to all forms of neopaganism, including descriptions of 135 newsletters and journals, 75 groups, and numerous festivals and gatherings.

The listings and descriptions in the 1990 Iris Sacred Circle's "Goddess Spirituality Catalog" provide a succinct look at the content of the gospel of Goddess feminism as it makes its appeal to women today. The sixteen-page catalogue, hand-lettered and "printed on 100% recycled paper, for the love of mother earth," is "dedicated to Goddess, to the healing of our mother earth, and to the liberation of all beings, within a positive, pagan way of enlightenment." Some of its entries are as follows:

Ancient Mirrors of Womanhood, by Merlin Stone. "Goddess Lore from many cultures and throughout the ages."

The Chalice and the Blade, by Riane Eisler. "Powerfully reconstructs the Goddess culture and the global shift to patriarchy."

Daughters of Copperwoman, by Anne Cameron. "Stories and legends . . . of a secret matriarchal society whose roots go back to ancient times."

Daughters of the Moon Tarot Deck, by Ffiona Morgan. "With images of Goddesses, matriarchs, and amazons."

Dreaming the Dark, by Starhawk. "A very inspiring work of pagan thealogy" with "an important herstory of the Burning Times."

The Great Cosmic Mother, by Monica Sjöö and Barbara Mor. "Best case yet for discounting the sway of patriarchal religions and returning to the matriarchal vision."

Healing the Wounds, ed. Judith Plant. "Weaving together the strengths of ecology and feminism . . . ecofeminist spirituality."

Ishtar Rising, by Robert Wilson. "In the last 3000 years, the Goddess has descended to hell – gradually at first as patriarchy emerged . . . and then with catastrophic speed after Christianity arose to damn the female half of humanity to sub-human status – and now the Goddess is beginning to rise again."

The Many Faces of the Great Mother, by Diane Brown. "A Goddess coloring book for all ages."

Motherpeace Round Tarot Deck, by Vicki Noble and Karen Vogel. To "help to awaken the Goddess within."

The Mother's Songs, by Meinrad Craighead. "Inspired by God the Mother."

The Politics of Women's Spirituality, ed. Charlene Spretnak. "Essays on the rise of women's spirituality within the feminist movement."

The Sacred Hoop, by Paula Gunn Allen. "A feminist reclaiming of Native American traditions, showing that Native American cultures are essentially gynocratic."

Womanspirit Rising, ed. Carol Christ and Judith Plaskow. "A reader in feminist spirituality . . . now classic."

Banana flower essence. "Develops in men those good qualities traditionally named 'feminine.'"

Blue corn flower essence. Develops a "spiritual relationship with Mother Earth."

Hyssop flower essence. "Eliminates guilt."

"Barely Lace" music cassette. "Original songs about the sacred Mother, and the magical female."

"A Circle Is Cast" music cassette. "Hauntingly beautiful earth-centered spiritual songs from a feminist chorus, celebrating Goddess and our earth connections."

"Emergence" music cassette. "Joyful Goddess songs (inspired by dolphins!)."

"Eye of the Womb" music cassette. "Use of primal rhythmic energy as a creative expression of women's spirituality and as a bridge between politics and faith."

"From the Goddess" music cassette. "Well-known Goddess chants" capture "the essence of pre-Christian feminist traditions."

"The Queen of Earth and Sky" music cassette. "Songs
of love, magic, and Goddess religion, from a feminist
witch."

The catalogue ends with this prayer: "May Goddess bless
and guide Iris Sacred Circle. . . . So mote it be."

It should be clear that Goddess feminism is a well-
defined subculture and that many women have been
attracted to it. "The attractiveness of the Goddess to
women was inevitable," Adler believes. She says, "It is not
surprising that spiritual feminists, in their explorations of
the hidden and distorted history of women, have been
attracted by the idea of a universal age of goddess worship
or a universal stage of matriarchy."[98] This raises the following question: specifically what is there about Goddess
spirituality (including its principal form, witchcraft) that
appeals to feminists?

A. Its Radical Nature

One thing about the Goddess that appeals to feminists
is its sheer radicalness. The more a course of action shocks
the patriarchal establishment, the more some feminists
like it; and few things would be more shocking than for an
otherwise respectable woman to call herself a witch! A
former Roman Catholic nun, a co-editor of the book *Lesbian Nuns,* says, "I like to call myself a witch because the
word carries such patriarchal taboo."[99]

This appeal is especially powerful to lesbian separatists,
says Adler, since they have already made the biggest break
with society at large. They feel a kinship or identity with
the antiestablishment mythical images associated with the
Goddess, such as Virgin Huntresses and Great Mothers.
Embracing Goddess spirituality helps them to accomplish
their goal of removing themselves entirely from the mainstream of our male-contaminated society. In Adler's judgment "the feminist Craft and the movement toward

feminist spirituality seems to have a larger percentage of lesbians" than either the feminist movement as such or neo-paganism as a whole.[100]

B. Its Symbolism of Female Power

Another obvious appeal of Goddess spirituality to feminists is the centrality of its female imagery, especially its emphasis on female power. This helps to counter the influence of thousands of years of male-god imagery with its legitimizing of male dominance and power. The ascendancy of the Goddess transfers power to the female instead. Women collectively are viewed as power figures, and individual women are infused with a personal sense of power.

In 1978 Carol Christ wrote an essay entitled "Why Women Need the Goddess," which is included in her book *Laughter of Aphrodite.*[101] The most important point in that essay, she says, "is that Goddesses are about female power." This is why the ancient Goddess images are appealing to women: they reflect female power; they symbolize "the legitimacy of female power as a beneficient and independent power." To acknowledge the Goddess within is to affirm, "Female power is strong and creative." To acknowledge the Goddess within is to declare independence from male power and from male figures as saviors.[102]

In feminist thinking the patriarchal concept of power is "power over," or one person exercising power over another person. The idea of the Goddess within is a liberating concept for women, because it replaces the concept of "power over" with "power from within." It provides a spiritual basis for women's sense of autonomy and independence. A witch named Mary Lee George says this is why witchcraft is appealing to women. "Feminist witchcraft offers a woman a new definition of power. The patriarchial definition of power is to have power over someone else. But in feminist witchcraft power is from within myself."[103]

Goldenberg agrees that this concept of the Goddess as a

psychic power immanent within the individual is attractive to feminists. It gives them a sense of their own divinity and of their supremacy over men. She notes that in some witchcraft rituals the participants salute each other with the expression, "Thou art Goddess" (or "Thou art God," if it is a man). This means that "the Goddess is acknowledged as an *internal* presence in the women who are worshiping her." Thus "witchcraft is the only Western religion that recognizes woman as a divinity in her own right."[104] And even though a man is also divinity ("Thou art God"), in feminist witchcraft "the Goddess is valued more highly than the God, with the result that women have a higher position in the power structure."[105]

Goldenberg relates an example of the ability of the Goddess to inspire women with a sense of power. She describes an episode at the first national all-woman conference on women's spirituality, held in April 1976 in a church building in Boston. On opening night two speeches on the theme "Womanpower: Energy Re-Sourcement" led to a spontaneous and very animated demonstration. The women began to chant, "The Goddess Is Alive – Magic Is Afoot"; and they "evoked the Goddess with dancing, stamping, clapping and yelling. They stood on pews and danced barebreasted on the pulpit and amid the hymnbooks." This was an act of defiance against the patriarchal religion and the male god represented by the church building, and an act of power in the name of the Goddess. Goldenberg says, "Proclaiming that the 'Goddess Is Alive' in a traditional church setting is proclaiming that woman is alive, that being female is divine. . . . At this opening of the Boston conference the Goddess represented fierce pride in female physical presence."[106]

The Goddess thus becomes a motivating force for women, moving them to take charge of their own lives.

C. Its Ecological Concern

Another aspect of the appeal of Goddess spirituality to

feminists is their common concern for the future of the planet Earth in view of recent anti-ecological trends such as the pollution of the environment and the waste of natural resources. This has already been explored in an earlier section on the significance of the Goddess for feminism. There we saw how feminists project nothing but disaster for the environment and for civilization in general if the patriarchal, masculine mentality continues to dominate our culture. Some feminists who are deeply concerned about this problem feel it can be solved by converting the world to think and act in accordance with the "kinder, gentler" feminine traits and virtues. In pursuit of this goal they find ready-made allies among peoples of the Goddess.

According to one of its priestesses, all neo-pagans "view the earth as the Great Mother who has been raped, pillaged, and plundered, who must once again be exalted and celebrated if we are to survive."[107] Feminists have a built-in sympathy for this view of the Earth. They see a parallel between the oppression of women and the rape of nature.[108] In drawing this parallel they personify the Earth as the Great Mother or as Gaia and think of it as a living being. It is an easy step for feminists then to identify themselves with this living organism called Earth, and to consider their destinies to be one. The Goddess concept not only gives this oneness with the Earth a theoretical basis but also interprets the whole scenario in terms of divinity, thus adding a sense of extreme urgency to the problem and a sense of extreme guilt for failure to deal with it.

It will be remembered that in Goddess spirituality the Goddess is not thought of as a separate and distinct being who exists apart from the universe, but is actually identified with the universe itself and with all things in it. The Goddess is the life-essence that permeates all things, including women themselves. The Goddess is within nature; the Goddess *is* nature. Thus nature is divine and holy. Carol Christ says, "For me Goddess has always been more than a symbol of female power. Goddess symbolizes my profound conviction that this earth, our source and ground, is holy."[109] If it is holy, we must revere it and venerate it. If we can thus view this earth as the Goddess herself, we will surely cease pillaging it and will begin to respect it and clean it up. Because of our mystical oneness with nature, we will see that harming it means harming ourselves.

Goddess spirituality thus gives feminists a basis upon which or a framework within which to pursue their struggle for the integrity of the environment as a natural corollary to their struggle for women's rights. Someone has coined the term *ecofeminism* to describe this union of the two crusades.

D. Its Celebration of Sexuality

A final reason why Goddess spirituality appeals to feminists is its emphasis on and celebration of sexuality. It will be remembered from the discussion of secular feminism in the preceding chapter that one of the feminists' main goals is sexual autonomy. That women do not have complete control over their own bodies is seen to be the result of male oppression or patriarchal norms relating to marriage and family. According to the reconstruction of history in terms of the Goddess, this all began when male gods and patriarchy displaced the reign of the Goddess several thousand years ago. A key factor in this displacement was the idea that the male god rules over the earth but is separate from the earth, a "sky-god." This was the beginning of the ontological dualism of spirit and matter and the anthropological dualism of spirit and body. Human beings began to think of their god-like spirits as their true and pure essence, and their physical bodies as being evil. This was also the beginning of all kinds of negative thoughts and repressive norms with regard to sexuality. "Sexuality, under the rule of the Father-God, is identified with his Opposition," which includes nature and woman.[110]

Another key factor in the patriarchal seizure of power was the Hebrews' creation of the story of the Fall in Genesis 3, a story in which the woman is portrayed as the cause of all the ills of human existence. As a result women in general are blamed for the Fall and are made to feel guilty for being women and to be ashamed of their bodies and their sexuality.

The way to liberation from this kind of oppression, in which women's bodies and sexuality are held hostage, is the return to the Goddess. In Goddess religion there is no transcendent, spiritual deity who sits high on a throne in judgment on all things physical. The Goddess *is* the Earth; she *is* nature; she *is* the physical; she *is* the body. Her divine energy permeates the whole physical world and blesses all things physical and all bodily processes and functions. She is easy, undemanding, life-giving, body-affirming. In the light of the divine Goddess the body is sacred, and sexuality is not only sacred but is unrestricted by the false norms arising from the false dualism.[111] In Goddess religion sexuality and spirituality are one – especially in women: "For women there is no separation between sex and spirit."[112]

Carol Christ says this is another reason why women need the Goddess, because the Goddess symbol is an affirmation of the female body, over against "the misogynist antibody tradition in Western thought . . . symbolized in the myth of Eve who is traditionally viewed as a sexual temptress, the epitome of women's carnal nature."[113] This includes a positive attitude not only toward sex as such but also toward other functions unique to female sexuality, such as menstruation, childbirth, and menopause.

This understanding of sexuality in Goddess religion is well summed up by Starhawk in the following quotation:

In the ethics of immanence, sexuality is also sacred, deeply valued, not just as the means of procreation, but as a power that infuses life with vitality and pleasure, as the numinous means of deep connection with others. Sexual integrity means honestly recognizing our own impulses and desires and honoring them, whether or not we choose to act on them. If we value integrity, we must also value diversity in sexual expression and orientation, recognizing that there is no one truth, or one way, that fits everyone.[114]

A key idea here is the lack of absolute norms and the acceptance of all kinds of sexual expression including gay and lesbian. "When the ethics is based on integrity instead of authority," says Starhawk, "no one has the right to interfere with another's sexual choice."[115]

Thus by invoking the Goddess one of feminism's main goals is achieved, i.e., sexual autonomy, or more precisely, "female sexual autonomy."[116]

E. Conclusion

In summary, the main elements of Goddess spirituality that appeal to feminists are its sheer radicalness, the symbolism of female power, its ecological concern, and its celebration of sexuality. Since most radical feminists are already interested in these things, it is no wonder that those who desire a spiritual underpinning for their cause are drawn to the Goddess.

Endnotes

1. Los Angeles *Times* (April 10, 1978), I:3, 19, as cited in "To Manipulate a Woman," a pamphlet published by Concerned Women for America, 370 L'Enfant Promenade, Suite 800; Washington, D.C. 20024.

2. Margot Adler, *Drawing Down the Moon: Witches, Druids, Goddess-Worshippers, and Other Pagans in America Today*, revised ed. (Boston: Beacon Press, 1986), pp. 178, 185. Most of the text of this book (including these quotations) remains unchanged from the 1979 edition.

3. Rosemary Radford Ruether, *Sexism and God-Talk: Toward a Feminist Theology* (Boston: Beacon Press, 1983), p. 268.

4. Mary Daly, *The Church and the Second Sex*, Colophon edition, "With a New Feminist Postchristian Introduction by the Author" (New York: Harper, 1975), p. 5. See also Daly, *Beyond God the Father: Toward a Philosophy of Women's Liberation*, new paperback edition, "With an Original Reintroduction by the Author" (Boston: Beacon Press, 1985), pp. xii-xiii.

5. Daly, *The Church and the Second Sex*, pp. 17-18.

6. Ibid., pp. 20, 37.

7. Naomi R. Goldenberg, *Changing of the Gods: Feminism and the End of Traditional Religions* (Boston: Beacon Press, 1979), p. 10.

8. Ibid., pp. 10-13.

9. Mary Daly, *Gyn/Ecology: The Metaethics of Radical Feminism* (Boston: Beacon Press, 1978), p. xi.

10. Adler, *Drawing Down the Moon*, p. 182.

11. Ibid., p. 202.

12. Merlin Stone, *When God Was A Woman* (New York: Dial Press, 1976), p. xii.

13. Ibid., pp. 1-2.

14. Ibid., pp. 18, 22.

15. Ibid., pp. xix-xx.

16. Monica Sjöö and Barbara Mor, *The Great Cosmic Mother: Rediscovering the Religion of the Earth* (San Francisco: Harper & Row, 1987), p. 8.

17. Ibid., pp. 50, 171.

18. Ibid., pp. 265-266.

19. Ibid., p. 235.

20. Ibid., p. 50.

21. Ibid., p. 429.

22. Adler, *Drawing Down the Moon*, p. 190.

23. Ibid., pp. 190, 229.

24. Riane Eisler, *The Chalice and the Blade: Our History, Our Future* (San Francisco; Harper & Row, 1987), pp. 24ff.

25. Adler, *Drawing Down the Moon,* pp. 194, 229. Carol Christ speaks of these "millennia of Goddess religion in which Goddesses were not subordinate to Gods and women had social and religious power" in *Laughter of Aphrodite: Reflections on a Journey to the Goddess* (San Francisco: Harper & Row, 1987), p. 65.

26. Riane Eisler, *The Chalice and the Blade,* pp. 6, 21ff., 27.

27. Ibid., pp. xvii, 24-28.

28. Ibid., p. 28.

29. Charlene Spretnak, "Gaia, Green Politics, and the Great Transformation," in *The Womanspirit Sourcebook,* ed. Patrice Wynne (San Francisco: Harper & Row, 1988), p. 89.

30. Stone, *When God Was A Woman,* pp. xiii, 62-68, 196.

31. Eisler, *The Chalice and the Blade,* p. xxiii.

32. Ibid., pp. 43-44, 48.

33. Sjöö and Mor, *The Great Cosmic Mother,* pp. 12, 235.

34. Christ, *Laughter of Aphrodite,* pp. 50, 119.

35. Eisler, *The Chalice and the Blade,* p. xviii.

36. Sjöö and Mor, *The Great Cosmic Mother,* p. 430.

37. Diane Stein, *The Kwan Yin Book of Changes* (St. Paul: Llewellyn Publications, 1985).

38. *Llewellyn New Times* (November/December 1985), pp. 10-11.

39. Another catalogue advertises a book called *A Feminist Tarot* by Sally Gearhart and Susan Rennie; the book "shows that this traditional deck is inherently feminist." Another book is *The Goddess in Your Stars,* by Geraldine Thorsten: "The only feminist astrological guide, this eye-opening book re-interprets the familiar sun signs according to the original meanings assigned to them by ancient pre-patriarchal societies." Also, Barbara Walker's *I Ching of the Goddess* "recovers the ancient matriarchal roots of this oracle." ("Goddess Spirituality Catalog," 1990 ed., published by Iris Sacred Circle, P.O. Box 68, Burlington, VT 05402, pp. 2-3)

40. Stone, *When God Was A Woman,* p. xxv.

41. Goldenberg, *Changing of the Gods,* p. 9.

42. Adler, *Drawing Down the Moon,* p. 205.

43. Starhawk [Miriam Simos], *Dreaming the Dark: Magic, Sex and Politics,* new ed. (Boston: Beacon Press, 1988), pp. 4, 11.

44. Daly, *Beyond God the Father,* pp. 33-34.

45. Daly, *Gyn/Ecology,* p. xi.

46. Daly, in her 1985 "Original Reintroduction" to *Beyond God the Father,* pp. xvii-xviii.

47. Starhawk, in *Dreaming the Dark,* p. xii, refers to "the Goddess, the universe." Sjöö and Mor declare that "the Goddess *IS* the world" *(The Great Cosmic Mother,* p. 418.)

48. Sjöö and Mor, *The Great Cosmic Mother,* p. 420. In the original this whole paragraph was italicized.

49. Ibid., p. 50.

50. Ibid., p. 421; Eisler, *The Chalice and the Blade,* p. 75.

51. A statement by the feminist witch Z. Budapest, quoted by Adler, *Drawing Down the Moon,* p. 192.

52. Merlin Stone, "Introduction," *The Goddess Re-Awakening: The Feminine Principle Today,* ed. Shirley Nicholson (Wheaton, IL: Theosophical Publishing House, 1989), p. 19.

53. Hallie Inglehart, *Womanspirit: A Guide to Women's Wisdom* (San Francisco: Harper and Row, 1983), p. 97.

54. Fran Rominsky, "goddess with a small g," *WomanSpirit,* I:1 (Autumn Equinox 1974), p. 48; cited in Adler, *Drawing Down the Moon,* p. 205.

55. A statement by a feminist witch named Joan Keller-Marsh, quoted in Donna Steichen, "From Convent to Coven: Catholic Neo-Pagans at the Witches' Sabbath," *Fidelity* (December 1985), 5:32.

56. Carol Christ, *Laughter of Aphrodite,* p. 117.

57. Ibid., p. xi.

58. Stone, "Introduction," *The Goddess Re-Awakening,* p. 19.

59. Starhawk, *Dreaming the Dark,* p. xxviii. See also Inglehart, *Womanspirit,* p. 97.

60. Adler, *Drawing Down the Moon,* pp. 189, 191-192.

61. Goldenberg, *Changing of the Gods,* p. 95.

62. Daly, *The Church and the Second Sex,* p. 38.

63. Daly, *Beyond God the Father,* p. 13.

64. Carol Christ, *Laughter of Aphrodite,* p. 139. Starhawk says, "Male imagery of God authenticates men as the carriers of humanness and legitimizes male rule" *(Dreaming the Dark,* p. 6).

65. Carol Christ, *Laughter of Aphrodite,* pp. 118-119. See pp. 59ff.

66. See Eisler, *The Chalice and the Blade,* pp. 190-194.

67. Sjöö and Mor, *The Great Cosmic Mother,* pp. 392-393.

68. Ibid., pp. 230-234.

69. Eisler, *The Chalice and the Blade,* pp. xx, xxiii.

70. Ibid., pp. 175, 184.

71. Daly, *Gyn/Ecology,* p. 9.

72. Adler, *Drawing Down the Moon,* p. 211.

73. Ibid., chapter 8, pp. 178-229.

74. Ibid., p. 178.

75. Goldenberg, *Changing of the Gods,* chapter 7, pp. 85-114.

76. Starhawk, *Dreaming the Dark*, p. 13.

77. Adler, *Drawing Down the Moon*, p. 11.

78. Goldenberg, *Changing of the Gods*, p. 96.

79. Starhawk, *Dreaming the Dark*, p. xxvi.

80. Adler, *Drawing Down the Moon*, pp. 178, 206, 207.

81. Ibid., pp. 228-229.

82. Ibid., pp. 178, 216, 226.

83. Ibid., pp. 215, 225-226, 228.

84. Adler, p. 216.

85. Sjöö and Mor, *The Great Cosmic Mother*, pp. 425-432. They declare that "the wiccan nature, or witchcraft, is the original nature of all women" (p. 207).

86. Daly, *Beyond God the Father*, p. xv.

87. Goldenberg, *Changing of the Gods*, p. 91.

88. Steichen, "From Convent to Coven," p. 32.

89. Starhawk, *The Spiral Dance: A Rebirth of the Ancient Religion of the Great Goddess* (San Francisco: Harper and Row, 1979).

90. "Goddess Spirituality Catalogue," p. 5.

91. Ibid., p. 3.

92. For more details about Budapest see Adler, *Drawing Down the Moon*, pp. 186-189. For a first-hand report from a Bible believer on what it is like to sit in on one of her lectures, see E. Michael Jones, "Witchcraft at Indiana University," *Fidelity* (May 1987), 6:20ff. For a report from the feminist perspective see Goldenberg, *Changing of the Gods*, pp. 94-96.

93. Zsuzsanna E. Budapest, *The Holy Book of Women's Mysteries* (Berkeley, CA: Wingbow Press, 1989). This is a revised one-volume edition of an earlier two-volume work.

94. "Goddess Spirituality Catalogue," p. 3.

95. Adler, *Drawing Down the Moon*, p. 228.

96. Stone, "Introduction," *The Goddess Re-Awakening*, pp. 3-4.

97. Patrice Wynne, ed., *The Womanspirit Sourcebook* (San Francisco: Harper and Row, 1988).

98. Adler, *Drawing Down the Moon*, pp. 189, 203.

99. Cited in E. Michael Jones, "What Lesbian Nuns Can Teach Us About Vatican II," *Fidelity* (December 1985), 5:19.

100. Adler, *Drawing Down the Moon*, p. 184.

101. Carol Christ, *Laughter of Aphrodite*, chapter 8, pp. 117-132.

102. Ibid., pp. 111, 113, 121.

103. Cited in Nancy M. Cross, "What's Christian About Christian Feminism?", *Fidelity* (December 1985), 5:11.

104. Goldenberg, *Changing of the Gods*, pp. 87, 88-89, 98.

105. Ibid., p. 103.

106. Ibid., pp. 92-93.

107. Adler, *Drawing Down the Moon,* p. 180.

108. Starhawk, *Dreaming the Dark,* p. xv.

109. Carol Christ, *Laughter of Aphrodite,* p. 209.

110. Starhawk, *Dreaming the Dark,* p. 8. The identification of dualism and antisexuality as one of the most evil results of the ascendancy of the male god is one of the main points in Sjöö and Mor's book, *The Great Cosmic Mother.* See, e.g., pp. 230-234.

111. See Adler, *Drawing Down the Moon,* p. 181.

112. Sjöö and Mor, *The Great Cosmic Mother,* pp. 53-54, 195, 291, 377. This is true because female sexuality is more highly evolved than male sexuality, they say. This is why "it is women who must take the lead in further human evolution." Only they can show us the way once more to "a sexual-spiritual religion, the celebration of cosmic ecstasy" (p. 54).

113. Carol Christ, *Laughter of Aphrodite,* p. 123.

114. Starhawk, *Dreaming the Dark,* p. 41.

115. Ibid., p. 42.

116. Sjöö and Mor, *The Great Cosmic Mother,* p. 407.

4 GODDESS FEMINISM AND THE BIBLE

In the last chapter we attempted only to describe the nature of Goddess feminism. What remains now is to evaluate it in the light of the Bible. Thus this chapter could be called "Goddess Feminism and Biblical Faith." The following points will be made: Goddess feminism is deliberately antibiblical; it has a perverted understanding of the Bible; it is just another form of rebellion against God's moral law; and it is idolatry in the form of self-worship.

I. DELIBERATELY ANTIBIBLICAL

The first point is that Goddess feminism makes no attempt to reconcile itself with Biblical teaching. In fact it deliberately sets itself over against the Bible in almost every way. It is self-consciously antibiblical; it is the self-proclaimed enemy of Biblical faith. This fact is seen in a list of twelve aspects of modern witchcraft which Golden-berg rightly says are contrary to Biblical belief:

1. Female deities.

2. No body and soul dualism. It "does not denigrate the human body."

3. Viewing nature as sacred. It "sees other forms of life as equal to the human form."

4. Value of the individual will. "There is no guilt attached to asserting one's will and to rallying deities to one's aid."

5. Spiraling notion of time. Time is "circular and repetitive."

6. Cyclic notion of bodily growth and decay. "The body's growth and decay [i.e., death] is accepted as inevitable and not depressing – definitely not a consequence of sin."

7. No original sin. There is no "concept of a covenant against which one can sin."

8. No division of good and evil. There is an "absence of dogma for dividing the world into moral absolutes."

9. Absence of a sacred text. "A pluralism of beliefs is encouraged."

10. No rigid law of discipline. It rejects "the Judaeo-Christian notion of the need for law." Each person is "considered self-regulating and self-governing."

11. Sex. This is "one aspect of life which the Craft does not consider to be in need of elaborate restrictions. . . . Witchcraft lets sex follow its own laws to a very large degree."

12. Play. "Rituals always have fun and jokes."[1]

With this list as a background we shall now see how God-dess spirituality fits Old Testament religion and New Testament Christianity into its reconstruction of world history.

A. *The Goddess and Old Testament Religion*

We have seen how Goddess feminists totally reconstruct history by positing a prehistoric era of universal Goddess religion and matriarchy (or at least partnership), a religion which was then overthrown by emerging patriarchies which worshiped male gods and exalted men. According to this reconstruction the religion of the Hebrews was a vital part of the reaction against the Goddess and one of the most influential forms of patriarchal religions to be established (though by no means the first[2]). Old Testament religion, which is interpreted totally in terms of evolution rather than revelation, is thus cast in the role of a villain, as one of the main causes of the dethroning of the Goddess and of the subjection of women to thousands of years of degradation and oppression.

Whatever the origin of the Hebrews, it is agreed that they at least were strongly influenced by the invading Indo-Europeans who began the long process of replacing the Goddess with the patriarchal system. Merlin Stone argues that the Levites, the ones mainly responsible for Yahweh religion, were directly related to the Indo-Europeans.[3] In any case the Hebrews moved into the land of Canaan, violently suppressed the existing Goddess worship, and established Yahweh as the one true God.[4]

As Sjöö and Mor tell it, "The Old Testament is the record of the conquest and massacre of these Neolithic people by the nomadic Hebrews, followers of a Sky God, who then set up their biblical God in the place of the ancient Goddess." By sacking, burning, and destroying the communities of the Moon Mother Astarte, "the Hebrews established themselves on the land, along with the worship of their Sky-and-Thunder God Yahweh." It was a continuous struggle because their own people kept backsliding into worship of the Great Mother, "for she had originally been the Goddess of the Hebrews themselves." This is because "Yahweh, like all male gods, was first the bisexual Goddess herself"; but

117

"he" was turned into a male God by his priests and warrior followers, who were simply deifying their own ego. "Yahweh, the pastoral god of cattle breeding, warfare, moralistic wrath, and misogyny, is the newly militant, self-aggrandizing and righteous male ego enthroned as God the Father, enemy of the Mother." His "constant fight against matriarchal religion and custom is the primary theme of the Old Testament."[5]

In their treatment of this era the Goddess feminists always portray the pagan idols of the Old Testament as the "good guys" (gals?). The heathen deity Ashtoreth or Astarte or Asherah was just the Canaanite version of the Great Goddess widely worshiped elsewhere under many other names.[6] She is the one whose worshipers were constantly being slain and whose sacred groves were consistently obliterated by the followers of Yahweh. "Yahweh's absolute hostility to the *asherah* was the political hostility of the nomadic-pastoral Hebrew people, or their priesthood at least, to the settled matriarchal cultures and their Goddess beliefs."[7]

Though Goddess worship was dominant then and even present among the Hebrews, it is claimed that the Biblical records "were edited to slander the worshipers of Gods and Goddesses other than Yahweh as followers after 'abomination.' "[8] This suppression and the allegedly slanted records thereof tend to infuriate modern Goddess folks. Carol Christ says they "cannot fail to be outraged when we discover that the 'idols' castigated by the prophets of Israel and Judah and by other biblical writers may have included the Goddesses whose histories and images we seek to reclaim."[9]

As the Goddess followers see it, one of the worst consequences of the Yahweh revolution was the introduction of a dualistic world view. The problems that threaten to destroy the world today are here "because of profound mistakes made in Bronze Age patriarchal ontology – mistakes about the nature of being, about the nature of human being in the world." These mistakes can be summed up in one concept: "ontological dualism."[10]

Goddess ontology is decidedly monistic, making no metaphysical distinction between the deity and the natural world or between a world of spirit and the physical universe. It sees the human individual as likewise monistic, i.e., as only a physical body with no separable mind or spirit. (As summed up above, this was the second aspect of witchcraft's antibiblical "thealogy," namely, *no body and soul dualism*.) Since the Goddess herself is either equated with physical existence or is intimately embedded in all its parts, all of nature is regarded as holy and sacred. This is true of the human body and all its natural activities, especially sexual activity. It is all "very good," because of this monistic union with the Goddess.

But Goddess spirituality sees the Hebrews and their Yahweh worship as guilty of separating deity from the physical world and thus desacralizing nature. Because the transcendent Father-God is spirit only, he is good; and because he is separate from matter, matter is regarded as evil. Under the "new male God . . . creation now comes to be seen as evil," thus laying the basis for such concepts as sin and for alienation from the deity, from the world, and from each other.[11] Since human beings are both spirit and matter, they can choose to follow spirit and be good or indulge in the physical and be evil. Since sexual activity is obviously physical, it is evil. Since Yahweh religion identified women with sexuality, women themselves were regarded as evil.[12] Goddess feminists declare that the result (if not goal) of such a spirit-flesh dualism is "the denigration of the female body," since in such dualisms men are equated with the spirit side while women are equated with "the despised body."[13]

Thus began the long history of the oppression of women and the repression of sexuality, which were continued and intensified by Christianity since it inherited this Yahwistic dualism.

> . . . Christianity deepened the split, establishing a
> duality between spirit and matter that identified
> flesh, nature, woman, and sexuality with the Devil
> and the forces of evil. God was envisioned as male —
> uncontaminated by the processes of birth, nurturing,
> growth, menstruation, and decay of the flesh. He was
> removed from this world to a transcendent realm of
> spirit somewhere else. Goodness and true value were
> removed from nature and the world as well. . . .[14]

Sjöö and Mor likewise see Christianity as just a continuation of this hated ontological dualism, with its pure-spirit
creator being separated from the evil earth made of impure
matter, its "dualism of God and Devil," and its tragic and
life-negating emphasis on "sin."[15]

According to the way Goddess feminists understand the
Old Testament, a principal result of the Yahwistic dualism
was a negative view of sex. In Goddess worship sex was
sacred; in Yahweh worship sex is evil. "The Bible God and
his religion are based on a violently asexual, or antisexual
morality never before seen on earth. Sex — the source of life
and pleasure of love — becomes the enemy of God." It was
"the opinion of the Hebrew patriarchs that human sexual
activity is basically vile and of the gutter, ultimately of the
Devil." Yahweh himself "is the only male God in the history
of the world who never made love to a female or to the
earth." In Christianity Yahweh's asexual son "counsels his
male followers to eschew sex and femaleness forever if
they want their spirits to reach heaven." In short, "Both
Old Testament and Christian priests saw physical love as
the archenemy of the spirit; it was Anti-Christ, it was
Satan."[16]

Merlin Stone agrees that the Hebrews reversed the attitude toward sex which existed in Goddess worship, but she
says it was the result of purely political motives, particularly the desire to make men rather than women the ones
who determined family identity and thus controlled inheri-

tance and ownership of property. In the Goddess system
sexual activity was basically unrestricted, especially since
it was a sacred aspect of Goddess worship itself. Thus children were often of uncertain paternity, but this did not
matter since the culture was matrilineal, i.e, descent and
inheritance passed down through the female line. But the
Levite-led Hebrews replaced the matrilineal with a patrilineal system, putting all things under the control of men.
But this required specific knowledge of the identity of the
father of any given child. This led the Levites to set up
laws restricting all sexual activity to marriage, with sex
outside of marriage (especially for women) being regarded
as evil. "Thus they developed and instituted the concept of
sexual *morality* – for women." The whole system of marriage and sex-within-marriage-only and the nuclear family
was created to ensure patriarchy and male dominance over
women. In this sense the Hebrews and Christianity after
them can be called anti-sexual. "Sex, especially non-mari-
tal sex, is considered to be somewhat naughty, dirty, even
sinful."[17]

I suggest that it was upon the attempt to establish
this certain knowledge of paternity, which would then
make patrilineal reckoning possible, that these
ancient sexual customs [promiscuity in service of the
Goddess] were finally denounced as wicked and
depraved and that it was for this reason that the
Levite priests devised the concept of sexual "morality": premarital virginity for *women*, marital fidelity
for *women*, in other words total control over the
knowledge of paternity.[18]
. . . It was surely apparent to Levite leaders that if
a religion existed alongside their own, a religion in
which women owned their own property, were
endowed with a legal identity and were free to relate
sexually to various men, it would be much more difficult for the Hebrew men to convince their women that
they must accept the position of being their husband's

property. Hebrew women had to be taught to accept the idea that for a woman to sleep with more than one man was evil. . . . Thus premarital virginity and marital fidelity were proclaimed by Levite law as divinely essential for all Hebrew women, the antithesis of the attitudes toward female sexuality held in the religion of the Goddess.[19]

But how could women be convinced to accept this revolutionary view of themselves and of their sexuality? Herein lies the origin, according to Goddess feminists, of what they consider to be one of the most destructive myths ever to be created by men, namely, the "myth" of Eve and the Fall of mankind. As they see it, this story was made up specifically to discredit the Goddess and to identify women and sex as evil, thus justifying the new sexual "morality" and ensuring male dominion and control.

"Feminists and Neo-Pagans," says Adler, "naturally feel that the story of Adam and Eve, as commonly interpreted, has probably done more to debase and subjugate women than any other such tale in Western history."[20] Carol Christ agrees, calling the story of Eve "the fountainhead of a woman-hating tradition within biblical religion."[21] By projecting guilt upon women and making them the "primordial scapegoats," says Daly, this "primordial lie" justifies women's inferior place in the universe.[22] The tragedy is compounded by the fact that the story has had and continues to have such a widespread and profound influence on society. Daly agrees with Elizabeth Cady Stanton that this "myth of feminine evil" is a foundation for "the entire structure of phallic Christian ideology," and she argues that its "malignant image" of women "retains its hold over the modern psyche" and continually "undergirds destructive patterns in the fabric of our culture."[23]

Though some such as Daly may grant that this effect was unintentional, many feminists have expressed the belief that the story of Eve and the Fall was written for the specific purpose of destroying Goddess religion and establishing male dominance over women. This is a theme relentlessly pursued by Merlin Stone in *When God Was A Woman*. She describes this "myth" as "yet another assault upon the Goddess religion" and as "designed to be used in the continuous Levite battle to suppress the female religion." She says that "this whole fable was designed and propagated to provide 'divine' sanction for male supremacy and a male kinship system." Thus this "seemingly innocent myth of Paradise . . . was actually carefully constructed and propagated to 'keep women in their place,' the place assigned to them by the Levite tribe of biblical Canaan."[24]

It is alleged that Goddess symbolism is carefully worked into the story in such a way that Goddess worship is discredited and Yahweh morality is established. Stone says that "at each turn, in each sentence of the biblical myth, the original tenets of the Goddess religion were attacked."[25] For example, the tree of knowledge of good and evil is said to represent the sacred tree of the Goddess,[26] and the serpent is supposedly always related to the Goddess as a source of divine counsel. "It was surely intended," says Stone, "that the serpent, as the familiar counselor of women, be seen as a source of evil and be placed in such a menacing and villainous role that to listen to the prophetesses of the female deity would be to violate the religion of the male deity in a most dangerous manner." Eisler says,[27]

> . . . The fact that the serpent, an ancient prophetic or oracular symbol of the Goddess, advises Eve, the prototypical woman, to disobey a male god's commands is surely not just an accident. Nor is it an accident that Eve in fact follows the advice of the serpent: that, in disregard of Jehovah's commands, she eats from the sacred tree of knowledge. Like the tree of life, the tree of knowledge was also a symbol associated with the Goddess . . . .
> From the perspective of that earlier reality, the

orders of this powerful upstart God Jehovah that Eve
may not eat from a sacred tree . . . would have been
not only unnatural but sacrilegious. Groves of sacred
trees were an integral part of the old religion. . . .

So in terms of the old reality, Jehovah had no right
to give such orders. But having been given them, neither Eve nor the serpent, as representatives of the
Goddess, could be expected to obey.[28]

Thus when Eve heeds the serpent and eats of the fruit of
the tree, this is a clear act of Goddess worship. When she
is called into account and condemned for worshiping the
Goddess, this is a warning to every woman to forsake
every deity but Yahweh and every man but her own husband. The message is clear: the Goddess is dethroned, and
women are a source of evil. As Eisler says, "The horrible
consequences of Eve's disobedience of Jehovah's orders
were more than just an allegory about humanity's 'sinful-
ness.' They were a clear warning to avoid the still persistent worship of the Goddess." Indeed, "the vilification of
the serpent and the association of woman with evil were a
means of discrediting The Goddess." The whole story thus
had the political purpose of establishing the male God and
his male worshipers as supreme.[29]

In this context it is generally agreed that Eve's partak-
ing of the forbidden tree involved sexual knowledge in
some form, since sexual activity was central in the worship
of the Goddess. Hence what was forbidden by Yahweh was
"eating of the paradise fruit of sexual consciousness." But
Eve ate anyway, and she tried, "with the magic aid of her
serpent, to persuade Adam to partake with her of the nar-
cotic fruit and sexual rites leading to ecstatic illumination
and rebirth."[30] "According to the Bible story, the forbidden
fruit caused the couple's conscious comprehension of sexuality," says Stone. "We are told that, by eating the fruit
first, woman possessed sexual consciousness before man
and in turn tempted man to partake of the forbidden fruit,
that is, to join her sinfully in sexual pleasures."[31] Thus,

says another, "The banishing of the snake is the banishing of the goddess and, symbolically, of Eve's free and autonomous expression of her sexuality." The condemnation placed upon Eve was "a clear condemnation by Yahweh of female sexuality exercised freely and autonomously."[32]

The general purpose of those who constructed the "myth," though, was to establish male dominance. This is how it has been understood ever since it was written. As the result of Eve's act, "it was decreed by God that woman must submit to the dominance of man — who was at that time divinely presented with the right to rule over her — from that moment until now."[33] Stone declares that the New Testament writers "repeatedly utilized the legend of the loss of Paradise to explain and even prove the natural inferiority of women." They "continually presented the myth of Adam and Eve as divine proof that man must hold the ultimate authority."[34]

Thus do the Goddess feminists thoroughly reject Old Testament religion as one of the decisive instruments in the suppression of original Goddess spirituality, with special denunciation being reserved for the "myth" of Eve. In light of this, the Goddess feminists see themselves as having the responsibility of "reversing Genesis, turning the myth on its head by validating and freeing their sexuality, by theologizing out of their own experience."[35] They call upon one another to look upon Eve in a positive way and to claim her as their own. Their battle cry is "Eve and the serpent were right!"[36]

B. The Goddess and Christianity

Since it has such a negative view of the Old Testament, we are not surprised to see that Goddess feminism also does not hesitate to attack the Christianity of the New Testament. The latter is seen as the culmination of Old Testament religion and is regarded as even more antigoddess than its predecessor. Carol Christ says that feminists do not blame "Jews" as such for the death of the Goddess. Rather, "if any one group is to be 'blamed' for the suppression of the Goddess in Western culture, 'the Christians' seem to me to be a more likely candidate."[37]

For one thing, Christian theology is seen as continuing and intensifying the Hebrews' spirit-is-good, matter-is-evil dualism. Thus it is ontologically flawed from the beginning.[38] Out of this dualism arose the very idea of sin as something associated with our very existence in this material world, and thus also the idea of our need for salvation out of this world. "Upon the machinery of sin and salvation the whole Christian ontology rests. The figure of Christ that the church is based on *is* this machinery; i.e., Christ depends on human sin for his existence." Because of these "concepts of Original Sin and the need for 'salvation' from fleshly life . . . Christianity is perhaps the most nihilistic religion yet to appear on earth." Because of these "almost entirely necrophilic and destructive" ideas, "the world has been hell under two thousand years of Christianity."[39] Daly sums it up succinctly but bluntly: "I propose that Christianity itself should be castrated by cutting away the products of **supermale arrogance: the myths of sin and salvation.**"[40]

In feminist thinking "the first and ultimate world-saver is the female." The original and true ideas of salvation were part of Goddess worship, and thus are "many millennia older than the doctrines of Christianity, which simply coopted them, because of their universal resonance and power, and attributed them to a male God."[41] This last point of course is one of the basic objections to Christianity: it has a *male* redeemer. It "offered redemption through a single being of the male sex. Christ must redeem us from being born out of a woman. His power to do so comes from the fact that he is the son of a male God."[42] Christ and Yahweh must go "because of the very basic quality of maleness," says Goldenberg. "Jesus Christ cannot symbolize the

126

liberation of women. A culture that maintains a masculine image for its highest divinity cannot allow its women to experience themselves as the equals of its men. In order to develop a theology of women's liberation, feminists have to leave Christ and the Bible behind them."[43]

Daly agrees that "the idea of redemptive incarnation uniquely in the form of a male savior" is futile, because "a patriarchal divinity or his son" certainly cannot "save us from the horrors of a patriarchal world." Thus it is necessary to have an Antichrist, which is nothing less than the women's movement itself. "Seen from this perspective the Antichrist and the *Second Coming of women* are synonymous. This Second Coming is not a return of Christ but a new arrival of female presence, once strong and powerful, but enchained since the dawn of patriarchy." Liberated women are the real saviors of the world and of Jesus himself.[44]

All the crucial aspects of the life and work of Christ and thus of the Christian gospel are attacked and denied by Goddess feminists. They attack the Virgin Birth as a denial of sexuality, especially female sexuality. Having Jesus conceived by this antisexual means is a way of dealing with "the messy femaleness of Mary."[45] In reference to Mary, Carol Christ refers to "the patriarchal fear of female (and ultimately all) sexuality implicit in her title as Virgin."[46] This "antiseptic birth" sets Jesus apart from women and sexuality and thus is a denial of life, a devaluation of life in this world.[47] Even more seriously, it is a denial of the value of the female will as such. The Virgin Birth was not a decision willed by Mary but one willed upon her in a kind of spiritual rape. "Within the rapist christian myth of the Virgin Birth the role of Mary is utterly minimal." She does nothing; she is "little more than a hollow eggshell." The Virgin Birth "myth" thus is just another deliberate effort "to remove creativity from women and re-establish it in the realm of male domination and control."[48]

127

Mary is wife, mother, and child to the same male power-figure. She is utterly meek, abject, passive. In her, the ancient power of the Goddess is captured, chained, used, cannibalized . . . domesticated and tranquilized. It is no accident that Mary is portrayed as giving birth in tranquility and bliss, as a reward for her asexuality and total submission. . . .[49]

Also attacked is the central Christian reality of the death of Christ on the cross. Whatever the cross itself came to mean for Christians, Goddess feminists say it is just a pale copy of the Cosmic Tree or Sacred Tree of the Goddess. It is an imitation of the many pagan images of the dying god, especially the "Neolithic rites of the vegetation deity . . . who is sacrificed on the Mother Tree for the renewal, or rebirth, of the life of the world. The Passion, the self-sacrificing ritual of Christ, does not have its roots in intellectual ideas but in the primordial passion of the Great Mother," who died to ensure the new growth of spring. Thus "Jesus Christ was the last vegetation deity of the Near Eastern world."[50]

The very idea of the "saving blood" of Christ is just a patriarchal substitute for the blood that is the true source of life, women's menstrual blood. "There is power in the blood – of the woman."[51] The wounds of Christ are "false male imitations of menstruation and childbirth," which are the real thing. Christ on the cross is a "male parody of the female experience – of menstrual bleeding, of childbirth, of ontological physical suffering for the human race." On the cross Christ "as a transvestite or female-imitation sacrifice to an asexual and jealous Father God" simply "acts out a female role: the erotic-dramatic role of bleeding and childbirth." As a "deified male martyr" Jesus takes over "this female experience into his own power and glory," while "women, who really do these things, have been forced to hide the signs of our bleeding and childbed 'crucifixions' as unclean processes, and badges of corruption, inferiority,

128

and shame."[52]

By denying its true saving and life-giving power, feminists are able to depict the cross as a symbol of nothing more than pain and cruelty. This is significant for them since they portray Christianity as one of the main patriarchal religions that destroyed the Goddess, thus turning the world's value system on its head. Gone is the gentle, life-exalting chalice-image of the Goddess cradling the divine child in her arms. This has been replaced by a blade-image of domination and destruction, namely, "the omnipresent theme of Christ dying on the cross" in "exaltation of pain, suffering, and death."[53] In Daly's bold and blasphemous terms, Goddess religion's "Tree of Life became converted into the symbol of the necrophilic S and M Society," a torture cross.[54]

In case anyone thinks that the resurrection of Christ refutes the charge that the cross makes Christianity "necrophilic," this is not how Goddess feminists interpret it. In fact, the idea of the resurrection of Christ only reinforces in their minds the notion that Christians are "worshiping a god of death."[55] Christianity's dualism already separates its transcendent deity from this tangible world; and his resurrection out of this world separates him even more from this physical matrix of true reality. The resurrection is thus a denial of life. "At death, Christ does not return to the Mother Earth like earlier vegetation deities, to renew and fructify us all. Christ is a vegetation deity who refuses to be recycled. Instead, he ascends to heaven to sit as a judge at his Father's side." This "nihilistic denial of the value of earthly life . . . has contributed greatly to the biophobic insanity of the past two thousand years of human existence."[56] The assertion "He is risen" is rooted in the false denial of finitude and death, which are good and natural and which can be affirmed without fear in the arms of the Goddess, who is our Mother Earth. "We must learn to love this life that ends in death," but this will happen only when we give up dualistic ideas such as the resurrection and return to the Goddess.[57]

In sum, Goddess feminism sees Christianity and the Christian gospel as its very opposite in just about every way. Sjöö and Mor cite Jesus' words in John 2:4, "Woman, what have I to do with thee?" Their answer: "Nothing, apparently."[58] E. Michael Jones reports on a lecture given by the witch Z Budapest at Indiana University at South Bend. She was introduced by another witch, Professor Gloria Kaufman, teacher of women's studies at IUSB. The introduction, says Jones, was "a diatribe against both Judaism and Christianity"; and "the thematic thread that bound the afternoon together" was "hatred for the Christian religion, specifically the Catholic Church." According to Jones, it was clear that this is the very "ideological glue" that holds the whole "pseudoscience" of women's spirituality together.[59]

C. The Goddess and the Liberation of God

Our point in this section is that Goddess feminism is deliberately antibiblical. We have seen how it attacks the basic content of both the Old and New Testaments. In the final analysis its hope is nothing less than to replace Biblical religion with the religion of the Goddess.

Some people depict Jesus as a revolutionary prophet and Christianity as a revolutionary religion. But if Christianity wants to be truly radical, says Goddess feminism, it will return to paganism.

To be truly revolutionary, Christianity would have to dissolve itself. It would have to dissolve its male-dominated and celibate hierarchies, and the social class systems from which it derives its worldly power. It would have to renounce and dissolve totally the world-hatred, the flesh-hatred, the ontological misogyny which has so long provided it with fanatic energy. It would have to renounce most of the Old Testament,

130

most of the New Testament, and all of Revelation, which dooms us to a grotesque apocalypse. It would have to throw out Genesis to return us radically to an image of God based on the pre-Biblical universal perception of a Great Mother – a bisexual being, both female and male in spirit and function. . . . But, as we said, if the Christian church ever changed itself this radically, it would become pagan. To realize its most radical vision, Christianity can only reinvent paganism. . . .[60]

But since Biblical religion will probably not cooperate by committing suicide, it becomes the task of the Goddess followers to kill it. Naomi Goldenberg states her conviction thus: "We women are going to bring an end to God. As we take positions in government, in medicine, in law, in business, in the arts and, finally, in religion, we will be the end of Him. We will change the world so much that He won't fit in anymore." In this way, she says, "the feminist movement in Western culture is engaged in the slow execution of Christ and Yahweh."[61] "Every woman working to improve her own position in society or that of women in general is bringing about the end of God. All feminists are making the world less and less like the one described in the Bible and are thus helping to lessen the influence of Christ and Yahweh on humanity." Thus shall "we watch Christ and Yahweh tumble to the ground."[62] After relating the term *Christian* to the term *cretin* ("deformed idiot"), Daly describes the Goddess revolution thus: "Revolting/re-considering requires deicide; leaving the State of Idiocy implies the death of the cretin god."[63]

In October 1986 about 2500 people (mostly women) met in Washington, D.C., for a conference on "Women in the Church." It was supposed to be a gathering of Catholics, but according to Donna Steichen it was "a consciousness-raising session for Church revolutionaries." She calls her report on the conference "The Goddess Goes to Washington," since many of the speakers were preaching Goddess

feminism. And even though they may not have fully understood "that the ultimate feminist objective is the obliteration of Christianity," says Steichen, "a stunning majority
thunderously applauded calls to defy the magisterium,
repudiate Judeo-Christian theology, and work as 'guerril-
las' toward a religious *coup d'etat* that would replace God
the Father with Goddess, the Mother." In short, the message proclaimed at the conference was "the choice of the
serpent over the Creator."[64]

Thus the Goddess feminists view their women's movement as nothing less than the "liberation of God." They are
liberating God from his Biblical father-image. "They will
never forget – nor will they let God forget – that such a
God is the symbol and source of their oppression." They are
struggling so hard with God that both they and God will
become new. They are listening for the still, small voice to
say to them, "God is a woman like yourself; she, too, has
suffered and ceased to exist through the long years of
patriarchal history." Women will then make a new
covenant with that sister God and her sister earth,
"promising to liberate her and the earth as they liberate
themselves."[65]

II. PERVERTED INTERPRETATION
OF THE BIBLE

There can be no doubt that Biblical faith and Goddess
spirituality stand in direct opposition to one another on
most crucial issues. The two are not just different; they are
incompatible. This would be true even if Biblical faith were
being properly described and fairly contrasted with Goddess religion.

The fact is, however, that the ideas and data attributed
to the Bible by Goddess feminists are often *not* the correct
interpretation of Biblical teaching. Much of what has been
related above as "what the Old and New Testaments teach"

132

is a seriously perverted understanding of Scriptural doctrine. The parodies and caricatures set forth, which are sometimes maliciously blasphemous, are designed to make Christianity sound as evil as possible, but in fact they bear no resemblance to truth whatsoever. Ronald and Beverly Allen are correct when they say that "if one does not really care what the Bible teaches, it is possible to claim that it teaches whatever one desires."[66] They make this statement in reference to Merlin Stone's work, *When God Was A Woman.*

The point of this section is to identify some of the more crucial of these perverted interpretations, most of which will be obvious to anyone with even a partially objective familiarity with Scripture. We are not hoping to convert any feminists by doing this; we are simply calling on them to be more careful and fair in their description of the Bible's teaching. Also we are concerned that their perverted explanations of the Bible may turn some honest seekers away from its Way, its Truth, and its Light.

A. Specific Examples of Misinterpretation

The most serious and most obvious errors of interpretation have to do with the central doctrines of sin and salvation. The doctrine of sin deals with the negative state of affairs into which we have fallen and out of which we need to be redeemed. What does the Bible say about the nature of this negative state that makes salvation necessary, and the nature of the salvation itself?

We will remember that the Goddess world view is monistic. This natural world is all that exists, with the Goddess herself either being identified with nature or permeating all its parts. Thus all aspects of the physical world, including the human body, are not just good but are even sacred. But according to Goddess feminists, the Biblical world view, like all patriarchy, is dualistic. This means that the world of divinity or spirit exists separate from or totally apart from this natural world. This is God's absolute transcendence, meaning that he is absolutely outside of and unrelated to what is going on around us. The things of this world – matter itself, the earth, nature, flesh, the body, sexuality – are impure and evil and debased and unreal; they are identified with the Devil himself. This is the world view known as ontological or metaphysical dualism, and to Goddess feminists it is the fundamental error of the Bible.[67]

Thus man's basic plight or "lostness," according to the feminists' interpretation of the Bible, is his involvement in the evil circumstances of this natural world.   His salvation comes from disengaging himself as much as possible from his material environment until finally he can be rescued from it altogether into the world of exclusively immortal spirit. This is the sort of theology "in which this earth, this body, and this life are despised, and in which the spiritual goal is to transcend the flesh and its desires and to seek a life after death in which the limitations of finitude are overcome."[68] Salvation thus understood as rescue from this world is a negation of the value and goodness of physical existence.

Without going into a lot of detail, we can emphatically declare that this is definitely *not* the world view of the Bible; and it is *not* the Bible's teaching about lostness and salvation. A number of pagan philosophies and religions do embrace this world view, but it is *not* the Biblical view.

The world view taught in the Bible is a kind of dualism, to be sure; but it is not a matter/spirit dualism in which spirit is good as such and matter is evil as such. It is rather a Creator/creature dualism, in which the eternally infinite and holy God brings finite beings into existence out of nothing. It is absolutely false, though, to think that the Bible represents the finite creation as somehow impure or evil just because it is finite and separate from God. The very fact that it is created by the holy and omnipotent God renders the creation ontologically pure. A thing does not have to be identified with or permeated with divinity in order to be good.

The Creator to be sure *is* transcendent, but this is not a matter of his being absent from his creation as if it were unworthy of his presence. Indeed, the Creator is continually and universally present within his creation, working within it and taking pleasure in it. God's transcendence or separateness simply means that his essence or being is *different* from the creation. He alone is infinite, uncreated spirit; everything else is a creature and thus finite though good.

The Creator/creature dualism is not a matter/spirit dualism, but the creation itself *is* a kind of dualism of matter and spirit. That is, part of the creation is spiritual in essence, in some ways similar to the divine being but by no means identical with it. This includes the world of angels, all of whom were created good in the beginning but some of whom sinned (2 Peter 2:4) and became Satan and his angels or evil spirits; and it includes every human being's soul or spirit, which is different from his body and can be separated from it but is not intended to be. The other part of the creation is the physical or material universe, or every particle of matter that exists. This includes the physical body of every human being. Now, what is crucially important to understand is this: unlike the matter/spirit dualisms of pagan philosophies and religions, the matter and spirit of the Biblical world view are both finite and distinct from God, yet both are ontologically pure and good.

What, then, is the nature of man's predicament, the state of "lostness" from which he needs saving? Here again is a fundamental error in the Goddess interpretation of the Bible. Evil is seen as a metaphysical problem, that is, as a problem arising from the very nature of stuff or the very way it exists. The Goddess feminists represent the Bible as teaching that the very physicalness or nonspiritualness of this world (including human bodies) makes it evil and something to be saved or rescued from. But this is absolutely false. In the Bible man's problem is not metaphysical but ethical. That is, his problem is not what he *is* but what he *has done*. His predicament is not caused by his being made out of the wrong stuff but by his making the wrong choices. His problem is sinful choices, not physical existence.

Man's sinful choices have had a negative effect both upon himself individually and upon the world as a whole. A sinner is evil, not because the stuff out of which he is made is impure, but because his thoughts and his actions are impure. He exists in a state of distortion and deterioration, in that his spirit is weak in the face of temptation and his body is invaded by disease and death. But these imperfections are not caused by finitude and physicalness; they are the results of the sinner's evil choices. The negative results of such choices go far beyond the life of the individual who makes them. Indeed, the whole universe is distorted and corrupt and "evil" as a result of human sin (Romans 8:19-23; Galatians 1:4). Thus man does not need to be saved from the finiteness and physicalness of this world; he needs to be saved from the sinful state of his heart and from the distorting and condemning consequences of his sins.

This salvation is not redemption from a finite, physical world into an infinite and immortal realm of pure spirit. In fact, Biblical salvation is not redemption *from* this world but *of* this world. Redemption is not just individual but is also cosmic; in the end the whole universe will be cleansed of the distorting and decaying effects of human sin, the result being a "new heavens and a new earth" (Romans 8:19-23; 2 Peter 3:13). "The resurrection of the dead" is not just the transfer of our saved spirits into some nonphysical heaven; it is the restoration of our redeemed and changed bodies to a gloriously restored earth (Romans 8:23; 1 Corinthians 15:51), which will be our eternal home. Rather than devaluing life upon this earth, Biblical teaching and the Christian gospel give it the highest possible value by making it the object of the redeeming work of Christ.

Since Goddess feminism misrepresents the whole framework of Biblical teaching concerning sin and salvation, we should not be surprised at its complete misunderstanding of the person and work of the Savior (though we may be deeply offended by its blasphemies). For example, to describe the Bible's view of the incarnation as "the *only* time in the history of the universe that spirit ever entered into matter"[69] shows a lack of understanding of the Biblical world view as described above, as well as a misunderstanding of the nature of the incarnation itself. It is true that what happened at Christ's incarnation was unique, but it was not just an event in which "spirit entered into matter."

Likewise, it is ludicrous to describe the Biblical picture of both the death and resurrection of Jesus as indicative of a necrophilic, nihilistic world view and as glorifying cruelty, suffering, and death. Again, this misrepresentation grows out of the false perception of the Bible's world view as a spirit-is-good/matter-is-evil world view. The ultimate goal of both the cross and the resurrection of Jesus is *life* – eternal bodily life on the redeemed and renewed earth.

The feminists' persistent accusation that the Bible teaches that sex is evil is also partly related to this confusion about the Biblical world view as a view that degrades the body. They say the Bible "saw physical love as the archenemy of the spirit"; "in Christianity, the only love-ecstasy allowed is beyond the body."[70] Whether for this or other reasons, they picture the Bible as regarding "sex as evil and dangerous"; as "basically vile and of the gutter, ultimately of the Devil"; "somewhat naughty, dirty, even sinful"; and as "the enemy of God." Jesus "counsels his male followers to eschew sex and femaleness forever if they want their spirits to reach heaven."[71]

All this of course is totally false. The Bible never speaks of sex as such as evil; it only condemns sex outside its intended boundaries of marriage. Sex within marriage is a good and positive gift of God, as the Song of Solomon attests (see Hebrews 13:4). Sex outside of marriage is wrong not because of its physical nature but because it violates God's purpose for it. The feminists also err regarding this purpose; they say the Bible says sex must be for procreation only.[72] But the Bible nowhere makes this kind of statement. Rather, it clearly implies (e.g., Genesis 2) that sexual union has to do with the relational needs of husbands and wives as such.

This leads to one final area of misrepresentation to be mentioned here, namely, the nature of the Fall in Genesis 3 and Eve's part in it. In keeping with their obsession with sexuality, Goddess feminists picture the forbidden fruit in Genesis 2 and 3 as sexual awareness or sexual activity.[73] But this is nowhere stated or implied in the text, and is contradictory to the Creator's instructions to Adam and Eve to "be fruitful and multiply" (Genesis 1:28). The feminists also err in representing the Bible as placing a lot of emphasis on Eve's role in the Fall as the source of male supremacy. Stone says the New Testament writers "continually" and "repeatedly utilized the legend of the loss of Paradise to explain and even prove the natural inferiority of women."[74] This is an absurd notion. The incident is used exactly one time, in 1 Timothy 2:14, as a secondary reason why women are not allowed to teach or exercise authority over men, but that is the extent of it. In the New Testament Adam is given as much if not more blame for the Fall than Eve (see Romans 5:12ff.).

B. General Observations

We have looked at several specific examples of how Goddess feminists misinterpret Biblical teaching, some of them quite gross. How is it possible that they could make such serious mistakes? Here we shall make several observations of a general nature that may provide some insight into their misuse of Scripture.

First, we must remember that these feminists are approaching the Bible from the standpoint of naturalistic evolution and not revelation. Thus they assume that everything in the Bible can be explained in terms of some purely human purpose or motivation. The records and stories and theories are there not because they are true but because some writer or editor had some ulterior (and usually base) motive for putting them there. This assumption allows for all kinds of free-wheeling speculation as to the sources and hidden meanings behind particular passages of Scripture. For example, since the Bronze Age (Old Testament) tribes were shepherds and cattle raisers, "their new patriarchal ideas of God and of human intercourse derived from cattle breeding." That is, they "stupidly and brutally tried to restrict human sexual activity precisely to that of the beasts," i.e., for reproduction only.[75]

Second, we must remember that these feminists themselves have a very specific and self-serving agenda; they have a viewpoint from which they are working and a thesis they intend to establish. Thus they have developed "eyes" with which they can see things no one else may be able to see. As Carol Christ says, "Women's imagination is by no means subject to the authority of the past. Instead, modern women joyfully discover what is useful to us in the past and reject what is not." They select or reject, "using feminism as a principle of selection." Referring specifically to the pre-biblical Goddess era, she says, "We seek to remember a past where women were not slaves. What we cannot remember we invent joyfully."[76] For example, who but a Goddess feminist would define the name *Adam* as meaning "son of the red Mother Earth"?[77] Who but the Goddess feminists would claim the Levite priests "were originally serpent priests – i.e., *Levi*: 'great serpent,' as in Leviathan"?[78] Who but they would describe the Virgin Mary as "a pale remnant of the Great Goddess," and the Virgin Birth as a deliberate attack on female sexuality?[79] These are just a few examples of how interpretive ele-

139

ments seem to be invented because they lend support to the Goddess hypothesis.

This leads to a third point, namely, that the Goddess feminists constantly draw highly speculative connections between elements of the Goddess religion and elements of Biblical religion, which they contend was in a way evolving out of yet trying to replace the former. We have already seen how many aspects of Bible history and doctrine are said to have their origins in Goddess piety, for example, the story of the Fall and the cross of Jesus.

Fourth, many of the feminist misrepresentations of the Bible seem to be a result simply of a very shallow or surface knowledge of what the Bible actually says. For example, what are referred to as the Old Testament's "sensual and ecstatic songs of earthly love" [presumably the Song of Solomon] are attributed to King David (who derived them from the ancient love rites of the shepherd king and the Goddess Ashtoreth!).[80] Another interpretation suggesting shallow understanding is the idea that the Bible has a "dualism of God and Devil" who are "eternally at war with each other and eternally irreconcilable."[81] Another example is an attempted quotation: "In 1 Samuel 21:4 it is said, 'Men are holy who stay away from women.' "[82] Such a loose and casual approach suggests a lack of any really serious attempt to represent the Bible fairly.

A final point is that sometimes false post-biblical interpretations of the Bible are equated with Biblical teaching itself. This is especially true of some of the erroneous views of sex attributed to the Bible, such as the view that sex is in itself impure and the only legitimate use for it is procreation.[83] Such notions have been held by various theologians in Christian history (e.g., Augustine), but are not correct Biblical interpretation. In fact no notable individual or church group today would hold to such views, and to represent them in a so-called scholarly work as "the Biblical view" is irresponsible.

I believe that the evidence warrants the conclusion that

Goddess feminism's use of the Bible reveals wholesale misunderstanding and very slanted interpretations that ignore the true and obvious meaning of its teaching. Such a prejudiced and perverted approach to Scripture gives us a legitimate reason to question the objectivity and fairness with which it examines data from other sources as well.

III. REBELLION AGAINST GOD'S MORAL LAW

A third main point to be noted in relation to Biblical faith is that Goddess feminism is a form of rebellion against God's moral law as revealed in Scripture. Totally apart from the issue of the role of women as such, these feminists mock the law of God and declare that it has no meaning or authority for them. This is seen in several ways.

A. An Absence of Absolutes

First of all, Goddess feminists declare that there are no absolute rules to govern human behavior. That is, they adopt a relativistic or situational ethic. Starhawk says, "There is no external authority, no set of absolute truths, that can tell us precisely how to determine the meaning of our personal commitment" to the dance of life and death. "There is no one truth, or one way, that fits everyone."[84]

Three of the anti-Christian tenets of witchcraft listed by Goldenberg express this rejection of ethical absolutes. One says there is an "absence of dogma for dividing the world into moral absolutes." Another says that witchcraft has no sacred text, which allows for relativism and "a pluralism of beliefs." Another says there is "no rigid law of discipline," or "no higher moral law" for keeping anyone in check.[85]

Rather than submitting to rules made by God or anyone else, the Goddess followers feel they are free to make up their own rules. The *autonomy of the female will* is one of their primary values. Carol Christ states it thus:

> In a Goddess-centered context . . . the will is valued. *A woman is encouraged to know her will, to believe that her will is valid, and to believe that her will can be achieved in the world,* three powers traditionally denied to her in patriarchy. In a Goddess-centered framework, a woman's will is not subordinated to the Lord God as king and ruler, nor to men as his representatives. Thus a woman is not reduced to waiting and acquiescing in the wills of others as she is in patriarchy. . . .[86]

Goldenberg says that in feminist witchcraft, "since each woman is considered a Goddess, all of her creations are in a sense holy. . . . Thus, not only are the inner dynamics of a woman's psyche seen as religious processes, but she is perceived as capable of evaluating these processes herself. Each is the priestess of her own religion."[87]

The contrast between the Biblical way and the Goddess way is well summed up in this statement by Lynn Marsh: "The patriarchal principle is 'Thou shalt,' or 'Thou shalt not.' The Goddess says, 'You may, perhaps; play, discover, find out for yourself.' She is my mentor."[88] This is an accurate description of a main difference between the two systems. While the Bible is much more than a list of ethical absolutes, it certainly includes them. The Goddess followers, however, will have none of it. Instead they will have their autonomy, their rebellion against the moral law of the Creator God.

B. Denial of the Concept of Sin

A second aspect of this rebellion is similar to the first, namely, Goddess feminism denies the very concept of sin. This was seen in Goldenberg's list of twelve ways that witchcraft differs from Christian teaching. One of these was the denial of original sin, and even the denial of any kind "of a covenant against which one can sin." Also, it denies any distinction between good and evil.[89] This denial of sin is seen also in Daly's list of false gods or idols that must be dethroned before the women's revolution can succeed. One of these "idols" is "the God who is the Judge of 'sin,' who confirms the rightness of the rules and roles of the reigning system, maintaining false consciences and self-destructive guilt feelings." Women have suffered from this false god, and their "growth in self-respect will deal the death blow to this as well as to the other demons dressed as Gods."[90]

Feminists consider "sins" to be repressive rules made up by the fathers of patriarchal religion just to keep women in check. They constitute a "male-constructed 'morality.' "[91] (We may remember Merlin Stone's view that the Levites invented the concept of "morality" when they made up rules to limit women's sexual activity.[92]) Sjöö and Mor equate "God's will" with "the male primate will to control female reproduction."[93]

Daly tries to trace the word *sin* to the Latin word meaning "to be." Therefore "to sin" means "to be." Only by doing what the fathers have called sin can a woman have authentic being. The things that are labeled as sins are the things that offer the greatest experience of being. Thus women must pursue "courageous sinning against the Sins of the Fathers."[94] "Clearly, the ontological courage of feminists, our courage to be, implies the courage to be WRONG. Elemental be-ing outside the fathers' rule(s) is Sinning; it requires the Courage to Sin."[95] Christianity gives us a choice. We can either follow a "dead script" about Jesus, or we can "sin" and experience that true experiential being that exists "in the renegade spaces outside the established religion, utterly outside and beyond its terms."[96]

In such ways do the Goddess feminists mock the very concept of sin and in so doing display their rebellion against God's moral law.

143

C. Demand for Sexual Freedom

A third aspect of Goddess religion's rebellion against law is its demand to be free from all rules and restrictions regarding sexual activity. When one reads their literature it is easy to get the impression that the Goddess feminists are actually obsessed with the idea of sexual freedom or sexual autonomy. It is a goal that seems to be at the very top of the list of "women's rights."

This idea of unrestricted sex is another of the anti-Christian tenets of witchcraft listed by Goldenberg. "Sexuality is but one aspect of life which the Craft does not consider to be in need of elaborate restrictions," she says. In contrast to Judaism and Christianity, "witchcraft lets sex follow its own laws to a very large degree. Sex, like ambition, is understood as having its own regulatory principle."[97] Daly makes this point clear: "It is important to repudiate the old dogmas concerning sexual behavior and it is also important to avoid setting up new ones."[98]

According to its devotees, Goddess religion has always been an ideological framework for sexual freedom. Up until its repression by patriarchy, Goddess religion not only allowed but even encouraged full and varied female sexual expression as a celebration of life and of the Goddess herself. But the patriarchal religions, including Judaism and Christianity, labeled such behavior as "sin" and limited it with a set of very restrictive laws. Thus rebellion against patriarchy in the name of the Goddess must include a battle for the restoration of female sexual freedom.

We have already seen several examples of this aspect of Goddess feminism. We have seen how Merlin Stone believes that the Levites sought to suppress female sexual freedom by inventing "sexual morality," in order to ensure male dominance.[99] We have seen how the same theme runs throughout the book by Sjöö and Mor. One of the primary assumptions of patriarchy, they say, is that "autonomous female sexuality poses a wild and lethal threat" to male-dominated world orders, "and therefore must be controlled and repressed." Thus "it was the male priesthoods of Father God religions who first wrote and enforced the new laws and new customs that stripped Neolithic women of all their ancient sexual autonomy, and made their sexual and reproductive functions the property of a dominating male elite." It was left to the Christian church, though, to impose "a form of marriage involving the greatest possible restriction of sexual feeling."[100] Z Budapest says it thus:

> The Goddess is intimately connected with religious sexual practices; when mating and pleasuring are observed in Her honor alone, giving up any and all sexual inhibitions of any current era. The patriarchal sexual mores are direct reversals of this religious sexual enjoyment. All taboos of Judaeo-Christianity were made against the values of the Old Religion.[101]

One of Goddess feminism's goals is to throw off all these "taboos" and to reinstate the uninhibited sexual scenario of the Goddess era. This would allow not only for pre-marital and extra-marital sex, but also for all kinds of sexual diversity (i.e., gay and lesbian homosexuality). Starhawk says, "If we value integrity, we must also value diversity in sexual expression and orientation, recognizing that there is no one truth, or one way, that fits everyone." There must be no physical or social coercion upon anyone "to focus their sexual drives in so-called acceptable channels." When "ethics is based on integrity instead of authority, no one has the right to interfere with another's sexual choice. 'All acts of love and pleasure are my rituals,' is a statement Witches attribute to the Goddess."[102]

As we might expect, Goddess feminists are very interested in defending lesbianism. In their effort to return to the spirit of the days of the Goddess, they note the probability that "the present-day Lesbian woman is the closest in character to ancient women." Indeed, "creative women and men in all ages have found rigid heterosexuality in conflict with being fully alive and aware on all levels."[103] Z Budapest offers a lesbian substitute for traditional marriage called "Dianic Trysting." The vow is worded thus: "Do you, [name], take this woman, [name], for your friend and lover for this life time, promise to care and love even if you love others in addition or not?" It will be noted that even this vow does not rule out promiscuous relationships with other women.[104] The spirit of rebellion is total.

D. Abortion as a Symbol of Female Autonomy

A final element of the feminist rebellion to be noted here is the emphatic demand for complete autonomy over the decision of whether to have an abortion or not. In some ways the so-called "right" to abortion is just another aspect of female sexual autonomy. It allows for the freedom of sexual indulgence without the fear of having to suffer the long-term consequences of pregnancy. But Goddess feminists (like all feminists) see abortion in the much broader context of female autonomy as such. They see it as a concrete symbol of their ideal of complete individual autonomy, the freedom to make their own decisions without having to follow any rules imposed upon them from outside themselves, especially from men or male Gods.

Laws against abortion, like all "moral laws," are regarded as the product of patriarchy; they are rules made and enforced by men "in a society which is male-controlled and serves male interests." Thus the real issue is "patriarchal authoritarianism," namely, whether men will continue to maintain control over women and over their bodies. Religious opponents of abortion usually claim they are concerned about the lives of the infants, but "their true concern is to maintain absolute control over the bodies of women, since it is upon this control that their entire religion is based." The so-called "pro-lifers" are not really pro-*life*. "Rather, they are pro-*control*; their obsession is the old

Bronze Age fundamentalist-patriarchal obsession to control female sex and reproduction."[105]

> . . . The biblical God, and the fundamentalist men who wave his holy book under the noses of pro-abortion women, are not involved in a religion of Life, but in a religion of male control. Fundamental to this religion, and this control, is a male's exclusive right to make life-and-death decisions. Abortion represents woman's right to make such decisions. And the fundamentalist men cannot bear the thought of sharing such ontological power with women. They oppose abortions not because they care mightily about the fetus – by their historic record, they show they never have – but they do care mightily about retaining this exclusive male power over life and death. For it is this power which keeps them in power.[106]

The women's movement says that this has to end, and that women must wrest control of their own bodies away from men. Henceforward, "women as individuals will make the decisions in matters most intimately concerning ourselves. I think that this, on the deepest level, is what authoritarian religion fears" in reference to the abortion issue, says Daly.[107] The real issue simply is male authority versus female autonomy.[108]

To some women there is much more involved than just having autonomous control over one's own body. They see it as a question of who will control the future of our planet. "When women begin to define our own lives, including being ontologically responsible for each life we choose to bring – or not bring – into the world, then women will become fully functioning *definers of the world*. And then we will be fully responsible for the kind of world . . . into which we bring new life."[109] Eisler presents a real doomsday scenario which will inevitably occur, she says, unless women regain full abortion rights. The world is plagued with all sorts of problems such as poverty, famine, pollution, and resource depletion; but all of these are traceable to one main problem – overpopulation. And overpopulation keeps worsening because in this world "women are viewed as male-controlled technologies of reproduction." Unless we want to rely solely on disease, hunger, and war, "giving top priority to reproductive freedom and equality for women is the only other way to halt the population explosion."[110] Thus the alternatives are women's autonomy over abortion, or increasing global disaster.

It all comes back ultimately to the question of autonomy, a point these women freely acknowledge. They resent being under any kind of external authority, especially when that authority is perceived as male on either the human or divine level. Their fanatical demand to be free from all restrictions on abortion is just part of the larger demand to be free from authority as such.

E. Conclusion

Whether the Goddess feminists or anyone else likes it or not, there is such a thing as absolute moral law. It is grounded in the eternally unchanging nature of God himself, and he reveals it to us by writing it on our hearts (Romans 2:14-15) and in the Bible. It is characteristic of sinners in general to despise God's law, for the law not only places them under condemnation for their sins but also inhibits them from sinning even more. Thus we are not surprised that sin is identified with lawlessness (1 John 3:4), which involves not just a breaking of the law but also a hatred of it and a spirit of rebellion against it.

This desire of sinners to be free from the law and its consequences is the root of all denials of God and of the Bible. Goddess feminists are no different from anyone else in this regard. It is typical of sinners in general that they reject absolutes and joyfully embrace ethical relativism. It is natural for all sinners to deny the very concept of sin. And it also seems typical that whenever ethical restraints are abandoned, the moral law concerning sexual behavior is the first to be trodden under foot.

Thus Goddess feminists are following a well-worn path when they walk away from God and reject his moral law. What is different about them is they are doing this self-consciously within the framework of pagan idolatry.

IV. IDOLATRY IN THE FORM OF SELF-WORSHIP

The God of the Bible, who is Yahweh, and who is Father and Son and Holy Spirit, is the one true and living God. The worship of any other so-called deity, whether it be a god or goddess, is condemned in the Bible as idolatry. Goddess feminism openly, boldly, and proudly stands for worship of the Great Goddess and deliberately rejects even the very reality of the God of the Bible. Thus they are guilty of idolatry in the first degree.

Any Bible-believer who reads the voluminous feminist material that details the prevalence of Goddess worship in ancient times cannot help but call to mind Romans 1:18-32. Here Paul speaks of those who knew God but did not honor him as God, but instead became futile in their speculations and became fools "and exchanged the glory of the incorruptible God for an image in the form of corruptible man and of birds and four-footed animals and crawling creatures. . . . For they exchanged the truth of God for a lie, and worshiped and served the creature rather than the Creator." No matter how much data Goddess feminism may amass concerning Goddess worship in the so-called "pre-patriarchal" era, it will not change the fact that it was all idolatry, a worshiping of the creature rather than the Creator. The fact that it existed or even prevailed does not make it normative or right. The same is true of any modern-day Goddess worship; it is still idolatry.

But we must note one important difference between ancient Goddess worship and that which exists in Goddess feminism today. It is apparent that the original followers of the Old Religion believed that their deities, their gods and goddesses, were distinct beings. They believed they were worshiping entities that really existed apart from themselves and that could personally interact with them. This is not true of modern Goddess feminists, however. As we have seen, they deny that the "Goddess" is an actual being who exists apart from themselves and the universe. In a monistic, pantheistic manner they identify the Goddess with the universe and with themselves. They speak of the "Goddess within," and they speak of themselves as being the Goddess.

Thus when these feminists speak about worshiping the Goddess, what they really mean is that they are worshiping themselves. Their emphasis on female power and the female will and female autonomy is nothing less than this, i.e., self-worship. They recognize no being higher than themselves and accept no authority outside themselves. Invoking the image of the "Goddess" is pure symbolism; it gives their self-deification a religious aura. In this way they differ from the secular feminists, but the difference is not significant. They both agree that the female will is the supreme factor in the universe, and they both bow before it in absolute reverence and devotion. One group chooses to speak of it as "the Goddess"; the other does not. It is idolatry in either case.

A primary expression of this idolatry or self-worship is the elevation of "women's experience" to the level of canonical authority. The number one rule for a feminist is this: female experience is the highest norm. A former Goddess follower says she "learned from wicca that a woman's will is sacred and that her true spiritual experience constitutes the new 'holy Scripture' that she should live by."[111] In her address at the "Women in the Church" conference in Washington, D.C., in 1986, Mary Jo Weaver declared, "What happens right here, right now, in this world, is revelation." Thus, "women's experience is a legitimate context for the continual self-communication of the Divine." We are "engaged in a new revelational encounter with the Divine, in and through women's experience." Dr. Weaver teaches in the religious studies department at Indiana University and, according to Donna Steichen, is "named with reverence among wicca-goddess feminists."[112]

Thus women's experience is the basis of all evaluations of existing institutions and conditions, and of all conclusions about the nature of true reality and good behavior. In other words, it is the basis of all the "theologizing" (or thealogizing) done by women. As Carol Christ says, "My theology, or rather thealogy, reflections on the meaning of Goddess, is rooted in my experience." Also, "I judge everything I learn from the past on the basis on [sic] my own experience as shaped, named, and confirmed by the voices of my sisters."[113] "Today we are creating feminist theory out of women's experience," says Daly.[114] All theology is grounded in experience, says Goldenberg. Patriarchal theology is based on male experience, but most male theologians just don't understand this. Feminists do understand it, though, and are deliberately making their experience their norm.[115]

V. CONCLUSION

In this chapter we have discussed the relation of Goddess feminism to Biblical faith. The contrast and the rivalry between them could hardly be more radical, and the hostility of Goddess feminists toward the Bible and Christianity could hardly be stronger. We have seen that the followers of the Goddess are self-consciously anti-biblical. They attack the Hebrew religion of the Old Testament and the Christianity of the New. Both are guilty, they say, of overthrowing the true religion of the Goddess and supplanting it with male-dominant, woman-hating systems. Thus their goal is to "liberate" the Goddess by working for the eradication of Biblical faith.

We have also seen that Goddess feminists have a perverted interpretation of the Bible. One might hope that if
they could come to a proper understanding of it, they
might be more kindly disposed to its teaching. This is not
likely, however. That is, it is not likely that they will come
to such a proper understanding; and even if they did, it is
not likely that this would change their attitude toward it
very much. At least this will be the case as long as they
continue to rebel against God's moral law and exalt their
own wills and experience to the level of self-worship.

At this point, then, we can only consider Goddess feminism to be a self-proclaimed and outspoken enemy of Biblical faith. It is important that we recognize this, because
there are some elements in Christendom that seem to be
becoming more open and susceptible to its doctrine, especially those who are already strongly feminist in their
thinking and who have a spiritual bent, but who are convinced that the traditional churches are not moving fast
enough in the direction of women's liberation. This is certainly more true of the liberal branches of Christendom
than the conservative.

Thus anyone who has any commitment to even the most
basic elements of the Christian faith needs to be reminded
that Goddess feminism and Biblical teaching are completely incompatible, period. This is true not only on the
theoretical level but on the practical level as well. The
relation between Goddess spirituality and witchcraft
cannot be forgotten. Modern witchcraft (wicca) may not
project the evil and sinister image of past centuries, but it
is still unabashedly occult and uses occult powers which
many Christians believe are derived from demonic spirits.
This only multiplies the dangers for anyone tempted to
flirt with Goddess feminism on any level.

It is not often that we encounter a movement or an ideology that is so open and frank in its opposition to God's
word. If we fail to denounce it, and to warn and guard one

another against it, our guilt and our shame will be all the greater for it.

Endnotes

1. Naomi R. Goldenberg, *Changing of the Gods: Feminism and the End Of Traditional Religions* (Boston: Beacon Press, 1979), pp. 111-114.

2. Carol Christ, *Laughter of Aphrodite: Reflections on a Journey to the Goddess* (San Francisco: Harper & Row, 1987), p. 87; Riane Eisler, *The Chalice and the Blade: Our History, Our Future* (San Francisco: Harper & Row, 1987), p. 95.

3. Merlin Stone, *When God Was a Woman* (New York: Dial Press, 1976), pp. 103ff.

4. Eisler, *The Chalice and the Blade*, pp. 44, 58, 92ff.

5. Monica Sjöö and Barbara Mor, *The Great Cosmic Mother: Rediscovering the Religion of the Earth* (San Francisco: Harper & Row, 1987), pp. 264-269.

6. Stone, *When God Was A Woman*, p. 9ff., 163ff.; Eisler, *The Chalice and the Blade*, p. 7.

7. Sjöö and Mor, *The Great Cosmic Mother*, p. 269.

8. Carol Christ, *Laughter of Aphrodite*, pp. 38-39. See also Stone, *When God Was A Woman*, p. 167.

9. Carol Christ, *Laughter of Aphrodite*, p. 84. Merlin Stone describes the Hebrews' treatment of idolatry and idolaters as "persecution of the religion of the Goddess" (*When God Was A Woman*, p. 193).

10. Sjöö and Mor, *The Great Cosmic Mother*, pp. 232, 422.

11. Ibid., p. 231.

12. Ibid., p. 365.

13. Carol Christ, *Laughter of Aphrodite*, pp. 126, 222.

14. Starhawk [Miriam Simos], *Dreaming the Dark: Magic, Sex and Politics*, new ed. (Boston: Beacon Press, 1988), p. 5.

15. Sjöö and Mor, *The Great Cosmic Mother*, pp. 342-343.

16. Ibid., pp. 270-275, 289.

17. Stone, *When God Was A Woman*, pp. 153-162, 181.

18. Ibid., p. 161.

19. Ibid., p. 182.

20. Margot Adler, *Drawing Down the Moon: Witches, Druids, Goddess-Worshippers, and Other Pagans in America Today*, revised ed. (Boston: Beacon Press, 1986), p. 200.

21. Carol Christ, *Laughter of Aphrodite*, pp. 140-141.

22. Mary Daly, *Beyond God the Father: Toward a Philosophy of Women's Liberation,* new paperback edition, "With an Original Reintroduction by the Author" (Boston: Beacon Press, 1985), pp. 46-47.

23. Ibid., pp. 45-48. Sjöö and Mor remark that "Eve is still Everywoman," and her story "is still treated with seriousness and respect in the Western political and cultural world" (*The Great Cosmic Mother,* p. 277).

24. Stone, *When God Was A Woman,* pp. 197-198, 222.

25. Ibid., p. 219.

26. Ibid., pp. 214-216, 220.

27. Ibid., pp. 199-211, 220-221.

28. Eisler, *The Chalice and the Blade,* pp. 88-89.

29. Ibid., p. 89. See also Sjöö and Mor, *The Great Cosmic Mother,* pp. 58, 276.

30. Sjöö and Mor, *The Great Cosmic Mother,* pp. 276, 289.

31. Stone, *When God Was A Woman,* pp. 220-221. See p. 217.

32. Madonna Kolbenschlag, in an address given at a women's conference in Washington, D.C., on October 10, 1986, as reported in Donna Steichen, "The Goddess Goes to Washington," *Fidelity* (December 1986), 6:41.

33. Stone, *When God Was A Woman,* p. xii.

34. Ibid., pp. 6, 225.

35. Kolbenschlag, as cited in Steichen, "The Goddess Goes to Washington," p. 42.

36. Adler, *Drawing Down the Moon,* pp. 200-201.

37. Carol Christ, *Laughter of Aphrodite,* p. 85.

38. Starhawk, *Dreaming the Dark,* p. 5; Sjöö and Mor, *The Great Cosmic Mother,* p. 342.

39. Sjöö and Mor, *The Great Cosmic Mother,* pp. 288, 343.

40. Daly, *Beyond God the Father,* pp. 71-72.

41. Sjöö and Mor, *The Great Cosmic Mother,* p. 170.

42. Ibid., p. 315.

43. Goldenberg, *Changing of the Gods,* pp. 8, 22.

44. Daly, *Beyond God the Father,* pp. 96-97.

45. Sjöö and Mor, *The Great Cosmic Mother,* p. 351.

46. Carol Christ, *Laughter of Aphrodite,* p. 178. Sjöö and Mor argue that the original meaning of "virgin" was not sexual chastity but sexual independence, i.e., the concept of a woman's having sex whenever and with whomever she liked. It was the later Christian translators who "distorted the meaning into sexually pure, chaste, never touched" (*The Great Cosmic Mother*), pp. 158-159.

47. Goldenberg, *Changing of the Gods,* p. 105.

48. Mary Daly, *Gyn/Ecology: The Metaethics of Radical Feminism* (Boston: Beacon Press, 1978), pp. 83-85.

49. Sjöö and Mor, *The Great Cosmic Mother,* p. 354.

50. Ibid., p. 286; Daly, *Gyn/Ecology,* p. 79.

51. See Alison Lentini, "Circle of Sisters: A Journey Through Elemental Feminism," *SCP Newsletter* (Fall 1985), p. 14. She seems to be excerpting this quotation from the summer 1976 issue of WomanSpirit.

52. Sjöö and Mor, *The Great Cosmic Mother,* pp. 185, 354. Feminists are anxious to create a positive image of menstruation for themselves, and this is one way they try to do it. "From hidden dirty secret to symbol of the life power of the Goddess, women's blood has come full circle" (Carol Christ, *Laughter of Aphrodite,* p. 126).

53. Eisler, *The Chalice and the Blade,* p. 103.

54. Daly, *Gyn/Ecology,* pp. 79-80.

55. Goldenberg, *Changing of the Gods,* p. 105.

56. Sjöö and Mor, *The Great Cosmic Mother,* p. 315. See Goldenberg, *Changing of the Gods,* p. 105.

57. Carol Christ, *Laughter of Aphrodite,* pp. 214-218.

58. Sjöö and Mor, *The Great Cosmic Mother,* p. 315.

59. E. Michael Jones, "Witchcraft at Indiana University," *Fidelity* (May 1987), 6:22.

60. Sjöö and Mor, *The Great Cosmic Mother,* p. 344.

61. Goldenberg, *Changing of the Gods,* pp. 3-4.

62. Ibid., pp. 10, 25.

63. Daly, *Gyn/Ecology,* p. 57.

64. Steichen, "The Goddess Goes to Washington, " pp. 34, 44.

65. Carol Christ, *Laughter of Aphrodite,* pp. 25-26. This is from a chapter entitled "Women's Liberation and the Liberation of God."

66. Ronald and Beverly Allen, *Liberated Traditionalism: Men and Women in Balance* (Portland, OR: Multnomah Press, 1985), p. 55.

67. Sjöö and Mor, *The Great Cosmic Mother,* pp. 231, 288-289, 342; Starhawk, *Dreaming the Dark,* p. 5.

68. Carol Christ, *Laughter of Aphrodite,* p. 217.

69. Sjöö and Mor, *The Great Cosmic Mother,* p. 342.

70. Ibid., pp. 289, 291.

71. Ibid., pp. 270, 275, 368; Stone, *When God Was A Woman,* p. 155.

72. Sjöö and Mor, *The Great Cosmic Mother,* pp. 290, 367.

73. Ibid., pp. 276, 289, 367; Stone, *When God Was A Woman,* pp. 217, 220-221.

74. Stone, *When God Was A Woman,* pp. 6, 225.

75. Sjöö and Mor, *The Great Cosmic Mother,* pp. 365-367.

76. Carol Christ, *Laughter of Aphrodite,* p. 154.

77. Sjöö and Mor, *The Great Cosmic Mother,* p. 276.

78. Ibid., p. 155.

79. Ibid., p. 351; Adler, *Drawing Down the Moon,* p. 203; Daly, *Beyond God the Father,* pp. 90-92.

80. Sjöö and Mor, *The Great Cosmic Mother,* p. 264.

81. Ibid., p. 342.

82. Ibid., p. 273.

83. Sjöö and Mor claim that the "basic tenets" of the Old Testament priesthood are "that (1) human sex is sacred only for reproductive purposes and (2) women have nothing to say about it except 'Yes, master'" (*The Great Cosmic Mother,* p. 365). Their whole book seems to be based on this false premise (cf. p. 5).

84. Starhawk, *Dreaming the Dark,* pp. 39, 41.

85. Goldenberg, *Changing of the Gods,* pp. 112-113.

86. Carol Christ, *Laughter of Aphrodite,* p. 128.

87. Goldenberg, *Changing of the Gods,* p. 93.

88. Lynn Pollock Marsh, as quoted in *The Womanspirit Sourcebook,* ed. Patrice Wynne (San Francisco: Harper & Row, 1988), p. 165.

89. Goldenberg, *Changing of the Gods,* p. 112.

90. Daly, *Beyond God the Father,* p. 31.

91. Daly, *Gyn/Ecology,* p. 30.

92. Stone, *When God Was A Woman,* pp. 161, 181-182.

93. Sjöö and Mor, *The Great Cosmic Mother,* p. 206.

94. Daly, *Gyn/Ecology,* p. 6.

95. Daly, *Beyond God the Father,* p. xxv.

96. Sjöö and Mor, *The Great Cosmic Mother,* p. 343.

97. Goldenberg, *Changing of the Gods,* p. 114.

98. Daly, *Beyond God the Father,* p. 125.

99. Stone, *When God Was A Woman,* pp. 161, 181-182.

100. Sjöö and Mor, *The Great Cosmic Mother,* pp. 6, 290, 365.

101. Zsuzsanna Budapest, in a speech at Indiana University at South Bend, as reported by E. Michael Jones, in "Witchcraft at Indiana University," p. 24.

102. Starhawk, *Dreaming the Dark,* pp. 41-42.

103. Sjöö and Mor, *The Great Cosmic Mother,* p. 67.

104. Z Budapest, cited in Jones, "Witchcraft at Indiana University," pp. 24-25. Jones comments, "In other words, you can be true to one person while having sex with another" (p. 25).

105. Daly, *Beyond God the Father,* pp. 108, 110; Sjöö and Mor, *The Great Cosmic Mother,* pp. 203, 373-4.

106. Sjöö and Mor, *The Great Cosmic Mother*, p. 376.
107. Daly, *Beyond God the Father*, p. 113.
108. Sjöö and Mor, *The Great Cosmic Mother*, pp. 377-78, 388.
109. Ibid., p. 378.
110. Eisler, *The Chalice and the Blade*, pp. 174-176.
111. Alison Lentini, "Circle of Sisters: A Journey Through Elemental Feminism," *SCP Newsletter* (Fall 1985), p. 16.
112. Steichen, "The Goddess Goes to Washington," pp. 35, 41.
113. Carol Christ, *Laughter of Aphrodite*, pp. ix, xi.
114. Mary Daly, *The Church and the Second Sex*, Colophon edition, "With a New Feminist Postchristian Introduction by the Author" (New York: Harper, 1975), p. 41.
115. Goldenberg, *Changing of the Gods*, pp. 115-117.

5 LIBERAL CHRISTIAN FEMINISM: GOALS AND NORM

The third major type of feminism is liberal Christian feminism. This type shares the same general goals of secular and Goddess feminism, but it pursues these goals from within the Christian framework and seeks to apply them to Christendom as well as to society as a whole.

Liberal Christian feminists reject the secular view that religion is no longer relevant for women as they struggle for freedom. They affirm the need for religious symbols and rituals and communities "to guide and interpret the actual experience of the journey from sexism to liberated humanity."[1] In this regard they agree with the Goddess feminists.

However, the liberal Christian feminists strongly disagree with their Goddess sisters regarding the value of the Bible and Christianity for the women's movement. The Goddess feminists agree that women still need a spiritual

159

base, but they reject Biblical faith as a viable form of women's spirituality because of its inherent patriarchy. They take the Bible to be totally oppressive and irredeemable for feminists.[2] In this sense they are called post-Christian and postbiblical.

Liberal Christian feminists agree that the Bible is androcentric and patriarchal, at least in part if not totally. But they disagree with the Goddess feminists as to whether or not it should simply be abandoned. As Letty Russell avows, "In spite of the patriarchal nature of the biblical texts, I myself have no intention of giving up the biblical basis of my theology."[3] This decision to remain within the boundaries of Christendom centers mainly upon Jesus Christ. "Those who would do Christian theology cannot abandon the story of Jesus of Nazareth."[4] Thus they take the view that the Biblical message can still be a force for feminism, despite its patriarchy. There are still "positive resources in the Biblical tradition" that can be rescued.[5] Thus it is not necessary for women "to develop a new religion and create new gods in order to liberate themselves."[6]

Elisabeth Schüssler Fiorenza agrees, despite the fact that she considers the Bible as a whole to be steeped in patriarchy. Postbiblical feminism gives up on Christianity too quickly, she says; it "too easily relinquishes women's feminist biblical heritage."[7] It is just not that easy for one to disengage herself from her roots. Besides, the Bible has been and still is very influential. It is not only a major source of women's oppression, but also a source of many positive experiences for women. For these reasons, "Western women are not able to discard completely and forget our personal, cultural, or religious Christian history. We will either transform it into a new liberating future or continue to be subject to its tyranny whether we recognize its power or not."[8]

This explains why this version of feminism is called *Christian*, but why is it called *liberal*? This has to do with its view of the nature of the Bible. Even though it accepts the Christian heritage and seeks to come to terms with the Bible's message about women, liberal Christian feminism does not accept the Bible as the revealed and inspired Word of God. (This is in contrast with the fourth type, evangelical Christian feminism, which will be discussed next.) It rejects the so-called "doctrinal approach," which "understands the Bible in terms of divine revelation and canonical authority," and most consistently "insists on the verbal inspiration and literal-historical inerrancy of the Bible."[9] Fiorenza declares that "biblical texts are not verbally inspired revelation," and that "a feminist hermeneutics cannot trust or accept Bible and tradition simply as divine revelation." She agrees with Elizabeth Cady Stanton that "biblical texts are not the words of God but the words of *men*."[10] Russell declares with emphasis that *"the Word of God is not identical with the biblical texts."* In fact, "the Bible is especially dangerous if we call it 'the Word of God' and think that divine inspiration means that everything we read is right."[11]

Thus the term *liberal* means "liberal Christian" as opposed to "conservative or evangelical Christian." For the sake of efficiency, henceforward this view will usually be referred to simply as liberal feminism.

Also for the sake of efficiency, this study will focus primarily on the writings of three leading representatives of liberal feminism, namely, Letty M. Russell, Rosemary Radford Ruether, and Elisabeth Schüssler Fiorenza. Russell was ordained in 1958 by the United Presbyterian Church, USA. She has served with the East Harlem Protestant Parish, the National Council of Churches, and the World Council of Churches. Most recently she has been Professor of the Practice of Theology at Yale Divinity School.

Ruether is the Georgia Harkness Professor of Applied Theology at Garrett-Evangelical Theological Seminary. She has also taught at Howard University, Harvard, and Yale divinity schools. She is a leading Roman Catholic feminist ("the diva of Catholic feminism"[12]), and has been a columnist for *National Catholic Reporter.*

Fiorenza, another Roman Catholic feminist, has been Professor of New Testament and Theology at the University of Notre Dame, as well as Talbot Professor of New Testament Studies at the Episcopal Divinity School in Cambridge, Massachusetts. Some of the groups she has worked with are the Women's Ordination Conference, Sisters Against Sexism, the Feminist Theological Institute, Women Scholars in Religion, Women in Theology, and Women Moving Church. When referring to her by her "last name," some call her Schüssler Fiorenza and others just Fiorenza. We have adopted the latter practice.

Our purpose here is not to cover the whole scope of liberal feminist theology, but to focus especially on its view of Biblical authority and interpretation.

I. THE AGENDA OF LIBERAL FEMINISM

Liberal feminist theology has two interrelated goals or agendas, says Ruether. One is negative: to unmask and critique the sexist bias and patriarchy of traditional theology. The other is positive: to rescue theology from sexism by reconstructing its basic foundations from the feminist perspective.[13] The latter goal involves the very essence of feminism, i.e., liberating women from male oppression and restoring them to a status of equality with men. Since these are *Christian* feminists, it also involves what is regarded as the restoration of equal roles for women in the church.

A. The Repudiation of Patriarchy

In agreement with the women's movement in general, liberal feminists describe all culture, including religious institutions, as thoroughly sexist, androcentric, and patriarchal. Sexism is "the distortion of humanity as male and

162

female into a dualism of superiority and inferiority," a "fundamentally male ideology" which provides "the support for male identity as normative humanity and the justification of servile roles for women." In short, "sexism is gender privilege of males over females."[14] Androcentric means literally "male-centered." It includes the idea that males are central in importance because they are superior to women. Fiorenza says that androcentrism is a mind-set or a way of thinking, while patriarchy is the social-cultural system itself or a way of acting. A patriarchal culture is a "system in which a few men have power over other men, women, children, slaves, and colonialized people."[15] The patriarchal concept of authority is domination over others,[16] thus its model for society is a "pyramidal system and hierarchical structure of society and church" which involve "graded subjugations and oppressions."[17]

The obvious result of patriarchy is the oppression of women. Men are the oppressors; women are the oppressed.[18] "*Patriarchy* as a male pyramid of graded subordinations and exploitations specifies women's oppression in terms of the class, race, country, or religion of the men to whom we 'belong.' "[19] It is a demonic caste system in which women "by birth, find themselves as a separate and inferior caste in relation to male social norms and privilege."[20] Unfortunately women have been culturally "programmed" to accept a life of subservience, male domination, dehumanization, oppression, and exploitation.[21]

Thus a major task of feminism is to unmask and repudiate this universal patriarchy. "Patriarchy is rejected as God's will. It is rejected as the order of creation or as a reflection of biological nature. Patriarchy is named as a historically contrived social system" by which ruling-class males have placed themselves in places of domination over women and others.[22] Such patriarchy or oppression is the very essence of evil, the new definition of sin. "Sexism is a root expression of sin."[23] It must be identified and branded as such for the sake of women and the world.

B. The Reaffirmation of the Integrity of Women

On the positive side the goal of liberal feminism is to liberate women from patriarchy and to reaffirm and restore their full partnership in the human race. As Fiorenza says, "The goal is women's (religious) self-affirmation, power, and liberation from all patriarchal alienation, marginalization, and exploitation."[24]

Except for the religious element, liberal feminists are no different from any others. They are feminists in the full sense of the word. In essence, "a feminist is one who advocates the human dignity and equality of women and men."[25] Feminism implies more than a verbal advocacy; it requires political action to bring about change. "Feminism is not just a theoretical world view or perspective but a women's liberation movement for social and ecclesiastical change."[26] This is how a *feminist* differs from a *female*, which is a term referring to biological characteristics, and from a *feminine* person, which is a term referring to culturally defined roles and characteristics.[27]

Liberal feminism is a facet of feminism in general; it is also a facet of the broad movement of liberation theology. Russell says, "Feminist theology today is, by definition, *liberation theology* because it is concerned with the liberation of all people to become full participants in human society. *Liberation theology is an attempt to reflect upon the experiences of oppression and our actions for the new creation of a more human society.*"[28] On the other hand, Ruether distinguishes feminism from liberation theology because she thinks the latter is basically a male effort.[29]

In either case the goal is the liberation of women. If oppression is the new definition of sin, then liberation is the new definition of salvation. This is a recurring theme in theology today, says Russell, namely, "that *salvation today* has to do with *liberation now* from all those things which keep humanity in slavery."[30]

Feminism is liberation *from* sexism and liberation *to* a

status of full equality. Equality is the central emphasis here. A feminist is one "actively engaged in advocating the equality and partnership of women and men in church and society," or women's "full partnership in humanity." The "radical goal" of feminist theology is "true partnership" in "co-humanity," and the eradication of "the basic polarity of *authority-submission.*" It seeks "a truly androgynous world where men and women [are] equal."[31] The "feminist critical consciousness" is the perception "that women and men are fully human and fully equal."[32]

Achieving this gender equality would require a complete paradigm shift (a term of which feminists seem particularly fond), a "shift from an androcentric to a feminist interpretation of the world."[33] The patriarchal paradigm of the hierarchical pyramid would have to give way to the feminist paradigm of mutual partnership. This concept of an ontological hierarchy of being has been applied to the cosmos as a whole. God is at the very top of the "great chain of being," and pure matter is at the bottom. In between are angels, humans, animals, plants, and such things as rocks. "Each level above is both morally and ontologically superior to that below it and is mandated to rule over it." The same thinking is applied to the human community: "Men rule over women . . . just as God rules nature." This is the model that has to go. It must be replaced by a non-hierarchical paradigm of mutuality in which no one is "beneath" anyone else.[34]

This would basically be a shift in the paradigm of authority, says Russell. The prevailing paradigm, she says, is authority as domination or authority-over. But this paradigm no longer makes sense to feminists, who advocate instead the concept of authority as partnership or interdependence. The pyramid gives way to the rainbow, which has no bottom or top but just diversity. Outranking gives way to enriching. Authority over community gives way to authority in community.[35]

By abandoning the hierarchical ontology in general, liberal feminists join the ranks of all those ecofeminists who have a monistic view of reality and a consequent reverence for all of nature. The "circle of interdependence" or "rainbow spectrum" embraces not only humanity but nature as well.[36] In the name of feminism Ruether rejects any "dualism of nature and spirit." Her "ecological-feminist theology of nature" excludes "the hierarchical chain of being and chain of command." It excludes "the hierarchy of human over nonhuman nature." We must "come to recognize the continuity of human consciousness with the radial energy of matter throughout the universe," and acknowledge "a 'thou-ness' in all beings." The "brotherhood of man" must be "widened to embrace not only women but also the whole community of life." We who reject androcentrism must also "criticize humanocentrism," or "making humans the norm and 'crown' of creation." This is another form of chauvinism, says Ruether.[37] (One of her new liturgies for Women-Church is an "Earth Day Celebration," which includes exorcising the spirits of pollution from earth, air, water, and society; and planting a tree.[38])

By pressing the paradigm of full equality of men and women to its limits, liberal feminists also join the ranks of the secular and Goddess feminists who have abandoned the Biblical norms for marriage, family, and sexual expression. New life-styles are needed, says Russell, in the areas of family and marriage. The traditional approach has not been working.

> Women and men are thus beginning to explore alternatives such as communal marriages, serial mating, single parent arrangements, cluster families, polygamy, homosexual arrangements. . . . To assert that only one arrangement, such as the nuclear family, is possible, is simply to deny the historical and social facts. . . . New forms of human sexuality might provide a basis for new life-styles and roles for women and men. . . .[39]

In a "truly androgynous world," she says, "each one could express his or her life-style in a variety of ways."[40]

Ruether's book of feminist liturgies also includes something called a "Coming-Out Rite for a Lesbian." Discovery of the fact that "one's sexuality is the good gift of God/ess provides the basis for celebration." The ritual is "based on the tradition of baptismal renewal rites," and includes a parody of "baptism" in which water is sprinkled or poured on the woman coming out and the following words are spoken: "Born of woman, beloved of woman, lover of woman, you are blessed. You are the light of the world."[41] This is in a chapter entitled "Healing Our Wounds: Overcoming the Violence of Patriarchy." The idea here is that patriarchy's opposition to homosexuality (i.e., homophobia) constitutes violence and creates unnecessary guilt and repression. Thus the ritual is included here, "because in homophobic society this event cannot be seen as the simple affirmation of a God-gifted sexual preference, but as the repudiation of past guilt and repression that have denied one's nature and a crying out against the homophobic society that has created this guilt and repression."[42]

In a happier context Ruether also includes a "Covenant Celebration for a Lesbian Couple," which is a parody of a marriage ceremony, complete with an exchange of rings and a communion service.[43]

Herein lies the fruit of the liberal feminist understanding of "liberation from patriarchy" and the restoration of the "full equality" of men and women.

C. The Restoration of Equal Roles for Women in the Church

Since liberal feminism works within the boundaries of Christendom, it is especially concerned to see that the feminist agenda is applied to the church. The church (in its various forms) is seen as a microcosm of culture as a whole. Culture in general is the embodiment of patriarchy's hierarchical pyramid of domination and submission; the church is exactly the same on a smaller scale. Thus when the paradigm of partnership is applied to the church, the result is the demand for equal access for women to ordination or to the decision-making process as such.

Russell devotes considerable attention to how authority is exercised in the church. She sees the church using the same hierarchical pyramid model that has prevailed in society in general. It entered the church through the influence of the ancient Greeks and Romans, being evident at least as early as the time of the Pastoral epistles.[44] The pyramid of domination has continued to determine church practices especially with regard to the role of women. Authority is exercised through hierarchical control; it is seen as authority-over. This very concept of authority, when it becomes the job description of the clergy, tends to exclude women. This is because "women do not fit at all well into this view of ministry." They are "not good representatives of authority, of 'father right.'"[45] Thus feminist theology must challenge the church to reject this "basic polarity of *authority-submission*," for "the church has no business continuing to order its life and thought in pyramids of domination."[46]

Another area in which the church has been persistently patriarchal is in its use of sexist or exclusive language, both in Scripture and in liturgy.[47] This, too, must be challenged.

The church is patriarchal and sexist also in that it often limits or even denies ordination to women. This is especially a problem for Catholic women, who are categorically denied admission to the priesthood; but some Protestant denominations have also made the ordination of women difficult if not impossible. Russell says that "ministry has been identified with an *all-male caste system* that dominates the work of most churches." This is an important issue, because to women it "is symbolic of the oppressive

168

structures of church life. It is also a key issue in the struggle of Christian women to find a dynamic sisterhood among themselves." If someone asks, "Why should *women* be ordained as clergy?", Russell replies that this question ought never to arise in the first place. The real question is this: "Why should *men* or anyone else be ordained to a special clerical status when all share the one calling of the whole people?"[48]

Russell sums up the patriarchal nature of the church thus: "It oppresses the lives of women by excluding them from decision-making and equality, and endorsing the cultural myths of their ontological inferiority." Thus it is not improper "to number the church among the oppressors, and to speak of it mainly as an institution *from* which we must be liberated."[49]

While some feminists think these problems warrant abandoning the church completely, the liberal feminists do not. Rather than abandoning it, feminists must work to change it. They must face the task of *"subverting the church into being the church."*[50] This requires "a radical redefinition of ministry and church," says Ruether.[51]

Letty Russell presents such a redefinition in her model of the church as a "household of freedom." This is a metaphor drawn from the Exodus experience in the Old Testament. The Israelite slaves lived in Pharaoh's "house of bondage," but then moved out as the people of God toward a new "house of freedom."[52] The patriarchal church is equated with the house of bondage; the church as restored by feminists is the household of freedom.

The central element in this renewed church is a new concept of authority, that of *partnership*. Partnership must replace the pyramid of domination. The "structures of oppression" must be "confronted and transformed into a situation of true partnership." This is the Christian gospel and the feminist ideal. This ideal is authority-in-community, not authority-over-community; it is servant ministry, not authoritative ministry. It is the ideal of shared leader-

169

ship, where no one is "in charge."[53] A key idea for understanding this concept is that authority is not power but empowerment, i.e., using one's own skills to enable or empower others to take their place in the partnership. "If authority is understood as *authorizing* the inclusion of all persons as partners, and power is understood as *empowerment* for self-actualization together with others, then the entire game of authority shifts."[54]

This paradigm shift with reference to authority will open the way for women's ordination. "In this perspective the question of women's ordination is not settled on the authority of 1 Timothy or any other particular text, but rather on the basis of a different theological understanding of authority."[55] In the partnership model there is no reason for *anyone not* to be ordained. The whole concept of ordination itself will be transformed,[56] as will the concept of ministry. New metaphors of ministry will be developed to do justice to authority as empowerment, metaphors that fit women better than patriarchal models. "Enabling the whole people of God to grow by functioning as the 'Mother' of a congregation may be a way of responding to God's call as women seek to carry out their ministries in Christian community."[57]

Women's ordination is crucial for liberal feminists because it is viewed as symbolic of the success of its total agenda. "A woman who is an ordained minister . . . becomes a sign of the longed-for future of liberation and equality."[58]

One thing the liberal feminists insist upon is that the restored church must not continue to use sexist or exclusive language. This is not just a goal to be sought, but is an important means to achieving the total goal of a partnership church. This is true because language as such has tremendous power; and when women are excluded from the language, they are excluded from power. This is an important cause of "women's condition of relative powerlessness."[59] Some argue that the male forms of words are

generic and thus include women, but Russell replies that
this is "generic nonsense." The plain fact is that women are
excluded by such language and are made invisible. The
language must be "desexed."[60]

This desexing of the language must be applied to liturgy
and hymns[61] as well as to Scripture itself. Regarding the
latter, even if the original texts were sexist, the translations do not have to be.[62] It is especially important that
language used of God be inclusive. This involves "imaging
God as transcendent of male sexual characteristics or as
inclusive of both male and female characteristics."[63] Whatever it takes, Ruether declares that "male language for the
divine must lose its privileged place." She herself when
writing uses the term *God/ess* "to combine both the masculine and feminine forms of the word for the divine while
preserving the Judeo-Christian affirmation that divinity is
one."[64]

In these and other ways, liberal feminists are seeking to
rebuild and restore the church as the household of freedom. They are not trying to destroy the house altogether;
even "the house of authority as such" is not seen as the
enemy of truth. "Rather, it is the master's house of patriarchal authority that needs replacement."[65] When this
happens, the church will then properly be "humanity
redeemed from sexism."[66]

Is there any historical model for such a restored church,
or is it merely an ideal existing in the minds of liberal feminists? Even though the church for most of its history has
been corrupted by patriarchy, the feminists say that in the
very beginning the church (i.e, the body of the followers of
Christ) existed as an egalitarian partnership. According to
Fiorenza's reconstruction of early Christian history, the
two earliest forms of Christianity were gender inclusive.
These were the Jesus movement in Palestine, and the
Christian-missionary movement in the Graeco-Roman
world. In both contexts "women had the power and authority of the gospel. They were central and leading individuals

in the early Christian movement."[67]

Jesus certainly was a feminist in the sense that he considered men and women to be equal.[68] He intended a non-sexist, androgynous, non-patriarchal church, but his followers subverted his plan or were unable to effect it.[69] As part of the Christian-missionary movement, Paul recognized women ministers and their gifts and encouraged them to preach and pray and work as fellow apostles.[70] The house churches with which Paul worked were egalitarian partnerships at first.[71]

Thus we have "a glimpse of the egalitarian-inclusive practice and theology of early Christians." There were no doubt many more. "These texts are the tip of the iceberg indicating a possibly rich heritage now lost to us." We just have to read between the lines for it.[72] We have enough, though, to provide a kind of model or prototype for reconstructing the church today according to the feminist ideal.

The process of restoring the church may seem exceedingly slow to many, and to others it may seem almost hopeless. The structures of patriarchy are very strong and not easily toppled. How is it possible, then, for liberal feminists to find the kind of ecclesiastical fulfilment they crave, and how is it possible for them to pursue the theological work that must undergird the restoration effort while languishing in the confines of an unsympathetic church? For some women the answer is a separate (but not separatist) church: a church by, of, and for women. Ruether says, "Christian feminists cannot wait for the institutional churches to reform themselves enough to provide the vehicles of faith and worship that women need at this time."[73] Thus they have started Women-Church.

In 1983 a group called Women of the Church Coalition sponsored a major conference in Chicago called "Woman Church Speaks." Over 1400 women, mostly Roman Catholic,[74] attended its group liturgies and workshops.[75] After that meeting a number of Women-Church groups sprang up around the country. Twenty-six of these formed a coalition called Women-Church Convergence, which sponsored a second national conference, called "Women-Church: Claiming Our Power," in Cincinnati in 1987.[76] Speakers for this conference included Elisabeth Schüssler Fiorenza, Rosemary Radford Ruether, and Gloria Steinem. Dozens of main sessions and workshops included the following: "Women's Political Power: Rocking the Boats of Church and State"; "Spirituality: Women Stretching the Circle"; "Sexuality: Healthy, Good and Holy"; "How To Start a Local Women-Church Group"; "Lesbians Keeping Faith: Is It Possible?"; "Images of the Divine: Women and Power"; "Interpreting Scripture: The Dilemma of Feminism and Fidelity"; and "Seeing Through Patriarchy."

The conference also included several "feminist liturgies." One was a bread-making session in which loaves of bread were made from flour of different colors, a symbolic protest against racism. The main liturgy was a feminist eucharist, in which, according to the program brochure, "the many breads which we have made are shared 'in memory of her' and in memory of us. In our praying and remembering, our singing and dancing we are Women-Church, at home."

Ruether's book, *Women-Church,* contains several dozen suggested liturgies and rites for use in all sorts of events, some traditional (such as funerals and baptism) and some uniquely woman-related (e.g., Rite of Healing for Wife Battering, Rite of Healing from Rape, Rite of Healing from an Abortion, Puberty Rite for a Young Woman, Menstrual Rituals, Menopause Liturgy, and the already-mentioned Coming-Out Rite for a Lesbian). Also included are some seasonal festivals, including Hallowmas: Remembrance of the Holocaust of Women;[77] Liturgy of Martyrs for Justice, in Solidarity with El Salvador; Ash Wednesday Liturgy: Repentance for the Sins of the Church; Summer Solstice Party; Hiroshima Memorial Day; and the already-mentioned Earth Day Celebration.

Why do feminists feel it is necessary to have their own separate church? Because only in these communities can they feel truly liberated from patriarchy and feel the full equality that the church is supposed to embody. To them these are truly spiritual needs that are simply not being met in the existing churches, which leave them feeling spiritually starved.

> Women in contemporary churches are suffering from linguistic deprivation and eucharistic famine. They can no longer nurture their souls in alienating words that ignore or systematically deny their existence. They are starved for the words of life, for symbolic forms that fully and wholeheartedly affirm their personhood and speak truth about the evils of sexism and the possibilities of a future beyond patriarchy. They desperately need primary communities that nurture their journey into wholeness, rather than constantly negating and thwarting it. . . .[78]

"Women-Church represents the first time that women collectively have claimed to be church and have claimed the tradition of the exodus community as a community of liberation from patriarchy."[79]

On a more practical level, these feminists "are beginning to recognize the need for autonomous bases for women's theologizing." That is, they need a place to share their collective experiences as oppressed women and reflect upon them together and work out their feminist theology together. "Thus the first step in forming the feminist exodus from patriarchy is to gather women together to articulate their own experience and communicate it with each other. . . . Women have to withdraw from male-dominated spaces so they can gather together and define their own experience."[80]

The women of Women-Church insist that this is not a separatist movement; it is not a complete withdrawal from the church and Christendom as is advocated by post-Christian and Goddess feminists. They still acknowledge the universal church and consider themselves to be one mani-

festation of it. Ideally Women-Church is a temporary expe-
dient that can be dissolved whenever the institutional
churches become what they ought to be. Thus it is necessary to keep lines of communication open with them to
work toward this end.[81]

D. The Construction of a Feminist Theology

As noted above, liberal feminists believe that Women-
Church is necessary because it gives them a secure
stronghold from within which they can work out their own
theology and hermeneutic. This is important to them,
because a crucial aspect of their agenda is the construction
of a feminist theology and especially a uniquely feminist
approach to the interpetation of the Bible.

Feminists need their own theology because existing theologies, especially within the Judeo-Christian tradition,
are sexist and biased against women. "God is imaged as
the great Patriarch. Male heads of families, in turn, come
to be regarded as the normative representatives of God. . . .
The woman is regarded as more responsible for sin than
the male." Also, "the redeemer is seen as normatively
male." In short, in patriarchal theology woman fares badly
in the doctrines of God, creation, sin, and redemption. This
is why feminist theology is needed. "Feminist theology
arises at the point where this sexist bias of classical theology is perceived and repudiated." The new feminist theology will be the true theology, because "redemption from
sexism is the authentic meaning and message of theology."[82]

The construction of a feminist theology is important to
liberal feminists not just in terms of the end result to be
produced, but also in reference to the theologizing process
itself. As Russell says, "Doing theology is itself an act of
freedom!" Instead of just accepting what has been delivered by the "fathers," women can engage in the very process of asking the questions and seeking their answers.

Instead of playing the supporting role of Martha, they can become directly involved in "matters of theological and social research and leadership in the church" – like Mary.[83]

But again this can only be done properly in the Women-Church context, because here is where God is making himself known today. "The locus or place of divine revelation and grace is therefore not the Bible or the tradition of the patriarchal church but the *ekklesia* of women and the lives of women who live the 'option for our women selves.' "[84] Thus Women-Church will be "the hermeneutical center of . . . feminist biblical interpretation."[85]

E. Conclusion

The liberal feminist agenda may thus be summed up as first, the repudiation of patriarchy; second, the reaffirmation of the integrity of women; third, the restoration of a non-sexist church; and fourth, the construction of a feminist theology.

This is a rather awesome agenda, and it raises two important questions that must be resolved before it can be addressed. One is the question of authority or the norm for truth. By what standard will matters of "faith and practice" be measured to determine if they are acceptable to feminists? This raises a second question, namely, the role of the Bible. Even though they accept the liberal view of the nature of the Bible, as discussed above, still the liberal feminists are pursuing their agenda as *Christian* feminists. Thus they are forced to deal with this question, i.e., what role can the Bible play in feminist faith and practice? The rest of our discussion of liberal feminism will be devoted to these questions.

II. THE BIBLE AND THE NORM FOR THEOLOGY

"The Bible and the Bible alone is our only rule of faith and practice." This is how traditionally conservative Protestants usually answer the question of the norm for theology. The *norm* is the rule or measure by which truth and falsehood are decided in matters of faith (i.e., theology), and the rule by which right and wrong are decided in matters of practice (i.e., ethics and worship). Traditional Protestants say the norm must be the Bible, since it is the supernaturally inspired Word of God and therefore inherently true. All other claims to truth must be judged by it.

Every attempt at theology must have some kind of norm. Since liberal feminism is one aspect of liberalism in general and is closely related to liberation theology, we can expect its approach to a theological norm to be similar to theirs. This is certainly the case. For one thing, theologians of these stripes do not speak so much of "faith and practice" as they do of "theology and praxis." *Praxis* is basically the same as practice. It is the action or application that flows out of theological reflection and thus brings about change in society. Praxis is actually what theology is all about. The liberation theologies especially are not so much concerned with *orthodoxy* (right doctrinal statements) as they are with *orthopraxy* (right action, i.e., the practice of liberation).[86]

But something has to be the final judge of what is right or true in both areas. A serious question for liberal feminists is, how does the Bible fit in here? Can they in any sense consider the Bible as an authority or norm? This question is especially difficult for feminists who grew up in a Bible-based home. They have a residual loyalty to the Bible, but they also feel the driving force of their own experience as women struggling for freedom from patriarchal bondage. The problem is that often the two seem to be in conflict. This presents them with a fundamental dilemma: "Are they to be faithful to the teachings of the Hebrew scriptures and the Christian scriptures, or are they to be faithful to their own integrity as whole human beings?"[87]

A. The Norm Is Not the Bible

In the final analysis, liberal feminists decide against the

Bible as the basic theological norm. This decision would have to be made just from the perspective of their liberalism alone. Like all liberals, they deny what Fiorenza calls the doctrinal model of biblical interpretation, which "understands Scripture as verbally inspired, the direct revelation of God."[88] They consider the Bible in essence to be like any other book, a product of human authors and therefore subject to human fallibility and historical-cultural relativity. For this reason alone they could not accept the Bible as an exclusive "rule of faith and practice."

Related to this and in some ways even more important is another reason why liberal feminists reject the Bible as their theological norm. This time the decision is made from the perspective of their feminism itself, i.e., from their perspective as women struggling against the bonds of sexism and patriarchy. They conclude that the Bible in a real sense contradicts their own experience of how things are and how they ought to be. That is, the Bible not only does not support them in their experience, but actually favors and encourages the enemy, patriarchy. This patriarchal character of the Bible is the primary reason why liberal feminists reject it as their norm.

At this point the question is raised as to whether it is the Biblical text itself that is guilty of patriarchal sexism, or whether it is just the traditional interpretations that are patriarchal. There is no dispute concerning this latter option; all agree that the classical interpretations or the traditional major theologies have all been "distorted by androcentrism."[89] It may well be that if we could correct these sexist interpretations, we would find Biblical passages that contradict patriarchy and support feminism. For example, proper exegesis shows that many of Paul's supposedly sexist statements were not necessarily intended that way but have been distorted by later tradition. Thus it may be that the Bible can become a liberating word, once it is liberated from these sexist interpretations.[90]

However, unlike evangelical feminists, very few if any liberal feminists would be willing to take this approach to the Bible as a whole. That is, they will not say that the problem lies only in the interpretations and not in the text itself. On the contrary, as a rule they judge the text itself to be patriarchal in character and biased against women. This may be more the case with some texts than others, but the fact is that "all texts are products of an androcentric patriarchal culture and history."[91] Thus the whole Bible reflects the patriarchal taint to some extent. The fact that the Bible is not the words of God but the words of *men* goes beyond the simple contrast between divine and human authorship. It indicates *male* authorship and results in male bias through and through. Fiorenza says, "The Bible is not only written in the words of men but also serves to legitimate patriarchal power and oppression insofar as it 'renders God' male and determines ultimate reality in male terms, which make women invisible or marginal."[92]

This view that the Bible is a sexist, patriarchal book is a central doctrine of liberal feminism. "It has become abundantly clear," says Russell, "that the scriptures need liberation, not only from existing interpretations but also from the patriarchal bias of the texts themselves." We would not expect it to be any different, since "the biblical texts were written in the context of patriarchal cultures." Thus the biblical message is in "patriarchal captivity" or "patriarchal bondage."[93] This is true of the very language of Scripture, which "without question . . . is androcentric," says Fiorenza.[94] But this is only what we should expect, since "the writings in the Bible took shape in a variety of cultures, but they were all patriarchal."[95]

Sometimes the question is raised as to whether the patriarchal bias is intentional or unintentional. If the Biblical writers were just products of their own cultures, would they not unconsciously (and thus unintentionally) reflect their cultures' views of gender roles? The feminists do not want to let the male writers off that easily, but rather accuse them of intentionally putting women in an inferior position in order to perpetuate their own male domination. At least certain Scriptural texts "are patriarchal in their original function and intention," says Fiorenza.[96] In her reconstruction of early Christian history from the New Testament texts, she assumes that the redactors and collectors of the texts changed them, edited them, and selected them in accordance with their theological intentions. She believes that "an active elimination of women from the biblical text has taken place." She says that "we can assume methodologically that the early Christian writers transmit only a fraction of the possibly rich traditions of women's contributions to the early Christian movement," because "the androcentric selection and transmission of early Christian traditions have manufactured the historical marginality of women."[97] This point about intentionality is driven home by Ruether:

> Feminist theology cannot be done from the existing base of the Christian Bible. The Old and New Testaments have been shaped in their formation, their transmission, and, finally, their canonization to sacralize patriarchy. They may preserve, between the lines, memories of women's experience. But in their present form and intention they are designed to erase women's existence as subjects and to mention women only as objects of male definition. . . .[98]

In their naming of the Bible as a patriarchal book, liberal feminists see themselves as following the tradition of Elizabeth Cady Stanton. Fiorenza has a lengthy discussion of *The Woman's Bible* in her book, *In Memory of Her*. She says Stanton set the stage for modern feminist hermeneutics by recognizing that "the Bible is not a 'neutral' book but a political weapon against women's struggle for liberation." Because of its political implications, *The Woman's Bible* proved to be very unpopular. Yet Stanton's work was necessary and her insights were valid, especially the insight "that the Bible is not just misunderstood or badly interpreted" but that "it *is* patriarchal and androcentric," that "men have put their stamp on biblical revelation," that "it is man-made because it is written by men and is the expression of a patriarchal culture."[99]

In a manner that would have made Stanton proud, Fiorenza labels her own approach to Scripture a "hermeneutics of suspicion." This hermeneutical principle "takes as its starting point the assumption that biblical texts and their interpretations are androcentric and serve patriarchal functions." Every act of feminist interpretation actually begins with this suspicion; it is taken for granted that every text is a potential enemy of women.[100]

> ... A feminist critical hermeneutics of suspicion places a warning label on all biblical texts: *Caution! Could be dangerous to your health and survival.* Not only is scripture interpreted by a long line of men and proclaimed in patriarchal churches, it is also authored by men, written in androcentric language, reflective of religious male experience, selected and transmitted by male religious leadership. Without question, the Bible is a male book. ... The first and never-ending task of a hermeneutics of suspicion, therefore, is to elaborate as much as possible the patriarchal, destructive aspects and oppressive elements in the Bible. ...[101]

This understanding of the Bible as an androcentric book written to serve the interests of patriarchy, along with their reluctance to renounce it altogether, leaves liberal feminists with only one viable course of action: the Bible itself must be liberated, both from sexist interpretations and from its own original androcentrism. "It is always in need of liberation from its own historical limitations as well as from those of the interpreters." Interpretations that reinforce patriarchal domination must be challenged.

"From this perspective the Bible needs to be liberated from its captivity to one-sided white, middle-class, male interpretation."[102] "Liberating the Bible from patriarchy is the first theological consideration," says Phyllis Trible.[103]

B. Women's Experience is the Norm

In liberal theology it is generally agreed that human experience is one foundation if not *the* foundation for theology and hermeneutics. "Human experience is both the starting point and the ending point of the circle of interpretation. The original texts themselves were rooted in experience, as is all later interpretation of them."[104] The new theologies of modern times, especially the liberation theologies, are being shaped specifically by the experience "of those struggling for full human personhood and dignity and reflecting critically upon their struggle." This struggle is "a lens of experience through which to understand the gospel message."[105]

What makes feminist theology different, then, is not the identification of experience as such as a theological norm, but the appeal to *women's* experience in particular. The sum and core of the consciousness that is called "women's experience" is "the conviction that women are fully human and are to be valued as such." This includes the principles of equality and mutuality. The point is that women feel this conviction so strongly that it becomes "the underlying principle for a feminist hermeneutic," one that has the power of a "moral imperative."[106]

It would appear that no principle is more widely endorsed among feminists than the normative character of women's experience. It is a viewpoint shared by all three types of feminism discussed thus far, secular, Goddess, and liberal. Liberal feminism differs from the other two only in that it recognizes the importance of *religious* experience (contrary to secular feminism), and in that it recognizes the validity of *Christian* religious experience (contrary to

Goddess feminism). The point of agreement is that *women's* experience is the starting point, the basis, and the norm for both theory and action, which in the case of liberal feminism means theology and praxis.

This principle and its normative function are affirmed by liberal feminists over and over, and in many different ways. One summary of the principle, as noted above, is "that women are fully human and are to be valued as such." This echoes Ruether's formulation, namely, that the critical or normative principle of feminist theology is "the promotion of the full humanity of women" or "the full personhood of women."[107] This is usually called the "feminist critical consciousness."

This critical principle functions as the authority, norm, or criterion for feminist faith and practice. As Ruether notes, "It has frequently been said that feminist theology draws on women's experience as a basic source of content as well as a *criterion of truth.*"[108] Russell refers to women's experience as "an authority in theology" and "a norm for the truthfulness of tradition."[109] It is assigned the quality and authority of revelation by Fiorenza, who says that "the 'church of women' in the past and in the present" is "the *locus* of divine revelation and grace." Feminist theology "locates revelation not in biblical texts but in the experience of women struggling for liberation from patriarchy."[110] Whatever is meant by inspiration also applies to women's experience. "Inspiration cannot be located in texts or books," says Fiorenza. Rather, feminist theologians insist "that the process of inspiration must be seen as the inspiration of those people, especially of poor women, struggling for human dignity and liberation from oppressive powers."[111] Such experience is the feminists' foundation or starting point: "Feminist theology begins with the experiences of women."[112] What all this means is clearly explained by Ruether:

> The critical principle of feminist theology is the promotion of the full humanity of women. Whatever

denies, diminishes, or distorts the full humanity of women is, therefore appraised as not redemptive. Theologically speaking, whatever diminishes or denies the full humanity of women must be presumed not to reflect the divine or an authentic relation to the divine, or to reflect the authentic nature of things, or to be the message or work of an authentic redeemer or a community of redemption.[113]

As Zikmund sums it up, "The development of a feminist critical consciousness has moved from the innocent assumption that women's experience was irrelevant to the conviction that it is normative."[114]

This emphasis on women's experience does not mean that *all* experience of *all* women qualifies as authoritative. The experience that counts is not just female (biological) or feminine (cultural), but feminist (political).[115] This refers specifically to the experience of patriarchal oppression and the struggle to be free from it. "Feminist theology is written out of an experience of oppression," says Russell.[116] Women experience oppression when they become critically aware of being victimized by male domination, when they become aware of the "falsifying and alienating experiences imposed upon them as women by a male-dominated culture, when they realize how patriarchy is subjecting them to "experiences of negation and trivialization." It is "women's experience of androcentric culture that we refer to when we say that women's experience is an interpretive key for feminist theology."[117]

This normative feminist experience must include not only awareness of oppression but also participation in the struggle against it. "The spiritual authority of women-church," says Fiorenza, "rests not simply on the 'experience of women' but on the experience of women struggling for liberation from patriarchal oppression," the "experience of women struggling for liberation and wholeness."[118]

This total reverence for this kind of *women's* experience is probably why there are relatively few men who may be identified as liberal feminists. Since only women can truly have this kind of experience, only women can truly engage in feminist theology and praxis. (This is contrary to evangelical Christian feminism, in which the final authority is still the Bible rather than women's experience, and in which many of the leading "feminists" are men.)

C. The Bible Is Judged by the Canon
of Women's Experience

The term *canon* literally means a measuring rod, a rule, a standard, a criterion by which other things are judged. In historical Christendom the term is used to refer to the books of the Bible because, as the divinely-inspired Word of God, they are the final and absolute standard of truth.

Liberal feminism also uses the word *canon*, but not for the books of the Bible. Instead it refers to women's experience as the canon or measure of truth by which all else is judged. "Feminist theological interpretation of the Bible . . . has as its canon the liberation of women from oppressive sexist structures, institutions, and internalized values," says Fiorenza. It "derives its canon from the struggle of women and other oppressed peoples for liberation from patriarchal structures."[119]

Liberal feminists specifically deny that the canon is the body of Biblical writings as such. If there is to be a written version of the canon, it will have to be a collection of writings by women reflecting on their struggle against patriarchy. This is what Ruether has attempted to provide in her collection of such texts in the book *Womanguides*. She declares that "feminist theology must create a new textual base, a new canon." Once the old patriarchal texts (i.e., the Biblical writings) have lost their normative status, "a new norm emerges on which to construct a new community, a new theology, eventually a new canon." Such a collection of texts would be "the accumulated heritage of a people's reflection on its experience in the light of questions of ultimate meaning and value. The texts provide norms for judging good and evil, truth and falsehood, for judging what is of God/ess and what is spurious and demonic."[120]

There is no doubt that Ruether considers *Womanguides* to be a beginning toward such a collection of normative texts. It contains a total of eighty-five selections in twelve categories, with an explanatory introduction for each category with brief introductions to the texts. Some of the categories are "Gender Imagery for God/ess," "The Origins of Evil," "Redeemer/Redemptrix: Male and Female Saviors," and "Foremothers of WomanChurch." The texts are chosen from a broad spectrum of backgrounds, from the most ancient to the most modern. Sometimes they represent the patriarchal perspective for the sake of contrast, but more often they reflect the feminist critical consciousness. The following is a list of some of the texts according to their backgrounds:

> SUMERIAN: "The Creation of Vegetation by the Mother Goddess"
> BABYLONIAN: "The Shaping of the Cosmos from the Body of the Mother Goddess"
> CANAANITE: "Ishtar, Shepherdess of the People"; "Anath, Savior of Baal, Restores the World"
> EGYPTIAN: "Isis, Queen of Heaven"
> GNOSTIC: "The Androgynous Unfolding of the Heavenly Pleroma"
> ROMAN CATHOLIC: "Christ as Mother: The Vision of a Woman Mystic"
> CULTIC: "The Father-Mother God of Christian Science"
> MARXIST: "The Rise of Private Property and the Demise of Mother-Right"
> *THE WOMAN'S BIBLE:* "Eve Exonerated: A Feminist Commentary"
> CONTEMPORARY FEMINIST: "A Jewish Feminist Midrash on Lilith and Eve"; "Unless a WomanChrist Comes, We Will All Die"; "The Parable of the Naked Lady"; "WomanChurch as a Feminist Exodus Com-

munity" (a canonical contribution by Ruether herself)
BIBLICAL: "Eve and the Snake in the Garden";
"Miriam, Priest and Prophet"

Ruether does not claim that her book is *the* new canon
since she does not consider it "closed" or completed. Other
suitable writings may be discovered or even produced in
the future. "New liberating experience is empowered to
write new stories, new parables, new *midrashim* on the old
stories. We, too, can write new texts to express our new
consciousness." Once these texts and stories have been
written, they may become authoritative in the feminist
community.[121]

Whether encoded in a book of texts or not, the crucial
point is that women's experience *is* the new canon – *"the
litmus test"* – by which all else is judged, including the
Bible itself. Fiorenza calls women's experience "the revelatory canon for theological evaluation of biblical androcentric traditions." Feminist theology "places biblical texts
under the authority of feminist experience insofar as it
maintains that revelation is ongoing," i.e., ongoing in the
feminist experience itself. This provides "a feminist scale of
values" that "enables us to make choices between oppressive and liberating traditions of the Bible without having
to accept or reject it as a whole. In this process of feminist
critical evaluation and assessment, the Bible no longer
functions as authoritative source but as a *resource* for
women's struggle for liberation."[122] "All Biblical texts must
be tested as to their feminist liberating content," and the
criteria for this testing "must be derived from a systematic
exploration of women's experience of oppression and liberation." In this way "the *ekklesia* of women has the authority
'to choose and to reject' biblical texts."[123]

Ruether has suggested a way for women to celebrate
their assumed power to stand in judgment over the Bible.
She has included in her book *Women-Church* a liturgy
called "Exorcism of Patriarchal Texts." In this liturgy "a

187

series of texts with clearly oppressive intentions" is selected. Some "suggested texts in need of exorcism" include Leviticus 12:1-5; Judges 19; Ephesians 5:21-23; and 1 Timothy 2:11-15. After each text is read, a bell is rung as the reader raises up the Bible, and the assembled group "cries out in unison, 'Out, demons, out!'" After all the selected texts have been read and thus "exorcised," someone says, "These texts and all oppressive texts have lost their power over our lives. We no longer need to apologize for them or try to interpret them as words of truth, but we cast out their oppressive message as expressions of evil and justifications of evil."[124]

D. Conclusion

The purpose of this section has been to explain what liberal feminism considers to be the ultimate norm for theology and praxis. The conclusion is that it rejects the Bible as the final authority and chooses instead to elevate women's experience of oppression and liberation to the level of canonical authority. Women's experience becomes the canon by which individual texts of Scripture are measured and then either accepted for use or rejected as evil. Clark Pinnock sums it up this way: "The starting point, therefore, is the modern experience of feminism itself. One starts from a commitment to feminism and proceeds from there to put the Bible in order."[125]

Endnotes

1. Rosemary Radford Ruether, *Women-Church: Theology and Practice of Feminist Liturgical Communities* (San Francisco: Harper & Row, 1986), pp. 2-3.

2. Elisabeth Schüssler Fiorenza, *Bread Not Stone: The Challenge of Feminist Biblical Interpretation* (Boston: Beacon Press, 1984), p. 7. See also Fiorenza, *In Memory of Her: A Feminist The-*

ological Reconstruction of Christian Origins (New York: Crossroad, 1987), p. xviii.

3. Letty Russell, "Authority and the Challenge of Feminist Interpretation," in *Feminist Interpretation of the Bible*, ed. Letty Russell (Philadelphia: Westminster Press, 1974), p. 138.

4. Russell, *Human Liberation in a Feminist Perspective – A Theology* (Philadelphia: Westminster Press, 1974), p. 58.

5. Ruether, *Sexism and God-Talk: Toward a Feminist Theology* (Boston: Beacon Press, 1983), p. 39.

6. Russell, *Human Liberation*, p. 80.

7. Fiorenza, *Bread*, p. 84.

8. Fiorenza, *Memory*, pp. xviii-xix.

9. Ibid., p. 4.

10. Ibid., p. xv; *Bread*, pp. x-xi.

11. Russell, "Introduction: Liberating the Word," in *Feminist Interpretation of the Bible*, p. 17; and "Authority," p. 141.

12. Suzanne M. Rini, "Dancing Around the Abyss: The Bishops Prepare a Pastoral on Women," *Fidelity* (September 1987), 6:43.

13. Ruether, "Feminist Theology and Spirituality," in *Christian Feminism: Visions of a New Humanity*, ed. Judith L. Weidman (San Francisco: Harper & Row, 1984), p. 11.

14. Ruether, *Sexism*, p. 165.

15. Fiorenza, *Memory*, p. 29.

16. Russell, *Household of Freedom: Authority in Feminist Theology* (Philadelphia: Westminster Press, 1987), p. 87.

17. Fiorenza, *Bread*, p. 5.

18. Russell, *Human Liberation*, p. 153: "women and men, oppressed and oppressor."

19. Fiorenza, *Bread*, p. xiv.

20. Russell, *Human Liberation*, p. 36.

21. Ibid., pp. 28-29; Russell, "Introduction," p. 17.

22. Ruether, *Women-Church*, p. 57.

23. Ruether, *Sexism*, p. 161; Russell, *Human Liberation*, pp. 62, 112-113; Fiorenza, "Feminist Theology," p. 27.

24. Fiorenza, *Bread*, p. xv.

25. Russell, *Household*, p. 18.

26. Fiorenza, *Bread*, p. 5.

27. Russell, "Introduction," p. 19; *Household*, p. 17.

28. Russell, "Introduction," p. 20.

29. Ruether, *Women-Church*, p. 2.

30. Russell, *Human Liberation*, pp. 105-106.

31. Ibid., pp. 19, 63, 146, 183.

32. Russell, "Introduction," p. 14.

33. Fiorenza, *Memory*, p. xxi.

34. Ruether, "Feminist Theology," pp. 18-20.

35. Russell, "Authority," pp. 143-144; *Household,* pp. 33-35.

36. Russell, "Authority," p. 144.

37. Ruether, *Sexism,* pp. 70, 85, 87; also Ruether, "Feminist Interpretation: A Method of Correlation," in *Feminist Interpretation of the Bible,* p. 116.

38. Ruether, *Women-Church,* pp. 267-273.

39. Russell, *Human Liberation,* pp. 151-152.

40. Ibid., p. 183.

41. Ruether, *Women-Church,* pp. 173, 178.

42. Ibid., pp. 109, 149.

43. Ibid., pp. 196-200.

44. Russell, *Household,* p. 25; Fiorenza, *Memory,* pp. 279, 285.

45. Russell, *Household,* pp. 21-22; also "Women and Ministry," in *Christian Feminism,* pp. 77-80.

46. Russell, *Human Liberation,* p. 146; "Women and Ministry," p. 91.

47. Russell, *Household,* p. 43.

48. Russell, *Human Liberation,* pp. 172-174.

49. Ibid., p. 155.

50. Ibid., p. 156.

51. Reuther, *Sexism,* p. 193.

52. Russell, *Household,* p. 37.

53. Russell, *Human Liberation,* p. 70; "Women and Ministry," pp. 82-85. See *Household,* chapter 2.

54. Russell, *Household,* 61.

55. Ibid.

56. Russell, *Human Liberation,* p. 177.

57. Russell, "Women in Ministry," p. 85.

58. Russell, *Human Liberation,* pp. 46-47.

59. Russell, *Household,* pp. 45-47.

60. Russell, *Human Liberation,* pp. 93-95.

61. See Sharon Neufer Emswiler and Thomas Neufer Emswiler, *Women and Worship: A Guide to Non-Sexist Hymns, Prayers, and Liturgies* (San Francisco: Harper & Row, 1974), pp. 26ff.

62. Russell, *Household,* pp. 47-48.

63. Russell, "Introduction," p. 13; see Ruether, "Feminist Theology," pp. 16-17.

64. Ruether, *Sexism,* p. 46, 67-69.

65. Russell, *Household,* pp. 63-64. In the expression "the master's house" the term *master* does not refer to God or Jesus but to an authoritarian, patriarchal master.

66. Ruether, *Sexism,* p. 152.

67. Fiorenza, *Memory,* pp. 36, 99-104, chapters 4 & 5.

68. Russell, *Human Liberation,* pp. 87, 138.

69. This was the view presented by several speakers at the Washington "Women in the Church" conference in October 1986. One declared that Jesus included women among his apostles, but patriarchal forces later concealed this fact. These data are reported by Donna Steichen in "The Goddess Goes to Washington," *Fidelity* (December 1986), 6:36-37, 40.

70. Russell, *Human Liberation,* pp. 87-88.

71. Russell, *Household,* pp. 39-40.

72. Fiorenza, *Memory,* p. 56; Ruether, *Sexism,* pp. 33-34.

73. Ruether, *Women-Church,* p. 4.

74. "These groups are particularly popular among Roman Catholic women because of their exclusion from ordination and decision making in that church" (Russell, *Household,* p. 96).

75. See Ruether, *Women-Church,* pp. 66-68, for a description of this conference.

76. The program for this meeting declares it to be "The Second National Conference" for Women-Church. Other conferences focusing on women in the church have been held, including the 1986 "Women in the Church" conference in Washington, D.C., mentioned several times in this book.

77. "This rite focuses on the burning time, the history of the holocaust of women, not only those killed as witches during the time of the Inquisition, but also the whole of patriarchal history which has turned women's lives into a burnt offering to reproduce the species" (Ruether, *Women-Church,* p. 116).

78. Ibid., pp. 4-5.

79. Ibid., p. 57. See Fiorenza, *Memory,* pp. 346-349.

80. Ruether, *Women-Church,* pp. 4, 59.

81. Ibid., pp. 39, 59-60; Fiorenza, *Bread,* p. 7.

82. Ruether, "Feminist Theology," pp. 9-12.

83. Russell, *Human Liberation,* p. 40.

84. Fiorenza, "The Will To Choose or To Reject: Continuing Our Critical Work," in *Feminist Interpretation of the Bible,* p. 128.

85. Fiorenza, *Bread,* p. xiv.

86. Russell, *Human Liberation,* pp. 55, 128.

87. Russell, "Authority," p. 137.

88. Fiorenza, *Bread,* pp. 25-28.

89. Ruether, *Sexism,* p. 37.

90. Russell, *Human Liberation,* p. 87; "Introduction," p. 11.

91. Fiorenza, *Memory,* p. xv.

92. Fiorenza, *Bread,* pp. x-xi.

93. Russell, "Introduction," pp. 11-12, 14.

94. Fiorenza, *Memory,* p. 43.

95. Russell, *Household,* p. 47.

96. Fiorenza, *Bread,* p. xii.

97. Fiorenza, *Memory,* pp. 49-52.

98. Ruether, *Womanguides: Readings Toward a Feminist Theology* (Boston: Beacon Press, 1985), p. ix.

99. Fiorenza, *Memory,* pp. 7-13; see also *Bread,* pp. 52-58.

100. Fiorenza, *Bread,* pp. xxii, 15.

101. Fiorenza, "The Will To Choose," p. 130.

102. Russell, "Introduction," pp. 12, 17.

103. Phyllis Trible, "Postscript: Jottings on the Journey," in *Feminist Interpretation of the Bible,* p. 147.

104. Ruether, "Feminist Interpretation," pp. 111-112.

105. Russell, *Household,* p. 32.

106. Margaret A. Farley, "Feminist Consciousness and the Interpretation of Scripture," in *Feminist Interpretation of the Bible,* pp. 44-45.

107. Ruether, *Sexism,* p. 18; "Feminist Theology," p. 12.

108. Ruether, *Sexism,* p. 12. Italics added.

109. Russell, *Household,* p. 17.

110. Fiorenza, *Bread,* p. xv; "The Will to Choose," p. 136.

111. Fiorenza, *Bread,* pp. 140, 147.

112. Ibid., p. x. See Russell, *Household,* p. 65: "Begin where you are to build up the new house from the foundation of your own experience and actions."

113. Ruether, *Sexism,* pp. 18-19.

114. Barbara Brown Zikmund, "Feminist Consciousness in Historical Perspective," in *Feminist Interpretation of the Bible,* p. 29.

115. Russell, *Household,* p. 17.

116. Russell, *Human Liberation,* p. 50.

117. Ruether, "Feminist Interpretation," p. 114.

118. Fiorenza, *Bread,* p. xvi. Also, "A feminist critical interpretation of the Bible . . . must begin with women's experience in their struggle for liberation" (ibid., p. 13).

119. Ibid., pp. 14, 60, 88.

120. Ruether, *Womanguides,* pp. ix-xi.

121. Ibid., pp. ix, xii, 247.

122. Fiorenza, *Memory,* pp. 32, 60; *Bread,* pp. xiii, 14.

123. Fiorenza, "The Will To Choose," p. 131.

124. Ruether, *Women-Church,* p. 137.

125. Clark Pinnock, "Biblical Authority and the Issues in Question," in *Women, Authority and the Bible,* ed. Alvera Mickelsen (Downers Grove, IL: InterVarsity Press, 1986), p. 52.

⑥ LIBERAL CHRISTIAN FEMINISM: INTERPRETATION AND USE OF THE BIBLE

It is obvious from what was seen in the last chapter that liberal Christian feminism does not have a very high view of the nature of the Bible. In light of this fact certain questions naturally arise. Does the Bible have any value at all for liberal feminists? How can they use it to help them to achieve their goals? What role can it play in feminist theology? Does the Bible have to be used at all, or can it be considered irrelevant?

At the very least, it is agreed that it cannot be ignored. In the spirit of Elizabeth Cady Stanton, modern feminists must take the Bible seriously because of the way it is used *against* women. *The Woman's Bible* was necessary in its day "because the keystone of misogynist religion and of women's oppression is the Bible." The situation is no different today. "The whole canon is to be taken seriously, especially because of the possibility of the Bible's use as a tool for the oppression of women."[1]

But the question still remains, does the Bible have any positive value for women today? Can it be rescued, reclaimed, liberated? It seems that we are still haunted by the ghost of Stanton. "The interpretative issues engendered by *The Woman's Bible* still determine the parameters of feminist biblical hermeneutics," says Fiorenza. "The discussion centers primarily around the revelatory authority of the Bible for today." The post-Christian feminists radicalize Stanton's position and reject the Bible altogether. But is this necessary? Can we preserve Stanton's insight – that the Bible itself is patriarchal and not just interpretations of it – and still "recover a feminist biblical heritage"?[2] As Russell puts it, "Thus the issue continues to be whether the biblical message can continue to evoke consent in spite of its patriarchal captivity."[3]

The answer to this question is a cautious but confident yes. Of all the forms of feminism, liberal Christian feminism is distinctive in this regard. Though they regard the Bible to be uninspired and patriarchal, liberal feminists still believe that it has some positive value for women. They believe that there is a *feminist* way of interpreting the Bible that can make it useful and relevant in the struggle for women's liberation. There *is* a feminist hermeneutic. "In spite of the patriarchal nature of the biblical texts," says Russell, "I myself have no intention of giving up the biblical basis of my theology." We can still speak of "a biblical message of liberation for women." "Perhaps it would seem more useful to give up on the Bible as a normative source of my theology, but I don't seem to be able to do that. The biblical witness continues to evoke my consent, even as I reject many of its teachings as well as its patriarchal context."[4]

As Ruether sees it, no one exists in a cultural and historical vacuum. We cannot deny our roots, our heritage; there is a real need "to situate oneself meaningfully in history." No matter how much we may have to discard as corrupted and invalid, we have a need "to look back to some original base of meaning and truth before corruption" in order "to know that truth is more basic than falsehood." "Glimmers" of this basic truth can be found submerged in a number of places, including the Bible.[5]

Fiorenza takes note of how Russell and Ruether, disagreeing with Stanton, affirm "that the Bible is not totally androcentric but also contains some absolute ethical principles and feminist liberating traditions." Though she does not agree with Russell's and Ruether's neo-orthodox methodology, Fiorenza does agree that liberal feminists must not relinquish their biblical heritage. They "cannot afford to disown androcentric biblical texts and patriarchal history as their own revelatory texts and history." They must reclaim it as their own.[6] This is possible because the Bible has not functioned *only* to legitimate the oppression of women.

> . . . It has also provided authorization and legitimization for women who have rejected slavery, racism, anti-Semitism, colonial exploitation, and misogynism as unbiblical and against God's will. The Bible has inspired and continues to inspire countless women to speak out and to struggle against injustice, exploitation, and stereotyping. The biblical vision of freedom and wholeness still energizes women in all walks of life to struggle against poverty, unfreedom, and denigration. It empowers us to survive with dignity and to continue the struggle when there seems to be no hope for success.[7]

Thus there is agreement *that* liberal feminists should continue to use the Bible as a valuable resource for liberation struggles. But this still leaves the question of *how* it should be used. "*How* can feminists use the Bible . . . ? *What approach* to the Bible is appropriate for feminists who locate themselves within the Christian community? *How* does the Bible serve as a resource for Christian feminists?"[8] Old approaches will no longer serve feminist purposes, because of the insight that the Bible is both "a source of revelatory truth" and "a resource for patriarchal subordination and domination." This fact "demands a new paradigm for biblical hermeneutics and theology."[9] This new paradigm for authority and interpretation must take account of the sexist nature of the Bible while at the same time allowing God to speak to women through it.[10]

The remainder of this chapter will be an attempt to summarize the feminist approach to Biblical interpretation, especially as represented by Russell, Ruether, and Fiorenza.

I. THE MODERN APPROACH
TO HERMENEUTICS

Before we turn to the question of feminist Biblical interpretation specifically, it will be necessary to discuss briefly several trends in the modern approach to hermeneutics.

A. The Priority of "What It Means"
over "What It Meant"

The first and most basic is the idea that what a text *means* for today, as determined by the interpreter, is more important than what it *meant* when written, as determined by the author. This is a reference to what are called the two poles or two horizons of Biblical interpretation, namely, the context of the writer and the context of the reader or interpreter.

This distinction is not new, though the terms may vary from time to time. Traditional hermeneutics has distinguished between the *primary sense* of Scripture, which is "what the author intended to convey, established by the grammaticohistorical method, and the *plenary sense*, which is "what the Bible has come to mean in the experience of Christian readers, generation by generation."[11] Some refer to the first of these as the *meaning* of the Bible, and to the second as its *significance*. To others it is the distinction between "what it means" and "what it means to me," or between what it meant "back there then" when it was written and what it means "here and now." Krister Stendahl refers to the former as exegesis and to the latter as hermeneutics. An exegete, he says, "interprets the biblical texts not only as to their historical meaning," which is exegesis; he also "pronounces judgment on how these texts are to be applied to a contemporary problem not envisaged by the early church," which is hermeneutics.[12] Fiorenza notes that Stendahl's distinction was widely accepted and still operates in biblical scholarship.[13]

A most serious question is which of these two horizons or contexts is more important for determining the actual and authentic meaning of Scripture for today. Traditionally, the former or primary sense has been taken as normative. The latter or plenary sense, i.e., any application to present-day situations, "is acceptable because it is consistent with the primary sense."[14] This is also the approach of a school of thought discussed by Stendahl called "realistic interpretation," whose scholarly ideal was "to creep out of one's Western and twentieth-century skin and reexperience the gospel as Peter and Paul and the nameless Christians and their opponents experienced it."[15]

This is basically the same as the view Fiorenza calls the objectivist or positivist historical model of exegesis. It seeks to achieve a purely objective, factual, and value-free understanding of the text as to what it meant at the time it was written. It "was modeled after the natural sciences and attempted to create a purely objective reconstruction of the facts." It "reconstructs as objectively as possible the historical meaning of the text, but on methodological grounds refuses to discuss the significance of the biblical text for the community of faith today."[16]

According to contemporary hermeneutical theory, one

problem with any approach that emphasizes an objective rendering of "what the text *meant*" is that it is practically impossible to know this, because of the historical relativity of the writer and inescapable subjectivity of the inter-preter. Biblical scholarship "can no longer articulate as its unqualified goal the intention to declare with scientific cer-tainty what the *text* meant, because this is virtually an epistemological impossibility."[17]

An even more serious problem, though, is the simple fact that this approach does not take into account the determinative nature of the role of the interpreter in the process of interpretation. Thus the trend today is to deem-phasize the horizon of the writer and to emphasize the horizon of the interpreter. Barbara Zikmund says, "In cur-rent biblical study it is almost as important to examine the contemporary situation of the reader as it is to know the particular milieu that produced a text many centuries ear-lier."[18] This is an understatement; in modern thinking the interpreter's context is *more* important for arriving at the authentic or "authoritative" meaning of a text. As Lewis Mudge says, "The question of how the text as a literary object contains meanings and conveys them *independently of authorial intention* now stands close to the centre of hermeneutical debate."[19]

One very consistent form of this view today is called structuralism, which "abandons all concern to keep the plenary sense in line with the primary sense. It may ignore all questions about the historical background of a text, its original life setting, and the course of its transmission; it may even be quite uninterested in the author's inten-tion."[20] Its concern is with "the meaning conveyed by a (biblical) text to those who read it rather than the meaning which the author intended to convey in the composition of the text." It concentrates on a text's present ability to convey meaning. "From this perspective a text does not have a meaning; it is meaningful in that it conveys mean-ing – indeed a gamut of meanings – to those who read it."[21]

Stendahl's view is similar to this, as can be seen from his attack on the "realistic interpretation" school.[22]

B. *The Relativity of All Interpretation*

A second trend in the modern approach to hermeneutics is to assert that the meaning of any text is *relative* both from the standpoint of the writer and from that of the interpreter. This should not be a surprise, since relativism is basic within the total world view of liberalism as such, as is evident in Stendahl's reference to the "relativities of ideologies."[23] To say that the Bible itself and Biblical interpretation are relative is simply consistent with the liberal world view.

To say that a Biblical text is relative from the writer's standpoint usually means that his perspective was so thoroughly a product of his time and culture that the text cannot be received as a norm for today. Even if the writer did intend to convey one specific meaning, and even if we could discern what it is, it is not binding on us. This means that we are not bound to abide by it as an authoritative command or example; it also means that we are not bound to stay with that particular interpretation but may look for new ones that are more relevant for today.

This is Stendahl's basic criticism of the school of realistic interpretation. "If something is a certain way in the New Testament, does that constitute the basic blueprint for our situation here and now?" he asks. Such "fidelity to the first century appears as a modern heresy," as "a new kind of biblicism. . . . For it is highly doubtful that God wants us to play 'First-Century Semites.'" That would be "a new twist to the slogan 'Back to the Bible': become like the first disciples, with their *concept* of man, their *concept* of the church, etc."[24] This is merely "a museum-minded conservatism" and an "archaizing deep freeze" that does not allow for discerning what is culturally conditioned. "It becomes a nostalgic attempt to play 'First Century,'" and results in "a permanent 'holding at minus x minutes' in the drama of the launching of the kingdom."[25]

To say that a Biblical text is relative from the writer's point of view is not necessarily new. What is distinctive of the modern approach to hermeneutics is that the text is also relative from the standpoint of the interpreter. This means that no one interpretation is inherent in the text, and that the reader may look for an interpretation that is relative or relevant to his or her own situation, even if it is different from the "original" meaning. As Mudge says, we are becoming "increasingly aware of the pluralism of contemporary contexts in which the Bible is interpreted. No longer can the hermeneutical presuppositions and practices of northern Europe and North America be considered normative in the Christian church."[26]

If, as we saw in the last chapter, experience is normative for hermeneutical method; and if experience is relative to cultures and groups of people, then interpretation itself will naturally be relative to each culture and each group. Russell says this is true of the way people view reality in general, and she gives an example from recent history. Then she says, "If this is true of recent world history, how much more is it true of the way we read the Bible?" We each have a "particular framework we use for understanding." That is, our understanding of anything, including the Bible, is "standpoint dependent." Russell prefers to say that this means that everything is "related" rather than "relative," but the distinction is meaningless. She says, "Because our understanding is related to our context, it matters a great deal who asks the questions and which believing community is struggling with the answers." The bottom line is that "the biblical message, like all messages, is 'situation variable' and can mean different things in different places."[27]

This freedom to reinterpret the Bible according to the reader's context is called the "pastoral-theological" paradigm of interpretation by Fiorenza. The idea is that each community may change and reinterpret according to the pastoral needs of the time. It is asserted that this is the very thing the Bible writers themselves did. For example, those who put the Gospels together "were free in their use of the Jesus traditions; they changed or reformulated them and reinterpreted them by bringing them into a different context and framework." They did this "in order to respond to the needs of the Christians of their own day."[28] Jesus did the same thing when he reinterpreted Isaiah 61 contrary to its original intention. In its own context Isaiah 61 promises "a nationalistic triumph of Israel over the Gentile nations." But according to Luke 4 Jesus gives the text a "dramatic reinterpretation," saying that it refers to "good news and healing that will come not to Israel but to the Gentiles and, indeed, to women and lepers among the Gentiles." Thus "if we today were to declare this same text, we too would have to reinterpret it in order to apply it to the outsiders and the despised of our time."[29] Fiorenza sums up this approach by saying that it "does not measure the theological validity of biblical texts, for their own communities, but evaluates them according to the theological insights and questions of the Christian community today."[30]

The illustrations cited in the previous paragraph show very clearly that in modern Biblical interpretation the horizon of the writer is secondary to that of the interpreter. The originally-intended meaning of the Jesus traditions or of Isaiah 61, according to this view, have been ignored and replaced by meanings more relevant to the interpreters' situations. Thus this second point, that the meaning of any text is relative, is just a variation of the first point, that what a text *means* today (as determined by the interpreter) is more important than what it *meant* when it was originally written.

C. The Bias of Every Interpreter

The same could be said of the third trend in the modern

approach to hermeneutics, namely, the assertion that all interpretation is biased. Even if an interpreter tried to be objective and to consider only the original intention of the writer, it would be impossible. One's interpretation will always be colored by his own personal feelings and unconscious presuppositions, as well as the context from within which he is working. These are the kinds of things that determine the questions a person brings to the text, and these questions always do more to shape interpretation than "what the text actually says."

This is taken as an accepted principle in the study of history in general. Historians always discuss the available historical evidence from within a particular frame of reference, one that "is always determined by their own philosophical perspective and values." This is especially true in the study of the Biblical texts. "Scholars no longer can pretend that what we do is completely 'detached' from all political interests. Since we always interpret the Bible and Christian faith from a position within history, scholarly detachment and neutrality must be unmasked as a fiction or false consciousness that serves definite political interests." "Therefore, understanding a text depends as much on the questions and presuppositions of the interpreter as on material explanation."[31] As Russell says, "The interpretative bias and understanding is build into the exegesis itself."[32]

This alleged bias of every interpreter is a point emphasized by liberation theology in general. "The various forms of liberation theology have challenged the so-called objectivity and value-neutrality of academic theology. The basic insight of all liberation theologies . . . is the recognition that all theology, willingly or not, is by definition always engaged for or against the oppressed. Intellectual neutrality is not possible in a world of exploitation and oppression."[33] Reading the Bible from the perspective of the oppressed, liberation theologians "note the bias in all biblical interpretation and call for clear advocacy of those who are in the greatest need of God's mercy and help: the dominated victims of society."[34] This so-called "advocacy stance" is based on the supposed inevitability of bias. Since bias is always present, a person may as well admit it and become an open advocate of the cause of the oppressed and marginalized.[35]

This, then, is the climate of hermeneutical opinion within which liberal feminism works today. It helps us to understand their own approach to Biblical interpretation, and their advocacy of a specifically feminist hermeneutic.

II. A DISTINCTIVELY FEMINIST HERMENEUTIC

The theory of interpretation described above actually makes possible the idea of a distinctively feminist hermeneutic. That is, if the crucial factor in interpretation is the context of the interpreter, and if all interpretation is admittedly relative and biased, then why should women not develop an approach to Scripture that is determined by and relative to their own situation as victims of patriarchal oppression standing in need of liberation?

This is exactly what feminist theologians are trying to do. Russell describes how since 1980 a group of feminists in the American Academy of Religion and the Society of Biblical Literature have been using the annual meetings to develop a project of feminist hermeneutics, trying to work out "the distinctive character of feminist interpretation." They have been asking such questions as these: "What is it that we are doing as feminists when we interpret the Bible? Is there something distinctive about this interpretation? If so, what is it?" They have been searching for "a feminist interpretation of the Bible that is rooted in the feminist critical consciousness that women and men are fully human and fully equal."[36]

The key to such a feminist hermeneutic, of course, is the

normative character of women's experience. Experience as such is the test of truth and meaning. If a particular text or interpretation does not "illuminate and interpret existence in a way that is experienced as meaningful," or if it "does not speak authentically to experience," then it must be either "discarded or altered to provide new meaning."[37] As Farley says, certain inner convictions are so basic that anything that contradicts them cannot be accepted. Biblical witness itself "cannot be believed unless it rings true to our deepest capacity for truth and goodness. If it contradicts this, it is not to be believed. If it falsifies this, it cannot be accepted."[38]

What is unique about feminist interpretation, then, is the *feminist* experience or feminist consciousness that tests and shapes it. This includes, says Farley, "some fundamental convictions so basic and so important that contradictory assertions cannot be accepted by feminists without violence being done to their very understandings and valuations." These convictions must "function in a feminist interpretation of scripture – discerning the meaning of the biblical witness as a whole and in its parts."[39]

Fiorenza explains that women must develop a "feminist hermeneutics of critical evaluation" which includes criteria for evaluating particular texts and interpretations. "Such criteria or principles must be derived from a systematic exploration of women's experience of oppression and liberation." These experience-based criteria will be designed to determine whether a text or interpretation "perpetrates and legitimates patriarchal structures," or whether it has "feminist liberating content."[40] Everything must be "assessed theologically in terms of a feminist scale of values."[41]

This involves the recognition that if the meaning of a Biblical text is relative to the interpreter as such, then when women do exegesis they must look for a meaning that speaks to their specific needs and is consistent with their unique experience as victims of male domination.

Feminist exegesis will actually begin with a different view of reality and will ask what interpretation is appropriate in light of that reality, i.e., in light of their own personal experience of oppression and liberation.[42]

This also means that feminist interpretation will be biased toward women. This is nothing to apologize for, since all interpretation is biased in one way or another. Hence feminists need to acknowledge their bias and consciously seek for meanings that are consistent with it. Along with liberation theologians, feminists must "refuse to hide their so-called 'bias' in the name of the universalism of theological ideas."[43]

In the name of such experiential relativity and bias, feminists are urged to achieve their hermeneutical goals by applying their creative imagination to the exegetical process. "Interpretation, like translation, is an imaginative reconstruction of meaning," says Russell. "For feminists this meaning comes alive most clearly through the community of struggle which seeks to overcome the domination and dehumanization of half the human race." "How does the Bible come to make sense in communities of faith? Not through a literal reading of the text but through . . . an 'imaginative construal.' "[44] One way to apply imagination to the exegetical task is to create new metaphors to represent Biblical realities. "A metaphor . . . is an imaginative way of describing what is still unknown by using an example from present concrete reality." This is Russell's purpose in her development of the metaphor of the "household of freedom" to represent what the people of God could and should be like when delivered from patriarchal captivity. She suggests that this be substituted for the metaphor of the kingdom or reign of God, which can be too easily misconstrued as an image of domination. Thus the "Lord's prayer" might be prayed, "For thine is the *household* and the power and the glory."[45]

In advocating the same thing Fiorenza speaks of "a hermeneutics of creative actualization" which "allows women to enter the biblical story with the help of historical imagination, artistic recreation, and liturgical ritualization." It "seeks to retell biblical stories from a feminist perspective, to reformulate biblical visions and injunctions in the perspective of the discipleship of equals, to create narrative amplifications of the feminist remnants that have survived in patriarchal texts." This can be done, for example, by retelling the story of the Passover or of the Last Supper, or by renaming the God of the Bible and the significance of Jesus.[46]

Another way that Fiorenza applies creative imagination to interpretation of the Bible is through her reconstruction of the history of the early church, which will be discussed later. The historical data in the Book of Acts, for example, is one-sided in its neglect of the actual contribution of women to the early missionary work of the church. Thus this part of the story "must be rescued through historical imagination," wherein we assume that the women who *are* mentioned are just the "tip of an iceberg" and thus just representatives of the full number. This is an "imaginative reconstruction," a "creative critical interpretation" which enables us to "challenge the blueprints of androcentric design, assuming instead a feminist pattern for the historical mosaic, one that allows us to place women as well as men into the center of early Christian history."[47]

Fiorenza attempts to sum up the distinctive feminist hermeneutic in the concept of "bread not stone." The idea behind this expression is that feminists should change the metaphor of Scripture from "tablets of stone," on which the unchanging word of God is engraved for all times, "into the image of bread that nurtures, sustains, and energizes women as people of God in our struggles against injustice and oppression." That is, the Bible is not to be taken as a "timeless archetype" containing forever-binding timeless truths; instead the Bible should be thought of as a "structuring prototype," an "open-ended paradigm that sets experience in motion," or a "formative root-model."[48] An archetype "establishes an unchanging timeless pattern, whereas a prototype is not a binding timeless pattern or principle. A prototype, therefore, is critically open to the possibility of its own transformation." Because the Bible is a prototype, it not only expects but requires us to transform its own models of Christian faith and community,[49] constructing models and interpretations that apply specifically to women struggling for liberation.

Those who object to this remolding of Scripture to fit feminist needs may cry out, "Scripture is fixed; you must not change the text. You cannot make it say what it does not say." To this objection Phyllis Trible replies that "a fixed, unchangeable text is neither possible nor desirable." Besides, the text is always being changed; and the warrant for such creative, situation-variable reinterpretation lies within the Bible itself. For an example, we need only note how the title *Adonai* was substituted for the sacred name of Yahweh, inevitably altering the meaning of the text.[50] As noted above, Ruether asserts that Jesus in Luke 4 changed the meaning of Isaiah 61. When feminists convert the prophetic message of the Bible into a feminist message, they are just following Scripture's own example, "whereby the text is reinterpreted in the context of new communities of critical consciousness."[51]

This, then, is the feminist hermeneutic. It is the application of the principle of women's experience to the Bible in such a way that the interpretation is altered to be consistent with their experience. This may mean that some texts are irretrievably patriarchal, which illuminates the feminist experience of oppression. But it may be that the meaning of some texts can be creatively and imaginatively reinterpreted so as to proclaim a liberating feminist message, whether that was the original intention of the author or not.

III. EXAMPLES OF FEMINIST HERMENEUTICS

Once the actual work of Biblical interpretation begins,

how does the feminist hermeneutic work? How can it be systematically applied to Scripture as a whole? This discussion usually takes the form of asking whether there is a certain "critical principle of revelation" or "interpretive key for feminists" that can be applied to specific texts in the Bible, to determine whether they are authoritative and meaningful for women today. This question is usually answered in the affirmative.

But this leads to a second question, namely, "whether the interpretive key for feminists should be located within the biblical canonical tradition or outside of that tradition."[52] Here there is some disagreement. Russell and Ruether are generally represented as affirming that the hermeneutical key is found in the Bible itself, with Fiorenza taking the position that it is not. After looking at the views of these three feminists, we shall see that there is really no basic difference among them.

A. Letty Russell

Although many feminists have rejected the Bible completely because of its patriarchal attitudes, Russell notes that Christian theologians, including herself, simply cannot give it up, especially its story of Jesus of Nazareth. "The biblical witness continues to evoke my consent," she says.[53] The crucial question remains, "*How* does the Bible serve as a resource for Christian feminists?"

Russell affirms that an interpretive key exists within the Bible that makes sense of the rest of the Bible and of women's experience of struggle for liberation. The Bible does have "a critical or liberating tradition embodied in its 'prophetic-messianic' message," which constitutes "a biblical message of liberation for women." This key is found specifically in the theme of "God's intention for the mending of all creation."[54] She continues,

The particular interpretive key that assists me in continuing to give assent is the witness of scripture to

God's promise (for the mending of creation) on its way
to fulfillment. That which denies this intention of God
for the liberation of groaning creation in all its parts
does not compel or evoke my assent (i.e., it is not
authoritative)....[55]

In this way the image of a "world beyond oppression as a
mended creation in which human beings, nature, and all
creation are set free from their groaning and are at home
with one another . . . functions as a hermeneutical key for
interpretation of scripture and tradition."[56]

The key text for articulating this theme is Romans 8:14-
27, especially the promise in verses 20-23. These verses
declare that although "the whole creation groans and suf-
fers" at the present time, it "will be set free from its slavery to corruption into the freedom of the glory of the
children of God." Russell expounds on this theme at length
in her early work, *Human Liberation in a Feminist Perspective.* She identifies this "groaning for freedom" especially with women's experience under male domination,
and declares that freedom is on the horizon.[57] This idea of
"the liberation of groaning creation" continues to serve as
her basic description of the hermeneutical key.[58]

In her book *Household of Freedom* Russell adapts the
idea of a mended creation to the metaphor of God as a
householder engaged in *"oikonomia,* or householding of the
whole earth." The "household of freedom" is a concept
drawn from the Old Testament Exodus experience, when
the slaves living in Pharaoh's "house of bondage" moved
out as the people of God toward a new "house of freedom."
The experience of women living under male domination is
equivalent to the "house of bondage." Liberation from this
bondage is described in several ways, including *rebuilding*
the house and *cleaning* the house.[59] These are the same
idea as mending the creation.

This mending or restoring of creation is the essence of
salvation, and its result is a state of *shalom.* Thus salva-

tion is a much broader concept than simply individual salvation in an afterlife, since *shalom* refers to wholeness and total social well-being, including full human personhood, in community with others in the present. In short, *shalom* is *"the restoration of created humanity."*[60]

The creation-mending or housecleaning work is accomplished by God through his Tradition (capital T), understood according to the literal meaning of the term. This is distinguished from tradition (small t), which is "the total traditioning process that operates in human history and society"; and traditions (with an s), which are "particular confessional patterns," liturgies, and polities within confessional groups. God's Tradition specifically is his handing over of Jesus Christ to men and women (see Matthew 17:22; Romans 8:31-32). "The Tradition refers to Christ as the content of the traditioning process by which God hands Christ over to men and women." Russell generalizes this to include not just Judas' betrayal of Jesus but also all missionary or evangelistic work in which Jesus is handed over to all generations and nations. Thus all people, both men and women, are invited to participate in this traditioning work of God, which restores *shalom* to the world. That is, he seeks "to be partner with all humankind in the mending of creation." He definitely intends women to be included as partners in this traditioning and mending process, which involves women's ordination and thus involves liberation for women even as they seek liberation for others. Thus, as Russell says, "a clear understanding of the central Tradition in Christ and of the nature of the human traditioning process" can help us discern "the liberating core of the Christian faith."[61]

This "liberating core" is what Russell singles out as the hermeneutical key for interpreting the Bible from the feminist perspective. Because of this core, the Bible can still be used by women. As Russell puts it, "The bible has authority because it witnesses to God's liberating action on behalf of God's creation."[62] Whatever contributes to the theme of this liberating, mending, restoring, and traditioning action is thus judged to be authentic Scripture.

B. Rosemary Radford Ruether

Rosemary Ruether's view is not essentially different from that of Russell. "Feminist readings of the Bible," she says, "can discern a norm within Biblical faith by which the Biblical texts themselves can be criticized. To the extent to which Biblical texts reflect this normative principle, they are regarded as authoritative." She calls this norm "the prophetic principle," also "the prophetic-liberating tradition" and "the prophetic-messianic tradition."[63] The basic theme of this prophetic-liberating tradition is simply the *liberation of the oppressed,* "God's defense and vindication of the oppressed." This "norm through which to criticize the Bible" is not an arbitrary or marginal idea in Scripture but is "the central tradition."[64]

This theme occurs in "the foundational myth of the Exodus," in which a slave people is liberated from the most powerful ruler on earth. Here it is significant that God does not take the side of the ruler but "takes the side of those who have been oppressed and forced into servitude and liberates them." This liberation theme also occurs in Old Testament prophetic renewal movements (as in Isaiah 10:1-2 and Amos 8:4-6) and in the teaching of Jesus (as in Luke 4:18-19). It also appears in the New Testament church, which defined itself as an "exodus community" which experienced "the ultimate exodus of the people of God from all historical conditions of servitude, demonic possession, sin, and death."[65]

One problem with this prophetic principle in Scripture is that it was never applied consistently and thoroughly in the various historical contexts. Ruether refers to this as "the deformation of prophetic themes into ideology."[66]

Another problem is that the Bible itself never applies this prophetic-liberating tradition to the most oppressed group of all, namely, women. Here it is important to see that the prophetic principle is not a "static set of 'ideas'" but is rather "a plumb line of truth and untruth . . . that has to be constantly adapted to changing social contexts and circumstances." Its content must be ever rediscovered and discerningly reapplied to new social situations. This is exactly what liberal feminism is doing; it is appropriating this norm *for women*.[67]

> . . . Feminism claims that *women too* are among those oppressed whom God comes to vindicate and liberate. By including women in the prophetic norm, feminism sees what male prophetic thought generally had not seen: that once the prophetic norm is asserted to be central to Biblical faith, then patriarchy can no longer be maintained as authoritative.[68]

In this way feminism's new application of the prophetic principle to women is simply continuing the pattern already established in the Bible itself.[69]

C. Elisabeth Schüssler Fiorenza

Fiorenza writes in full awareness of the attempts by Russell and Ruether to isolate from within the Bible itself a feminist hermeneutical principle for evaluating the Bible. She pictures her colleagues as using the "dialogical-pluralistic model" of Biblical interpretation, associating it with neo-orthodoxy. This approach seeks to identify a "canon within the canon," an absolute Archimedean point within the Bible by which the rest of it can be judged and tested. As used by feminists such as Russell and Ruether, this view claims "that certain texts or traditions are not deformed by androcentrism or have been critical of patriarchy in order to reclaim the Bible as normative and authoritative for feminists in biblical religion."[70]

Fiorenza rejects this approach, concluding that this sort

of search is futile because there *is* no pure canon or core tradition in the text. "We cannot," she says, "resort to an 'Archimedean point' – be it Tradition with capital T or 'prophetic-messianic traditions' as the revelatory or hermeneutic key for the scores of relative oppressive traditions and texts of the Bible."[71] She agrees with Stanton that all Biblical texts are thoroughly androcentric and patriarchal. She criticizes Stanton and other post-biblical feminists who abandon the Bible altogether, though, because this means abandoning all the women whose history lies embedded in the Biblical texts. Such a view "too easily relinquishes women's feminist biblical heritage." "Therefore, feminists cannot afford to disown androcentric biblical texts and patriarchal history as their own revelatory texts and history." We must stay with the Bible and continue to use it for the sake of the women who are there in its history. A feminist critical hermeneutics cannot abandon their memory, but "must reclaim its foresisters as victims *and* subjects participating in patriarchal culture."[72]

The true history of Biblical women, however, is not in the patriarchalized text but in the historical context which underlies the text and which gave rise to it, i.e., in the actual life and ministry of Jesus and the movement of women and men called forth by him. Thus in order to reclaim the place of these women, we must go behind the text and try to sort out and reconstruct the history which has been distorted by the Biblical writers and editors.[73]

Thus Fiorenza sets as her goal, especially in her book *In Memory of Her*, the reconstruction of women's history in the early Christian movement. She says that she will "attempt to reconstruct early Christian history as women's history in order not only to restore women's stories to early Christian history but also to reclaim this history" as "women's own past and to insist that women's history is an integral part of early Christian historiography."[74] Such a task involves no less than "an intellectual re-creation of early Christian beginnings."[75]

213

Fiorenza describes this task as "a critical hermeneutics of remembrance" that seeks to "move beyond the androcentric text to the history of women in biblical religion," which is much more significant than we are led to believe by the edited patriarchal texts. "Rather than abandoning the memory of our foresisters' sufferings and hopes in our patriarchal Christian past, a hermeneutics of remembrance *reclaims* their sufferings and struggles through the subversive power of the 'remembered past.'" It "proposes theoretical models for historical reconstructions that place women in the center of biblical community and theology."[76] The ultimate goal of such a task is "not just to undermine the legitimization of patriarchal religious structures but also to empower women in their struggle against such oppressive structures."[77]

Now the crucial question is, what is the *norm* according to which this or any other critical Biblical study must be done? As we have already noted, Fiorenza rejects the approach that says an authoritative norm can be found within the Bible. Thus the norm must be sought outside the Bible, and it is none other than *women's experience itself.* She suggests that "the revelatory canon for theological evaluation of biblical androcentric traditions and their subsequent interpretations cannot be derived from the Bible itself but can only be formulated in and through women's struggle for liberation from all patriarchal oppression."[78]

> What leads us to perceive biblical texts as oppressive or as providing resources in the struggle for liberation from patriarchal oppression or as models for the transformation of the patriarchal church into women-church is not a revealed principle or a special canon of texts that can claim divine authority. Rather it is the experience of women struggling for liberation and wholeness. . . .[79]

The canon used by feminist critical hermeneutics is the

liberation of *all* women from oppressive structures and patriarchal institutions. This critical criterion of evaluation must be applied to *all* biblical texts in order to determine whether or not they contribute to the social salvation, well-being, and freedom of women. I.e., "all biblical texts must be tested as to their feminist liberating content." In this way feminism interprets, retrieves, and evaluates biblical texts, accepting or rejecting them according to its own canon of liberation.[80]

Fiorenza criticizes Ruether and Russell for continuing to use the old archetypal paradigm of Biblical interpretation. Even though they apply it only to a part of the Bible (the "canon within the canon"), that still means that they accept certain texts or traditions as not being deformed by patriarchalism and as having absolute authority. But this is unacceptable.

A feminist critical interpretation of the Bible cannot take as its point of departure the normative authority of the biblical archetype, but must begin with women's experience in their struggle for liberation. In doing so this mode of interpretation subjects the Bible to a critical feminist scrutiny and to the theological authority of the church of women, an authority that seeks to assess the oppressive or liberating dynamics of all biblical texts. . . .

Its canon is thus derived "*not* from the biblical writings, but from the contemporary struggle of women against racism, sexism, and poverty as oppressive systems of patriarchy and from its systematic explorations in feminist theory." In this way "it places biblical texts under the authority of feminist experience."[81]

D. A Comparison of These Views

On the surface Fiorenza's approach to feminist Biblical

interpretation seems to differ from that of Russell and Ruether, who themselves perceive this to be the case.[82] In reality, though, there is very little if any difference between them.

Even though Fiorenza openly begins with women's experience as the canon by which to test Biblical texts, once a text has passed this test she describes it in ways that attribute to it a very special character. For example, she declares that "only the nonsexist and nonandrocentric traditions of the Bible . . . have the theological authority of revelation."[83] Again, "only those traditions and texts that critically break through patriarchal culture . . . have the theological authority of revelation."[84] These are the texts "that transcend critically their patriarchal frameworks and allow for a vision of Christian women as historical and theological subjects and actors."[85] Also, "*the* litmus test for invoking Scripture as the Word of God must be whether or not biblical texts and traditions seek to end relations of domination and exploitation."[86]

The point is that according to these statements there *is* a category of Biblical texts that transcend the Bible as a whole and which can be invoked in some sense as "the Word of God" and which have "the theological authority of revelation." The fact that these texts are identified by the criterion of women's experience is significant, but the result is essentially the same as that achieved by Russell and Ruether.

The truth is that the *process* by which this result is achieved is no different from that used by Russell and Ruether, either. This is seen when we look more closely at the views of the latter two. It is true that they locate a kind of canon or norm within the Bible itself, but the question must be raised as to how they select or identify this Biblical norm. The plain fact is that they *select* or *identify* it by applying to Scripture the even more basic and fundamentally ultimate norm of *women's experience* – exactly as Fiorenza does.

216

Though Russell calls God's mending of the groaning creation her interpretive key, she declares that "I arrived at this interpretive key through my own life story."[87] She says that this key had to pass the test of what is "seriously imaginable" for feminists: "For my part, I cannot imagine a God who does not seek to be partner with all humankind in the mending of creation." Thus she includes "this principle of interpretation as part of what is seriously imaginable in the paradigm of authority."[88] Even though she finds "a biblical message of liberation for women . . . in God's intention for the mending of all creation," this message "has authority in my life because it makes sense of my experience."[89] The critical feminist perspective says that "the biblical text can only be considered to function as God's word, compelling our faith, when it is nonsexist." Thus it is clear that the "feminist interpretation of the Bible" ultimately "is rooted in the feminist critical consciousness that women and men are fully human and fully equal."[90] It is clear from these statements that Russell's "biblical" norm is subordinate to and is the product of the more basic norm of women's experience.

The same is true of Ruether's "prophetic-liberating tradition." Operating prior to this and independently of it is "the critical principle of feminist theology," which is "the promotion of the full humanity of women." Whatever denies or diminishes the full humanity of women is nonredemptive; whatever promotes it is the authentic message of redemption.[91] This is called the "feminist critical principle" in distinction from the "biblical critical principle" of the prophetic-messianic tradition. There is a correlation or a parallel between the two, says Ruether.[92] But which is the ultimate test, even of the other? There can be no question that Ruether here gives the nod to the feminist principle, which is simply canonized women's experience. All codes must ultimately pass the test of experience, she says. Any interpretive key, such as the exodus theme, has its roots in some "foundational revelatory experience" and

217

must be evaluated again and again by continuing experience, especially women's experience.[93] In this way even the Bible must be "corrected" by the feminist critical principle.[94]

Thus it is quite obvious that Ruether's methodology is no different from Fiorenza's, in that both make women's experience the final norm for judging all of Scripture. This is seen even more clearly in the fact that Ruether sees Scripture as just one of *five* distinct areas of cultural tradition, *all* of which are measured by the feminist critical principle in search of "usable tradition." The other four are the marginalized or "heretical" Christian groups such as Gnosticism and Quakerism; the primary classical Christian traditions of Orthodoxy, Catholicism, and Protestantism; non-Christian or pagan Near Eastern (e.g., Canaanite) and Greco-Roman religion and philosophy; and post-Christian world views such as liberalism, romanticism, and Marxism. All five of these traditions are sexist, and all five must be judged and corrected by the feminist critical principle.[95] In such a program as this the Bible is methodologically no different from any other writings. If a special "prophetic principle" exists therein, it is discovered only through testing by the canon of the feminist principle. This is essentially Fiorenza's approach.

Also, the fact that in her book *Womanguides* Ruether begins the task of creating "a new textual base, a new canon" to "provide norms for judging good and evil, truth and falsehood"[96] shows that she already has in place a more fundamental canon that serves as the normative basis for selecting the entries for her "new canon." This, of course, must be the feminist critical principle, which is for her, as for Fiorenza, the truly ultimate norm.

The conclusion of this section is that all liberal feminists use the same hermeneutical key in their interpretation of the Bible, namely, women's experience of struggle for liberation from male domination. We have already noted Margaret Farley's explanation that certain inner convictions are so basic that anything that contradicts them cannot be accepted. Even Biblical witness "cannot be believed unless it rings true to our deepest capacity for truth and goodness. If it contradicts this, it is not to be believed. If it falsifies this, it cannot be accepted." Such convictions "serve as a kind of negative test for any revelation in knowledge. . . . These convictions must, then, function in a feminist interpretation of scripture – discerning the meaning of the biblical witness as a whole and in its parts and thus . . . whether it is to be believed." The most fundamental conviction shared by feminists is "the conviction that women are fully human and are to be valued as such," a principle that includes the closely related principles of equality and mutuality. This conviction is so basic, she says, that it "could well be formulated as the underlying principle for a feminist hermeneutic," an interpretative principle that is so normative that it gives rise "to an experience of a moral imperative."[97]

Russell's and Ruether's isolating of an interpretive key *within* the Bible is only a mask for their commitment to this more basic norm. Because Fiorenza openly begins at this point, she is being more honest with herself; and her methodology is less ambiguous and more consistent. But in the final analysis these three have the same general approach to Biblical interpretation, and their approach sets the pattern for liberal feminism as a whole.

IV. THE RESULTS OF FEMINIST HERMENEUTICS

What happens when the feminist critical principle is applied to specific texts or sections of the Bible? Certainly we can expect "a new interpretation of the Bible" from "women applying their experience and their feelings to the study of the Bible."[98] As Zikmund says, "The feminist critical consciousness which has emerged over the last century can unlock new meaning in Scripture."[99] Through such new interpretations much of the Bible can be rescued or reclaimed from patriarchy.

A. The Reconstruction of Early Christian History

One of the most ambitious rescue efforts is Fiorenza's attempt to rewrite or reconstruct early Christian history by applying her "hermeneutics of suspicion" and "hermeneutics of remembrance." According to the former she begins by assuming that the New Testament writings as a whole are androcentric and that the true role of women in the early church is suppressed and distorted therein, often deliberately. Then by applying her creative historical imagination, she delves beneath the surface of the patriarchal texts and "remembers" a version of Christian history that begins in egalitarian purity before eventually becoming corrupted by "gradual patriarchialism."[100] The following is a brief summary of her efforts as found in parts II and III of her book, *In Memory of Her.*

1. Early Egalitarianism

In its earliest days Christianity consisted of two separate movements, both of which were inclusive and non-patriarchal. One was the Jesus movement in Palestine, and the other was the Christian-missionary movement in the Greco-Roman world.

The Jesus movement was begun by Jesus himself as a renewal movement within Judaism and not as a "Christian" movement as such. It stressed the theme of the kingdom of God as good news for the marginalized groups among the Jews, i.e., the poor, the sick, and the outcast. It preached a discipleship of equals and thus had an attractiveness to women. It also proclaimed an inclusive wholeness and an everyday presence of God that can be experienced by every human being, women as well as men. Women were prominent leaders, especially in the continuation and expansion of the movement after Jesus' death.

The early Christian movement began in Syrian Antioch. It was likewise an egalitarian movement which challenged and opposed the dominant patriarchal ethos through the praxis of equal discipleship. From its beginning it admitted gentiles as equal members. Paul was not the originator of this movement; he joined it "in progress." The Pauline and post-Pauline writings (but not Acts!) show that women were prominent leaders and missionaries in this movement; they toiled for the gospel in their own right and not just as Paul's assistants. "Without question they were equal and sometimes even superior to Paul in their work for the gospel."[101]

Because of the Acts cover-up, women's actual contribution to the early Christian missionary movement is largely lost and must be rescued through historical imagination. The women who are mentioned must be taken not as exceptions but as representatives of what must have been a much greater number, since this movement "allowed for the full participation and leadership of women."[102] Many worked as traveling missionaries on an equal basis with Paul, e.g., Prisca, Phoebe, the apostle Junia, Euodia, and Syntyche. Others were leaders in the house churches that formed when the church was beginning in a certain city or district, e.g., Aphia, Prisca (again), Nympha, and Lydia. The house church was attractive to women because it was an association of equals and afforded them an equal opportunity for leadership. It was understood that the Spirit was given to all, and thus there was an equality in the power of the Spirit. All without exception were considered to be adopted by God and thus sisters and brothers. The climactic theological self-understanding of the Christian missionary movement was Galatians 3:28.

2. The Pauline Modification of Galatians 3:28

Paul did not originate Galatians 3:28. It was probably part of a pre-Pauline baptismal confession quoted by him. It intends to affirm "that in the Christian community all

221

distinctions of religion, race, class, nationality, and gender are insignificant. All the baptized are equal, they are one in Christ." It advocates the abolition of religious-cultural divisions and of domination involved in slavery or based on sexual divisions. It declares that "within the Christian community no structures of dominance can be tolerated."[103] "Insofar as this egalitarian Christian self-understanding did away with all male privileges of religion, class, and caste, it allowed not only gentiles and slaves but also women to exercise leadership functions within the missionary movement."[104]

Although Paul accepted this theology with its egalitarian view of women's leadership, he felt it was necessary to modify or qualify it in his letters to the church at Corinth because of the circumstances of the concrete pastoral situation that existed there. For example, in 1 Corinthians 11-14 he forbids certain practices that would be detrimental to the church's missionary work (e.g., women prophets' loose and disheveled hair, and wives' speaking in public). The prohibitions are based on the need for decency and order as perceived in that culture, not on any differences between male and female. "He wanted to prevent the Christian community from being mistaken for one of the orgiastic, secret, oriental cults that undermined public order and decency."[105]

Unfortunately, in his paternal zeal for his converts Paul introduced patriarchal imagery and language into the Christian community. This is seen especially in his reference to himself as the "father" of his converts. Though he intended only parental affection, he nevertheless opened the door for the reintroduction of patriarchal authority within the Christian community. "Thus Paul makes it possible for later generations to transfer the hierarchy of the patriarchal family to the new family of God."[106]

3. The Patriarchal Household
In the last decades of the first century several post-

Pauline texts claiming the authority of Paul appeared, namely, Colossians, Ephesians, and the Pastoral letters. These texts advocated the adoption of the Greco-Roman household pattern, which involved the subordination and submission of the socially weaker party.

At first this pattern was applied only to the family or the familial household, as in the household codes of Colossians 3 and Ephesians 5, and as in 1 Peter 2:11-3:12. The emphasis is on the submission of wives to their husbands, slaves to their masters, and children to their parents, with the father of the household being head over all. This social order, probably derived from Aristotelian ethics, was the norm in Greco-Roman culture. Because the early Christian message emphasized freedom and equality for women and slaves, it was viewed by pagans as a threat to the societal order and institutions of the patriarchal household. Thus as a strategy for survival, this patriarchal-societal ethos was gradually introduced into the church, replacing the genuine Christian vision of equality. Thus was the tension between the Christian community and pagan society lessened. Ephesians 5 goes further than the rest by making submission not just a survival strategy but a religious Christian duty.

4. The Patriarchal Household of God

The patriarchalization process was carried a step further when the Pastoral Epistles applied the Greco-Roman patriarchal household concept to the church as the household of God. The result was the patriarchalization of local church leadership and ministry, and the relegation of women's leadership to marginal positions within the sphere of women.

This was done for apologetic reasons, to order the Christian community in such a way that it would not be disruptive to the established social order. But it was also done for what were perceived to be inherent theological reasons, namely, that ministry and leadership are dependent upon age and gender qualifications. Only the older men were allowed to function as leaders and teachers of the whole church; women were required to restrict the use of their gifts to the leadership and teaching of other women. This led to the rise of a kind of auxiliary "church of women," who nevertheless were kept under the authority of the emerging male episcopacy.

5. Mark, John, and the Original Egalitarian Ideal

At the same time this patriarchalization process was taking place, the gospels of Mark and John appeared. In them the original ideal of Jesus is preserved, with its emphasis on altruistic service and egalitarian leadership. Contrary to the Greco-Roman pattern and the post-Pauline texts, they present children, slaves, and women as the paradigms of true discipleship and leadership. Mark's gospel includes an "indirect polemic against the male disciples" by presenting the women followers of Jesus as "examples of suffering discipleship and true leadership," and as the foremost ministers and apostolic witnesses. This is part of the Markan community's struggle "to avoid the pattern of dominance and submission that characterizes its social-cultural environment."[107]

In the gospel of John the footwashing scene sums up Jesus' whole ministry and revelation of God. This gospel never stresses the special leadership of the twelve. Instead it reiterates the theme of the discipleship of equals, with alternating leadership open to every member of the community and inclusive of women and men. The author of the gospel gives women an astonishingly prominent place in the narrative; at crucial points they emerge as exemplary disciples and apostolic witnesses.

Thus at the end of the first century two Christian traditions existed: post-Pauline/Petrine patriarchalism, and the original altruistic egalitarianism. The latter had women leaders; the former limited them to what was culturally acceptable. The former won out.

Yet this "success" can not be justified theologically, since it cannot claim the authority of Jesus for its own Christian praxis. . . . The discipleship and apostolic leadership of women are integral parts of Jesus' "alternative" praxis of agape and service. The "light shines in the darkness" of patriarchal repression and forgetfulness, and this "darkness has never overcome it."[108]

6. Conclusion

This is the essence of Fiorenza's reconstruction of the history of women in early Christianity. It is a primary example of the application of the feminist critical principle (the normative character of women's experience) to the Biblical texts. The texts are assumed to be patriarchally biased and culturally relative, and the historically imaginative reconstruction itself exhibits an approved opposite bias, presenting women in the best possible light.

B. The Meaning of Jesus

Another example of what happens when the feminist hermeneutic is applied to specific texts is the interpretation of the person and work of the man Jesus. In general the liberal feminists view Jesus in a very positive way, accepting him as a "feminist" in the sense that he considered men and women to be equal.[109] Ruether, for example, denies that Jesus came to ratify the status quo of male domination. Instead he came "to overturn it, to raise up women from their subjugated position"; he came "in judgment on oppressive and unjust social systems."[110] The Jesus of the synoptics is "a figure remarkably compatible with feminism" in that his criticism of religious and social hierarchy "is remarkably parallel to feminist criticism." Overall, Ruether sees Jesus as a primary example of the prophetic-messianic principle. He "renews the prophetic vision whereby the Word of God does not validate the existing social and religious hierarchy but speaks on behalf of the marginalized and despised groups of society."[111]

Contrary to the secular and Goddess feminists who reject Jesus just because he was a man, and contrary to conservative traditionalists who argue that Jesus' maleness is a pattern for male leadership, liberal feminists generally regard Jesus' maleness as irrelevant or as having no ultimate significance.[112] "Christ's work was not first of all that of being a male but that of being the new human." He is "a unique revelation of true personhood," not just true *man*hood. In this sense what once was called "incarnation" is better referred to as *humanization*.[113]

As the revelation of true personhood, Jesus' purpose and value for us is that of an example. Russell says, "For Christians the most important image of humanity is Jesus Christ who was incarnate in human flesh so that we might know God's intention for humanity." He came as "a representative of the new humanity."[114] As Ruether puts it, a true feminist Christology "must restore the understanding of Christ to its true function as paradigm of the liberated humanity." He presents to us both the image of God as liberator and the image of humanity as liberated.[115]

For feminists it is important to see that Jesus is not "the sole and exclusive model of Christ," but is only a paradigm of what all may become by imitating both his role as liberator and his role as liberated. "Christ, as redemptive person and Word of God, is not to be encapsulated 'once-for-all' in the historical Jesus. . . . Christic personhood continues in our sisters and brothers."[116] In imitation of Jesus, "*all* can become representative of a new personhood." The new humanity modeled by Jesus "is available to those who participate with him through faith" in God's work of liberation.[117]

Thus far this feminist Christology is little different from typical liberal Christology. A specifically feminist twist is provided when Russell declares that the concept of the *kingship* of Christ must be abandoned and replaced with the concept of Christ as liberator. This is necessary because "we are accustomed to rulership as top-down dominating authority," or the pyramid model of authority, which is a patriarchal corruption of the model of authority as empowerment. Christ's threefold work of prophecy, priesthood, and kingship is thus transformed by Russell into prophecy, suffering, and liberation. (The priesthood idea is that of Christ's suffering *with* us and *not* for us.) Russell grants that this view of Christ and the church may "seem one-sided," but "at least it promotes partnership in ministry among the whole people of God."[118]

This version of Christology is a clear example of how feminists when applying the feminist critical principle of hermeneutics feel free to adjust and revise the text in whatever way is necessary to promote the full humanity of women as they understand it.

C. Miscellaneous Examples

There are many examples of how the application of this critical principle enables feminists to see things in Biblical texts that others probably will not see. One is Russell's explanation of the true identity of Miriam in the Old Testament. "Although she was probably an independent leader in Israel, Miriam was made a sister of Aaron and Moses in the later tradition." Because she was such a prominent prophet and leader, the patriarchal revisers of Hebrew tradition felt it was necessary to diminish her by demoting her to just a sister of the main leaders of Israel and by depicting her as being punished with leprosy. But women today understand that this was just a patriarchal cover-up, and they "continue to reconstruct the past of their foremothers in order to gain strength to speak with authority of the future that God intends for all people."[119]

Another example of such "imaginative reconstruction" is Fiorenza's elevation of Martha of Bethany to the role of primary theologian of the Johannine community and possible author of the fourth gospel. The former is based on the nature of Martha's Christological confession in John 11:27 and its deliberate placement in the very center of the narrative. This shows that she "is responsible for the primary articulation of the community's christological faith," and thus is "the spokeswoman for the messianic faith of the community." Regarding the question of authorship, since in John 11:5 Jesus is said to have loved Martha and Mary and Lazarus, Martha may well be "the disciple whom Jesus loved"; and we may conjecture that her confession is deliberately repeated in John 20:31 "as the climactic faith confession of a 'beloved disciple' in order to identify her with the writer of the book."[120]

A final example is the common feminist interpretation of the incident in Luke 11:27-28, where a woman said to Jesus, "Blessed is the womb that bore You, and the breasts at which You nursed." Jesus replied, "On the contrary, blessed are those who hear the word of God, and observe it." To the non-feminist Jesus seems to be saying that *nothing* is more important than each individual's hearing and honoring the word of God, not even the significant role of motherhood, and not even Mary's uniquely supreme instance of motherhood. That the initiating comment referred to motherhood is incidental; whatever role might have been named (e.g., elder in Israel, physician), Jesus' reply would have been the same. That is, the point of his statement is in what he is affirming, not in what he is denying.

Women prompted by the feminist consciousness, however, have seen something entirely different in this incident. They see Jesus as deliberately and specifically "rejecting the stereotype of a woman as first of all a reproductive being." As Justo and Catherine González say, this is something that "only a woman could feel and point out."[121] That is, they zero in not on what Jesus is affirming but on what he is denying, and they imply that the *central purpose* of Jesus in his remark is to make a statement about the nature of women. Jesus saw the woman's comment as an opportunity for a "radical rejection . . . of the uterus image" of women, since in that culture the main justification for a woman's existence was to bear children. Thus he decided to address the question, "What is woman?" His reply says, *"She is one who can hear the will of God and do it."*[122] That is, Jesus' statement is interpreted as deliberately referring specifically to women and not to all people in general, in spite of the fact that in the text "Blessed are those" is in the masculine plural form. This is an excellent illustration of how the present context of feminist experience, rather than the originally-intended meaning of the author, is made the key to the hermeneutical task.

D. Unredeemable Texts

The goal of feminist hermeneutics is much more than just the simple interpretation of a particular text. Such interpretation is actually the means to an end, that end being the decision as to whether the given text can be rescued from its patriarchal framework and used by women in a positive way today, or whether it must be rejected because it is irredeemably androcentric. Despite the most heroic efforts to reinterpret them in harmony with feminism, in the end some Biblical texts are found to be so androcentric that they are simply discarded as unusable. As Sakenfeld says, there surely do remain "some negative texts concerning women for which no reinterpretation seems possible."[123] These are "texts that consciously intend to repress women, such as the story of Eve or 1 Timothy's dictum that women should keep silence," says Ruether.[124] These and other such oppressive texts are the ones she says should be identified as false and evil in her Women-Church rite, "Exorcism of Patriarchal Texts."[125]

Liberal feminists are ready to cast aside *any* Biblical

text, tradition, or doctrine that is perceived as irreconcilable with women s experience of the struggle for liberation, no matter how traditionally central it may have been. The sacred absoluteness of this feminist critical principle as the final authority for truth and falsehood is seen in Ruether's statement that even the cross of Jesus would be discarded if it were so perceived:

> ... Traditions die when a new generation is no longer able to reappropriate the foundational paradigm in a meaningful way; when it is experienced as meaningless or even as demonic: that is, disclosing a meaning that points to false or inauthentic life. Thus if the cross of Jesus would be experienced by women as pointing them only toward continued victimization and not redemption, it would be perceived as false and demonic in this way, and women could no longer identify themselves as Christians.[126]

V. CONCLUSION

Whereas Goddess feminists see themselves as liberating deity itself from patriarchalism, liberal feminists think of themselves as liberating the Bible therefrom. They affirm that for the most part the Bible can be thus liberated through the process of feminist hermeneutics; therefore Scripture can be used by women today. Thus the liberal Christian feminists still remain within the broad pale of Christendom. They refuse to follow their Goddess (post-Christian) sisters in abandoning the Bible, the Church, and the Christ.

In the final analysis, however, we must insist that there is no essential difference between Goddess feminism and liberal Christian feminism. This is true because on the deepest level they both accept the same ultimate authority and norm, namely, women's experience. As long as this is the case, the difference between them is formal only. Liberal feminists express their religious convictions in forms derived from the Christian tradition, albeit selected and sanitized according to their normative experience. Goddess feminists express their religious convictions in non-Christian (pagan, wiccan) forms. Only the forms are different; the beliefs and convictions are the same.

This is why liberal feminists remain friendly toward their Goddess/wiccan sisters, and open to paganism as a usable tradition for contemporary feminism. At the very least, as Russell points out, "even from within the Christian tradition, feminist theologians have come to recognize the legitimacy of encountering the divine as goddess."[127] She herself asserts that the plural Hebrew word for God, *Elohim,* reflects "the notion of God as combining all the characteristics of the male and female gods in the Canaanite pantheon which Yahweh now transcends, yet includes."[128]

But many liberal feminists go far beyond this. Fiorenza suggests that a feminist hermeneutics must be able to learn from post-Biblical feminists and should be able to "incorporate Wicca's feminist spiritual quest for women's power."[129] Fiorenza makes this remark in her criticism of Ruether, implying that the latter's view is not able to incorporate Wicca.

But this is not completely fair to Ruether. Even though she does not accept all aspects of Goddess feminism, Ruether does agree with it in accepting pagan religions (e.g., Canaanite) as one of her five sources of "usable tradition" for constructing a feminist theology.[130] This is what she means when she says that "feminism does not simply go back to earliest Christianity or Judaism, but it reaches back to lost options behind them."[131] True feminist theology should be inclusive rather than exclusive. This is Goddess feminism's main error: it totally excludes the Biblical tradition. But true feminism reaches out critically to both traditions: the Biblical religion in all its patriarchy on the one hand, and the pagan or Goddess religion with its matriarchal excesses on the other hand. Both are one-sided and need to be transformed into a new whole, with neither being excluded.

> . . . Feminist theology should not fall back on biblical exclusivism over against "paganism." It should not call for biblical religion as the "true" foundation of feminism over against non-Christian traditions. Rather it should raise questions about all religious exclusivism, including the reversed use of exclusivism by goddess religion to repudiate biblical religion.[132]

This openness toward pagan religions and Goddess feminism is no doubt why liberal feminism and Goddess feminism seem to be drawing closer and closer together on a practical level, even as they are already essentially the same on a theoretical level. This ecumenical attitude is usually evident in the occasional feminist conferences held either in the name of liberal Christian feminism and/or of Goddess feminism. For example, a Women and Spirituality conference held in Mankato, Minnesota, in October 1985 was well represented by both sides. Rosemary Radford Ruether was the keynote speaker. She called for more cooperation between Women-Church groups and witchcraft covens. Other speakers included Catholics, Protestants, Jews, a Hindu, lesbians, and "a profusion of professed witches." Three Sunday worship services were held: an ecumenical communion service conducted by a woman, a feminist communion service, and a Wiccan ritual conducted by two witches.[133]

A similar combination occurred at the "Women in the Church" conference in Washington, D.C., in October 1986. Though the conference was ostensibly Catholic, two of the main speakers were representatives of the Goddess.[134] In April 1985 a "Women's Inter-seminary Conference" hosted by the Association of Women Seminarians was held at Pittsburgh Theological Seminary. Two of the three main speakers were an American Baptist and a Presbyterian; the keynote speaker, Judith Plaskow, was a representative of the Goddess. Workshops spanned the interests of both liberal and Goddess feminists.

Though these events are evidence of a certain inner unity between these two kinds of feminism, important differences remain. Their willingness to be identified with the Christian tradition means that liberal feminists can never be truly at home in either the secular or the Goddess feminist camp.

Endnotes

1. Letty M. Russell, "Introduction: Liberating the Word," in *Feminist Interpretation of the Bible*, ed. Letty M. Russell (Philadelphia: Westminster Press, 1985), pp. 14, 16.

2. Elisabeth Schüssler Fiorenza, *In Memory of Her: A Feminist Theological Reconstruction of Christian Origins* (New York: Crossroad, 1987), p. 27.

3. Russell, "Introduction," p. 12.

4. Russell, "Authority and Challenge of Feminist Interpretation," in *Feminist Interpretation of the Bible*, pp. 138, 140.

5. Rosemary Radford Ruether, *Sexism and God-Talk: Toward a Feminist Theology* (Boston: Beacon Press, 1983), pp. 18, 20ff.

6. Fiorenza, *Memory*, pp. 27-31.

7. Fiorenza, *Bread Not Stone: The Challenge of Feminist Biblical Interpretation* (Boston: Beacon Press, 1984), p. xiii.

8. Katharine Doob Sakenfeld, "Feminist Uses of Biblical Materials," in *Feminist Interpretation of the Bible*, p. 55. Italics added.

9. Fiorenza, *Memory*, p. 30.

10. Russell, "Authority," pp. 140-41.

11. F.F. Bruce, "Interpretation of the Bible," *Evangelical Dictionary of Theology*, ed. Walter A. Elwell (Grand Rapids: Baker, 1984), p. 567.

12. Krister Stendahl, *The Bible and the Role of Women: A Case Study in Hermeneutics*, tr. Emilie T. Sander (Philadelphia: Fortress Press, 1966), pp. 8-9. See John Reumann's introduction, p. iii.

13. Fiorenza, *Bread*, p. 126.

14. Bruce, "Interpretation," p. 568.

15. Stendahl, *The Bible and the Role of Women*, p. 12.

16. Fiorenza, *Memory*, p. 5; *Bread*, pp. 28-30.

17. Fiorenza, *Bread*, p. 148.

18. Barbara Brown Zikmund, "Feminist Consciousness in Historical Perspective," in *Feminist Interpretation of the Bible*, p. 22.

19. Lewis S. Mudge, "Hermeneutics," *The Westminster Dictionary of Christian Theology*, ed. Alan Richardson and John Bowden (Philadelphia: Westminster Press, 1983), p. 252. Italics added.

20. Bruce, "Interpretation," p. 568.

21. Raymond F. Collins, "Structuralism," *The Westminster Dictionary of Christian Theology*, p. 551.

22. Stendahl, *The Bible and the Role of Women*, pp. 10ff.

23. Ibid., p. 20.

24. Ibid., pp. 17-18.

25. Ibid., pp. 22-23, 35-36.

26. Mudge, "Hermeneutics," p. 253.

27. Russell, *Household of Freedom: Authority in Feminist Theology* (Philadelphia: Westminster Press, 1987), pp. 29-31, 79-80. See also Ruether, "Feminist Interpretation: A Method of Correlation," in *Feminist Interpretation of the Bible*, pp. 118ff.

28. Fiorenza, *Bread*, pp. 32-33; see pp. 35-36.

29. Ruether, "Feminist Interpretation," pp. 121-122.

30. Fiorenza, *Bread*, p. 40.

31. Fiorenza, *Memory*, p. xvii; *Bread*, pp. 38, 62.

32. Russell, "Introduction," p. 15.

33. Fiorenza, *Memory*, p. 6; *Bread*, p. 45.

34. Russell, "Introduction," p. 12.

35. Fiorenza, *Bread*, p. 138.

36. Russell, "Introduction," pp. 13-14.

37. Ruether, "Feminist Interpretation," p. 111.

38. Margaret A. Farley, "Feminist Consciousness and the Interpretation of Scripture," in *Feminist Interpretation of the Bible*, p. 43.

39. Ibid., p. 44.

40. Fiorenza, "The Will To Choose or To Reject: Continuing our Critical Work," in *Feminist Interpretation of the Bible*, p. 131. See also Fiorenza, *Bread*, p. xiii, where this is called "*the* litmus test."

41. Fiorenza, *Memory*, p. 60.

42. Russell, "Introduction," p. 16.

43. Russell, *Household*, p. 30.

44. Russell, "Introduction," p. 17; "Authority," p. 141.

45. Russell, *Household*, pp. 37, 83.

46. Fiorenza, *Bread*, pp. 20-21.

47. Fiorenza, *Memory*, pp. 41, 167-168.

48. Fiorenza, *Bread*, pp. xiii-xvii.

49. Fiorenza, *Memory*, p. 33.

50. Phyllis Trible, "Postscript: Jottings on the Journey," in *Feminist Interpretation of the Bible*, p. 148.

51. Ruether, "Feminist Interpretation," pp. 121-122.

52. Russell, "Authority," p. 145.

53. Russell, *Human Liberation in a Feminist Perspective – A Theology* (Philadelphia: Westminster Press, 1974), p. 58; "Introduction," pp. 138, 140.

54. Russell, "Authority," p. 138.

55. Ibid., p. 139.

56. Russell, *Household*, p. 71.

57. Russell, *Human Liberation*, pp. 27ff., 41ff.

58. See Russell, "Authority," p. 139.

59. Russell, *Household*, pp. 26, 37, 64, 87.

60. Russell, *Human Liberation*, pp. 61, 107ff., 121, 133.

61. Ibid., pp. 74-79, 86-88; *Household*, pp. 49, 71.

62. Russell, "Feminist Critique: Opportunity for Cooperation," *Journal for the Study of the Old Testament* (February 1982), 22:68.

63. Ruether, *Sexism*, pp. 22-24; "Feminist Interpretation," p. 117.

64. Ruether, *Sexism*, p. 24.

65. Ibid., pp. 24-25; *Women-Church: Theology and Practice of Feminist Liturgical Communities* (San Francisco: Harper and Row, 1986), pp. 41-42, 45.

66. Ruether, *Sexism*, pp. 27ff.

67. Ibid., pp. 24, 27, 31.

68. Ibid., p. 24.

69. Ruether, "Feminist Interpretation," p. 122.

70. Fiorenza, *Bread*, pp. 11-13; *Memory*, pp. 14-17.

71. Fiorenza, *Memory*, p. 19.

72. Ibid., pp. xv, xix, 27-30.

73. Ibid., pp. 29, 41.

74. Ibid., pp. xiv, xix.

75. Ibid., p. 70.

76. Fiorenza, *Bread*, pp. 19-20.

77. Fiorenza, *Memory*, p. xx.

78. Ibid., p. 32.

79. Fiorenza, *Bread*, p. xvi.

80. Ibid., pp. 40-41, 92; "The Will To Choose," p. 131.

81. Fiorenza, *Bread*, pp. 12-14.

82. Fiorenza distinguishes her view from the others in *Bread*, pp. 12-13, and in *Memory*, pp. 14-21. Russell makes the same distinction in her chapter in *Feminist Interpretation of the Bible,* pp. 145-146.

83. Fiorenza, "Toward A Feminist Biblical Hermeneutics: Biblical Interpretation and Liberation Theology," in *The Challenge of Liberation Theology: A First World Response,* ed. Brian Mahan and L. Dale Richesin (Maryknoll, NY: Orbis Books, 1981), p. 108.

84. Fiorenza, *Memory,* p. 33.

85. Ibid., p. 30.

86. Fiorenza, *Bread,* p. xiii.

87. Russell, "Authority," p. 139.

88. Russell, *Household,* p. 49.

89. Russell, "Authority," p. 138.

90. Russell, "Introduction," pp. 14, 16.

91. Ruether, *Sexism,* pp. 18-19. She says that "the normative principle of feminist theology" is "the full personhood of women" ("Feminist Theology," p. 12).

92. Ruether, "Feminist Interpretation," pp. 116-118.

93. Ibid., pp. 111-112.

94. Ruether, *Sexism,* p. 22.

95. Ibid., pp. 20ff.

96. Ruether, *Womanguides: Readings Toward a Feminist Theology* (Boston: Beacon Press, 1985), p. ix.

97. Farley, "Feminist Consciousness," pp. 43-45.

98. Justo L. González and Catherine Gunsalus González, *Liberation Preaching: The Pulpit and the Oppressed* (Nashville: Abingdon Press, 1980), p. 81.

99. Zikmund, "Feminist Consciousness," p. 29.

100. Fiorenza, *Memory,* p. 84.

101. Ibid., p. 161.

102. Ibid., pp. 167-168.

103. Ibid., p. 213.

104. Ibid., p. 218.

105. Ibid., p. 232.

106. Ibid., pp. 233-234.

107. Ibid., pp. 320-323.

108. Ibid., p. 334.

109. Russell, *Human Liberation,* p. 138.

110. Ruether, "Feminist Theology and Spirituality," in *Christian Feminism: Visions of a New Humanity,* ed. Judith L. Weidman (San Francisco: Harper and Row, 1984), pp. 21-22.

111. Ruether, Sexism, pp. 135-136.

112. Ibid., p. 137. It is just one of the "historical accidents of Jesus' person" ("Feminist Theology," p. 21).

113. Russell, *Human Liberation,* pp. 71, 137-138.

114. Ibid., pp. 65, 133-136.
115. Ruether, "Feminist Theology," pp. 21-22.
116. Ibid., p. 22; *Sexism*, p. 138.
117. Russell, *Human Liberation*, pp. 136, 139.
118. Russell, "Women and Ministry: Problem or Possibility?", in *Christian Feminism: Visions of a New Humanity*, ed. Judith L. Weidman (San Francisco: Harper and Row, 1984), pp. 83-84.
119. Russell, *Household*, p. 19.
120. Fiorenza, *Memory*, pp. 329-330.
121. González, *Liberation Preaching*, p. 64.
122. Rachel Conrad Wahlberg, *Jesus According to a Woman* (New York: Paulist Press, 1975), p. 44.
123. Sakenfeld, "Feminist Uses of Biblical Materials," pp. 58-59.
124. Ruether, *Women-Church*, p. 136.
125. Ibid., p. 137. The "suggested texts in need of exorcism" that she lists here are Lev. 12:1-5; Exod. 19:1, 7-9, 14-15; Judges 19; Eph. 5:21-23; I Tim. 2:11-15; and I Pet. 2:18-20.
126. Ruether, "Feminist Interpretation," p. 112.
127. Russell, *Household*, p. 53.
128. Russell, *Human Liberation* , p. 99.
129. Fiorenza, *Memory*, pp. 18-19.
130. Ruether, *Sexism*, pp. 21-22, 38-41.
131. Ruether, *Women-Church*, p. 38.
132. Ruether, "Feminist Theology," pp. 14-15.
133. Donna Steichen, "From Convent to Coven: Catholic Neo-Pagans at the Witches' Sabbath," *Fidelity* (December 1985), 5:27-28.
134. Steichen, "The Goddess Goes to Washington," *Fidelity* (December 1986), 6:34, 40ff.

7 BIBLICAL FEMINISM: DESCRIPTION

Thus far we have discussed three types of feminism: secular, Goddess, and liberal Christian. This chapter begins our discussion of the fourth and final type, which will be called Biblical feminism. It could be called evangelical feminism, since the discussion will focus on the feminist movement that has intensified in modern American Evangelicalism since about 1970. It could also be called conservative Christian feminism, which would highlight both its kinship with and its differences from liberal Christian feminism. But the expression *Biblical feminism* is appropriately descriptive, because most of those who hold this view (1) accept the final authority of the Bible and (2) believe that feminism is the Bible's authentic teaching.

I. BIBLICAL FEMINISTS AND OTHER FEMINISTS

In this study of feminism and the Bible, two of the main issues have been Biblical *authority* and Biblical *interpreta-*

239

tion (hermeneutics), topics that are not always easily separable. These are the issues that set Biblical feminism apart from the other types.

A. *Biblical Authority*

Biblical feminism is distinguished from all other types by its view of Biblical authority. No other form of feminism accepts the Bible as the final authority in matters of faith and practice. Secular and Goddess feminists openly repudiate the Bible and make no attempt to relate positively to it. Liberal feminism does use the Bible, sometimes in a very positive way, but not as its final authority. The final authority for all these forms of feminism, as we have seen, is women's experience of struggle for liberation from male dominance.

But Biblical feminism does accept the Bible as its final authority, as its "only rule of faith and practice." This is because it is a movement within the general stream of orthodox, conservative Christendom, particularly Evangelicalism, which has been traditionally committed to a high view of Scripture. The Bible is considered to be the product of revelation and inspiration and is thus taken to be the true Word of God in human language. What it teaches about the role of women or about any other subject is true because of the very nature of the book.

This does not mean that all Biblical feminists have exactly the same view of Biblical authority. Some are more consistent than others on this point. In its most consistent form, Biblical feminism accepts the full authority of the whole Bible. All its affirmations are taken to be true, and there are no contradictions among them. In a word, the Bible is considered to be inerrant. Thus its authority is final, and all experience must be subordinate to it.

Some who fall within this general category are less consistent in their view of the Bible's authority, allowing for some errors and contradictions within it. Thus there is some shading toward the left, toward the direction of liberal Christian feminism.[1] However, even these regard the Bible to be of divine origin and to be generally authoritative, though they tend to be more openly swayed by the voice of women's experience than the more consistent Biblical feminists. This will be discussed further under point II below.

B. Biblical Interpretation

The second distinguishing feature of Biblical feminism is its approach to Biblical interpretation, or hermeneutics. Two aspects of this approach are relevant here. The first has to do with the "two horizons" of interpretation, that of the writer and that of the reader. This is a point of difference between Biblical feminists and their liberal Christian cousins. Whereas the latter tend to minimize the writer's intention and emphasize the reader's experience and perspective as the key to understanding a text, Biblical feminists usually agree that the true meaning of any text is determined by the writer's own originally intended meaning. The basic rule of interpretation, as Scott McClelland puts it, is this: "The primary meaning of a text is what the original author intended and what the original readers could have understood."[2] Acknowledging the two horizons (the "then and there" versus the "here and now"), Gordon Fee and Douglas Stuart say,

> The reason one must *not begin* with the here and now is that *the only proper control for hermeneutics is to be found in the original intent of the biblical text.* . . . This is the "plain meaning" one is after. Otherwise biblical texts can be made to mean whatever they mean to any given reader. But such hermeneutics becomes pure subjectivity, and who then is to say that one person's interpretation is right, and another's is wrong. Anything goes.[3]

241

As they say with emphasis, *"A text cannot mean what it never meant."*[4]

As Ruth Tucker and Walter Liefeld put it, "Evangelicals, however, including those who recognize the existence of what has been called two 'horizons' . . . still normally believe that what the Bible *teaches* is true and authoritative."[5] Reta Finger says, "We must look for the basic intention of each biblical writer. What did each of them really mean in that time and place?"[6]

The second aspect of Biblical feminism's hermeneutics is the fact that it interprets the Bible as teaching an egalitarian view of women. That this is the intended meaning of the relevant Biblical texts becomes plain when they are properly interpreted, it says. This is the aspect of Biblical interpretation that distinguishes this form of feminism from secular and Goddess feminism. These latter types say that the basic intention of the Bible is to teach patriarchy.

II. BIBLICAL FEMINISTS AND OTHER CONSERVATIVES

All conservatives, feminist and non-feminist, declare their acceptance of the authority of the Bible; and all attempt to honor its originally intended meaning as hermeneutically normative. But in spite of these important points of agreement, conservatives still seriously disagree over the subject of feminism. Strong voices are heard on each side of the issue, though it is unclear what the relative strength of each side is. In a *Christianity Today* editorial, Terry Muck notes that "if an article endorses women in leadership roles, many letters object and a few congratulate. If the article endorses a male hierarchy, many object and a few congratulate."[7] In a 1990 poll conducted by *Christianity Today*, to which nearly 750 subscribers and spouses responded, about 90% agreed or strongly agreed with the statement, "The Bible affirms the principle of male headship in the family." Over 90% agreed with the statement, "God made men and women to be equal in personhood and in value, but different in roles." Yet only about four out of ten would restrict women from being elders or being ordained.[8]

Neither do Biblical feminists agree among themselves on all points. Most seem to hold to an unrestricted egalitarianism in both home and church. The husband-wife relationship should be a total partnership, with no hierarchy or even headship in the traditional sense of the term. Also, a complete interchangeability of roles should exist within the church.

Some, however, hold to what may be called a modified or restricted egalitarianism. Grant Osborne, for example, concludes that the subjection of wives to their husbands is normative, but women may be ordained as pastors and leaders in the church.[9] John Stott accepts the principle of male headship, but believes this allows for a woman to be ordained for ministry as long as she is serving on a ministry team where a man is the team leader.[10] Donald Bloesch's view is similar to that of Stott.[11] (There may be some justification for calling such a view modified hierarchicalism, as Diehl does.[12] But strict egalitarians would probably have warmer feelings toward it than would strict hierarchicalists.)

What, then, accounts for the differences among conservatives over this question of feminism? Interestingly, the differences on this issue are again the result of different approaches to Biblical authority and Biblical interpretation.

A. Biblical Authority

Just as the issue of Biblical authority separates Biblical feminists from other kinds of feminists, so also is it one thing that separates some of them from conservative nonfeminists. As mentioned above, most conservatives have a very high view of the Bible. This is especially true of nonfeminists, most of whom accept the Bible as the inerrant

Word of God. Many if not most conservative feminists take the same position. However, *some* in the latter category have compromised their view on the authority of the Bible, because they believe that in a few places the Bible actually *intends* to teach patriarchy, and therefore it must be wrong in those places. The inerrancy of the Bible is thus seriously brought into question if not openly denied. This constitutes a step in the direction of liberal Christian feminism, where women's experience is elevated to a position of authority alongside if not over the Bible.

The examples of those Biblical feminists who take this view are quite well known by now. One is Paul King Jewett, whose 1975 book, *Man as Male and Female,* caused a bit of a stir among Evangelicals because of its affirmation of contradictions within Paul's writings on the subject of women. The gist of his view is that there was an inner conflict in Paul's mind because of his thorough rabbinic training on the one hand and his strong commitment to Christ on the other. When he thought in terms of the former, he thought of woman as subordinate to man; when he thought in terms of the new revelation of God in Christ, he thought of woman as equal to man in all things, as in Galatians 3:28. The two are not compatible and cannot be harmonized.[13] In 1 Corinthians 11 in particular, Paul bases his argument on the rabbinic understanding of Genesis 2:18ff. But, asks Jewett, is this understanding correct? He replies, "We do not think that it is." Thus by teaching female subordination here Paul contradicts the first creation narrative, the life style of Jesus, and his own teaching in Galatians 3:28.[14] This, says Jewett, "may be regarded as a disparity or incongruity within Scripture itself."[15]

A similar view is held by Virginia Ramey Mollenkott, a feminist who was widely influential in the earlier stages of the development of Biblical feminism. In an interview published in the May/June 1976 issue of *The Other Side,* Mollenkott describes how she met Paul Jewett at an earlier

244

evangelical conference on feminism at which she was the keynote speaker.[16] She reports how the night before he was to speak, they discussed "whether he dared say his thing on the Pauline self-contradictions." They decided he should not. But Mollenkott implies that she herself agreed with his views even then, and she certainly affirms as much in the interview. Concerning Paul she says, "There are flat contradictions between some of his theological arguments and his own doctrines and behavior."

She says that Paul admits that his opinions as stated in Scripture may be wrong. He argues from Genesis 2, where Eve is said to be created after Adam. This is not in harmony with Genesis 1, which says they were created simultaneously. Jesus argues from Genesis 1. "So Paul is in a way contradicting Jesus here."[17] In her book, *Women, Men, and the Bible,* she explains this further in a chapter called "Pauline Contradictions and Biblical Inspiration." She says that "the apostle Paul seems to contradict his own teachings and behavior concerning women, apparently because of inner conflicts between the training he had received and the liberating insights of the gospel."[18] She also mentions the conflict she sees between Genesis 1 and a literal understanding of Genesis 2.[19]

Basically she says the inerrantist faces a dilemma. On the one hand, Paul bases his argument for female subordination (in 1 Corinthians 11 and 1 Timothy 2) on a literal reading of the order of creation in Genesis 2. But a literal reading of Genesis 2 contradicts the simultaneous creation of Genesis 1. Thus one must say either that there is a contradiction between Genesis 1 and Genesis 2, or that Paul misreads Genesis 2 (through rabbinic eyes) and therefore comes up with an invalid argument and an invalid conclusion (i.e., female subordination). She opts for the latter: Paul was wrong. She harmonizes Genesis 1 and Genesis 2 by saying that Genesis 2 is poetical and is not intended to be taken literally in its chronology.[20]

It is rather remarkable that in spite of all this, Mol-

245

lenkott is not willing to say that she is claiming the Bible is guilty of any real error. When Harold Lindsell charged that her view of Genesis 2 means she cannot hold to an infallible Bible,[21] she indignantly replied that he should have checked with her before saying such a thing. Because Genesis 2 is poetry, there is no conflict. "Never have I denied that the Bible is the infallible rule of faith and practice," she said.[22] Even her view of Paul's erroneous thinking does not imply that the Bible is in error, she claims. "I hesitate to say that this record of Paul's position is an error in Scripture. It is just an honest record of a human being thinking out loud and working through his conflicts."[23] "Let us, then, courageously recognize that Paul's human limitations do crop up in his arguments undergirding female subordination, believing that these inner conflicts were recorded for our instruction in righteousness by the inspiration of God." Thus "the Bible was not in error to record Paul's thought-processes."[24]

The final example of Biblical feminists who seem to have a weak view of Scriptural authority is the book *All We're Meant To Be*, by Letha Scanzoni and Nancy Hardesty. As Susan Foh notes, their inconsistency on this point is "less explicit" (than Jewett's) in the first edition of their book in 1974.[25] However, it is much more clear in the 1986 revised edition. They affirm their commitment to Biblical authority.[26] Nevertheless they seem to accept the liberal party line concerning the patriarchal nature of the Bible. They point out that Scripture was written by men in patriarchal cultures, and "that the canon was defined by men, who left out many books now known to us to be more favorable to women." They endorse Fiorenza's hermeneutics of suspicion.[27] They suggest that Genesis 1 and 2 are contradictory.[28] They say Paul contradicts the main tenor of Genesis as well as himself.[29]

When confronted with these sorts of statements, conservatives in general – especially the non-feminists – are very uncomfortable with their implications with regard to Biblical authority. Mollenkott's attempts to harmonize her views of Paul and Genesis with a high view of the Bible, for example, are not seen as convincing. As non-feminists see it, this kind of approach just seems to confirm that feminism is not consistent with a high view of Biblical authority, especially one that involves a belief in the inerrancy of Scripture. In commenting on Jewett and Mollenkott, Clark Pinnock says, "Perhaps it is necessary to reject parts of the Bible in order to come up with the feminist belief. If it were not, why would these two engage in it?"[30]

In her 1980 book, *Women and the Word of God*, Susan Foh cites the individuals in the three examples discussed above and charges them along with Biblical feminism in general of abandoning Biblical authority. She says that "the biblical feminists see irreconcilable contradictions in the Bible's teaching on women." They "do not believe that God has given us his word true and trustworthy, the unchanging standard for beliefs and practice. Instead we have a hodgepodge of information . . . , and God has left us on our own to figure out which parts to obey and believe. Human reason becomes the final authority, the judge of Scripture."[31]

But it must be emphasized that there are many Biblical feminists who firmly reject viewpoints such as those of Jewett and Mollenkott, and who still hold to a high view of Scripture, including its inerrancy. They believe that feminism is completely compatible with such a view of the Bible when it is properly interpreted. Thus they disagree with Pinnock's suggestion that it is necessary to reject parts of the Bible to be a feminist. They also are critical of Foh for implying that all "biblical feminists" have the same view of the Bible as Jewett et al. Concerning Foh's generalizations, Tucker and Liefeld say,

. . . Remarks like these may be true of some feminists, especially those whom traditionalists call "radical," but there are many biblical feminists today of whom the statements are not only untrue but also a very serious misrepresentation. Such language can have the unfortunate effect of leading readers to conclude that anyone who holds to views other than Foh's regarding women's ministries has abandoned inerrancy and become apostate....[32]

It is true, as Tucker and Liefeld say, that many if not most Biblical feminists today hold a high view of Scripture. Thus if their view of Biblical authority is not what separates them from their non-feminist colleagues, what does? The answer lies in their approach to Biblical interpretation.

B. Biblical Interpretation

Hermeneutics is by far the thorniest issue facing any type of Christian feminism. In the last two chapters we saw how it is handled by liberal feminists. Now we shall try to understand how conservatives also wrestle with the problem. As we proceed we shall see that it is the issue that ultimately separates Biblical feminists from conservative non-feminists. As Robert Johnston rightly says, "Behind the apparent differences in approach and opinion regarding the women's issue are opposing principles for interpreting Scripture – i.e., different hermeneutics. Here is the real issue facing evangelical theology as it seeks to answer the women's question."[33]

1. The Distinction Between Prescriptive and Descriptive

It is difficult to boil the hermeneutical problem down to just a single issue, but I suggest that it may be summed up in this, namely, the identification of which texts concerning women are *descriptive* of first-century conditions and which are *prescriptive* for Christians today. Everyone agrees that some elements of some Biblical texts are descriptive only, i.e., they are not normative or binding for faith and practice today. But there is strong disagreement as to how this applies to texts which speak about women and their roles in the family, the church, and society.

What makes this a crucial point is the fact that, as Pinnock observes, "certain passages in the New Testament, to say nothing of the Old, cannot be feministically interpreted."[34] That is to say, certain passages do not support feminism *if we allow them to be considered as prescriptive for today.* Thus the general approach or rule of thumb for Biblical feminists seems to be this: any passage that supports hierarchicalism and goes against egalitarianism must be *descriptive,* and is not binding as eternal truth. Non-feminists, on the other hand, have not been able to accept the feminists' rationale for this de-absolutizing of certain key hierarchical texts, and thus they take these texts as prescriptive of a hierarchical relationship between men and women.

This hermeneutical problem among Evangelicals is usually discussed in terms of *culture,* i.e., determining which texts are cultural and therefore limited in application, and which texts transcend cultural limitations and are therefore normative for all times and places. This is how Grant Osborne, for example, sets up the problem. He says that most evangelicals would accept the principle that "both cultural and normative commands are found in Scipture, and we must decide which category an individual command fits before we apply it to this age."[35] Diehl says that "the *cultural* factor in biblical interpretation" is "one of the giant questions of biblical hermeneutics today," the one that overarches all the others. "How do we distinguish between culturally directed applications of biblical principles and the transcultural biblical principles themselves?"[36]

But the fact is that the issue of culture is just one aspect of the more general distinction between the descriptive and the prescriptive. It is probably the most difficult of these aspects, but it is not the only one. Three such aspects may be distinguished overall, i.e., three possible ways that a text may be descriptive. First, it may simply be describing the author's own fallible feelings or preferences; second, it may be describing what is required by a certain localized situation; and third, it may be describing what is required in the interest of cultural accommodation.

Regarding the first of these, it is possible that a text may be describing the writer's views and feelings without intending to make them binding on anyone else. The psalmists occasionally express such feelings, e.g., "My soul is in despair within me" (Psalm 42:6); "I am in distress; . . . my life is spent with sorrow" (Psalm 31:9-10). Ecclesiastes sometimes expresses the vain thoughts of its author, e.g., "The fate of the sons of men and the fate of beasts is the same" (Eccl. 3:19). On the basis of 1 Corinthians 7:10-12, 25 some think that Paul at times expresses only his own uninspired and nonbinding opinions.[37] Even though this is probably not what Paul meant even for his teaching in 1 Corinthians 7, some use this possibility as a kind of escape valve to let the prescriptive air out of certain Pauline passages that seem to contradict egalitarianism.

Here is one place where the issues of Biblical authority and Biblical interpretation overlap. Although most conservatives would regard the views of Mollenkott and others discussed in the previous section to be a weakening of Biblical *authority*, she and the others basically see it as just a different way of *interpreting* the Bible. Mollenkott specifically makes it very clear that she believes Paul's statements about women's subordination to be his own uninspired and erroneous opinion. She paraphrases 1 Corinthians 7:25 as saying, "I do not know the mind of the Lord on this, but I'll give you my opinion." Then she says, "I believe that Paul is here explicitly saying that on this point his opinion may be wrong." Referring to 1 Corinthians 11:16, she says, "If anything could tell us that not every word of Paul was intended to be taken as an absolute word of God for all times and places, this is it." She then applies this to Paul's statements about female subordination and de-absolutizes them.[38] Then she says, "I can do this without questioning the authority of Scripture."[39]

Not many Biblical feminists are willing to take Mollenkott's specific approach to the troubling Pauline passages, but in general they do agree that the key is deciding what is descriptive and what is prescriptive. They especially agree on the propriety of the second way that a text may be descriptive, namely, that it is describing what is required by a local and therefore limited situation. This localized problem is not necessarily caused by or reflective of a cultural practice, though it may be. The important point is that the problem may be something very specific and temporary; therefore the instruction may be intended to be limited to that situation only.

This seems to be Reta Finger's point when she says, "Not everything in the canon is life-giving for us today. Many writers had only their own Christian community in mind when they wrote."[40] This is also what Tucker and Liefeld mean when they say that "an attempt should be made to determine from the context of a passage what circumstances evoked it." For example, in reference to 1 Timothy 2:12, "Under what circumstances did Paul refuse to allow women to teach at Ephesus?"[41] This last citation zeroes in on the crucial application of this interpretive principle, since the most common way that Biblical feminists try to avoid the hierarchical implications of 1 Timothy 2:12 is to say that from the perspective of the twentieth century it is merely *descriptive* of what was required only at Ephesus because of the peculiar circumstances that existed there in the first century.

The third possible way that a text may be descriptive does have to do specifically with instruction required by certain cultural expectations. Almost everyone acknowledges this as a legitimate approach to certain Biblical texts. The common examples are foot-washing and the holy kiss. In reference to women, many would agree that the instructions concerning headcovering in 1 Corinthians 11 were occasioned by the cultural practices in the Middle East in the first century and are not intended to be permanently binding. In this sense they are descriptive, not prescriptive.

With reference to feminism the crucial question is how far can this point about culture be pressed regarding women's roles? Is the command regarding silence culturally limited? Are the prohibitions against teaching and having authority over men also cultural? Does the same apply to the command for the wife to be submissive to her husband? Even if these instructions are not directly required by cultural considerations, could cultural limitations be indirectly responsible for the circumstances that called them forth?

2. Suggested Guidelines for Making the Distinction

Whichever of these three types of descriptive statements one has in mind, *the* issue – perhaps the most serious one of all regarding Biblical feminism – is *how to distinguish* the descriptive from the prescriptive. Though this problem is usually stated in terms of culture alone, it really applies to all three possibilities discussed above, especially to the last two. To paraphrase Diehl's question, How do we distinguish between circumstantially or culturally limited Biblical instructions, and instructions that are intended to be permanently and universally binding? This is indeed "one of the giant questions of biblical hermeneutics today,"[42] especially where Biblical feminism is concerned.

What follows are some of the more common and relevant suggestions for distinguishing between the cultural and the normative, the descriptive and the prescriptive. These are the ones usually preferred by feminists themselves, since they believe that their application to certain crucial passages assures a feminist conclusion.

Specific vs. general. A frequently suggested rule is that

cultural or descriptive texts tend to be more specific, while the normative or prescriptive ones are more general. In seeking to recognize cultural applications in the New Testament, says Osborne, we must remember that "each of the epistles was written to meet a specific problem in the first-century Church." Thus we can look for "a temporary application to a specific problem."[43] Willard Swartley gives this rule: "The interpreter should give priority to theological principles and basic moral imperatives rather than to specific counsel on particular topics when these two contradict."[44] Or as some would put it, when these two appear to contradict. Johnston correctly notes, "Feminists have tended to emphasize the broader affirmations of the gospel" while non-feminists have "centered on specific passages of advice."[45]

Incidental vs. systematic. Scanzoni and Hardesty say, "Passages which deal with an issue systematically are used to help understand incidental references elsewhere." This would be giving priority to "the *locus classicus,* the major biblical statement, on a given matter," rather than "isolated proof texts."[46] Osborne agrees.[47]

Historical vs. didactic. Another suggestion for distinguishing cultural from normative is also given by Osborne: "Didactic passages must be used to interpret historical events." This refers not only to the historical sections of the New Testament (such as Acts), but also "to historical problems reflected in the epistles." The latter is especially crucial for the question of feminism, he says.[48]

Practical vs. doctrinal. Still another suggestion emphasizes the distinction between practical and doctrinal statements. "Passages which are theological and doctrinal in content are used to interpret those where the writer is dealing with practical local cultural problems" say Scanzoni and Hardesty.[49] Mollenkott likewise contrasts passages "which are associated with individual church problems" or "addressed to very specific cases" with passages that are "in a fully theological context" and thus set forth "God's ideal for all times and places."[50]

3. Problems with These Guidelines

Biblical feminists believe that these are the kinds of distinctions that enable us to tell whether a text is descriptive, i.e., limited by cultural or circumstantial factors, or prescriptive and normative for all times. They also believe that when these rules are applied, all passages supporting female subordination are found to be descriptive only, while only those supporting egalitarianism are prescriptive. To get right to the heart of the matter, they generally believe that *only* Galatians 3:28 can be viewed as a general, systematic, didactic, doctrinal statement, while all the others are specific, incidental, historical, or practical and thus not normative for today. As Scanzoni and Hardesty say, "Of all the passages concerning women in the New Testament, only Galatians 3:28 is in a doctrinal setting; the remainder are all concerned with practical matters," an opinion that is applied especially to 1 Timothy 2:12.[51]

To be even more specific, Biblical feminism stands or falls on whether or not it is successful in its effort to label 1 Timothy 2:12 as circumstantial and descriptive, and Galatians 3:28 as theological and prescriptive. The next chapter will deal with these passages in a more specific way. Here we shall only suggest some of the problems involved in the hermeneutical methodology used to make this sort of distinction in the first place.

The problem of distinguishing the cultural or circumstantial from the permanently normative is notoriously difficult. The suggested distinctions listed above are often applied, especially in the context of feminism. But the fact is that they are much more ambivalent and inconclusive than they may seem at first, and are ringed about with fallacious thinking.

The fallacy that seems to intrude most often into this discussion is called "the simple conversion of a universal affirmative." Stated formally it declares, "All A is B, therefore all B is A." With reference to our hermeneutical problem it takes the form, "All descriptive (e.g., cultural) statements are specific (or historical or practical), therefore all specific (historical, practical) statements are descriptive." This fallacy begins to intrude when in the context of this discussion someone finds it necessary to remind us that all of the epistles were occasioned by specific problems, or were written to deal with specific problems on a practical level. The conclusion will then be that a statement within such an occasional letter, such as 1 Timothy 2:12, must have been dealing with a specific problem and therefore must be descriptive, not prescriptive.

For example, Osborne says, "There are some considerations that argue for a recognition of cultural application in the NT itself. Each of the epistles was written to meet a specific problem in the first-century Church."[52] But even if we grant that each epistle was occasioned by specific problems, this does not in itself mean that those problems were culturally or locally unique. The problem of division in Corinth, for example, called for some very practical instruction from Paul, specifically applied in 1 Corinthians. Very few would doubt that it is intended to be normative for the whole church, however.

Fee and Stuart begin their discussion of cultural relativity with a reference to *historical particularity,* which means first of all that "the Epistles are occasional documents of the first century, conditioned by the language and culture of the first century, which spoke to specific situations in the first-century church." This leads them to suggest "that the recognition of a degree of cultural relativity is a valid hermeneutical procedure and is an inevitable corollary of the occasional nature of the Epistles."[53] But this will lead to fallacious thinking if this "inevitable corollary" concept is applied to *every* specific statement and practical application in these epistles just because they are occasional. The occasional nature of the epistles makes the presence of descriptive, non-normative statements within them possible, but not necessary, and certainly not all-inclusive.

In other words, it is a fallacy to assume that a command occasioned by a specific historical situation is not binding outside that situation. A specific situation may well occasion the reciting of a general principle. It depends on what is occasioning the command. It may not be a cultural or locally unique problem at all, but something involving inherent right and wrong. To equate cultural or descriptive with occasional and historical begs the question (another fallacy) and prejudices the argument, in this case in favor of feminism.

The distinction between the historical on the one hand and the didactic or doctrinal on the other can easily lead to the same kind of fallacy discussed above, especially when applied to the epistles. The distinction is probably valid if the historical is limited to historical *events*. But the fallacy intrudes when one tries to apply this in the same way "to historical problems reflected in the epistles," as Osborne recommends.[54] The report of an historical event in the book of Acts is quite different from Paul's didactic and theological instruction with reference to a specific problem, no matter how "historical" the latter may be.

The fallacy of begging the question seems to intrude quite often in the effort to set forth rules that can help to distinguish the cultural from the normative. "What we need," says Osborne, "is a series of covering laws to distinguish the eternal core from the cultural application in all the commands of Scripture and *then* apply these to the sections on women in the Church." Then he offers this specific principle to help with this distinction: "Teaching that transcends the cultural biases of the author and his readers will be normative."[55] But is this not the very thing that is in question, the very thing we are trying to decide, namely, which teaching transcends culture?

The same problem is found in Osborne's next specific

principle, "If a command is wholly tied to a cultural situation that is not timeless in itself, it will probably be a temporary application rather than an eternal norm."[56] Again this is the very thing the principle is supposed to help us decide, namely, whether a particular command is "wholly tied to a cultural situation." Thus it begs the question.

In discussing the role of culture with reference to Biblical interpretation Tucker and Liefeld say, "There is a qualitative distinction between the doctrines of faith and justification and the social role of women." But again, as they themselves state just two sentences earlier, this is the very issue to be decided: "The issue here is whether the role of women is a purely theological matter, like faith and justification, or whether in the ancient world the way women appeared and what they did in public had a social significance that doctrines per se did not."[57] It may be true that the role of women is not a *purely* theological matter, but it certainly was understood by Paul to be an aspect of the doctrine of creation and the doctrine of man. Also, we must point out that neither are the doctrines of justification and faith *purely* theological, as if they had no social significance for the ancient world.

In the list of guidelines offered by Fee and Stuart for distinguishing the culturally relative from the culturally transcendent, they suggest the following: "One should be prepared to distinguish between what the New Testament itself sees as inherently moral and what is not. Those items that are inherently moral are therefore absolute and abide for every culture; those that are not inherently moral are therefore cultural expressions and may change from culture to culture."[58] But is this not the very thing that is at stake, especially in reference to the texts about women? Is "women not teaching men" inherently moral or just an accommodation to a local culture or a local controversy?

One problem lurking beneath the surface in all the suggested rules for distinguishing the cultural from the normative in Scripture is the unexamined assumption that *no* cultural features will *ever* correspond to eternal truth. But if a particular practice or idea can be shown to be a common aspect of Jewish culture or Greco-Roman culture, does that in itself mean that such items cannot be eternally valid? Is it not possible that individual cultures may occasionally come up with something that overlaps the divine will on the subject? Thus it is quite presumptuous for us to assume that apostolic instruction on a subject such as the role of women is not normative even if that instruction is occasioned by specific problems in specific cultures.

In the preceding paragraphs we have been looking at some of the methodological problems involved in the well-meant attempt to come up with rules or guidelines for distinguishing the descriptive from the prescriptive elements in Biblical instruction. We have seen that some serious problems do indeed exist. But let us assume for the moment that the suggested guidelines are valid, i.e., that the cultural or descriptive elements are found in specific, incidental, historical or practical instruction; and the permanently normative elements are found in general, systematic, didactic or doctrinal instruction. Assuming the validity of this distinction, is it really so clear-cut that 1 Timothy 2:12 obviously belongs in the former category and Galatians 3:28 just as obviously belongs in the latter? Is this assumption not open to serious challenge? I believe that it is.

First Timothy is certainly an occasional letter, and it addresses certain specific problems. But it is foolish to think that because of this every specific command in the letter is historical or cultural and thus limited in application to Ephesus or the first century alone. The bulk of the general context of 1 Timothy 2:12 (chapters 2 and 3) is certainly intended to be universally applied. The immediate context (2:8-15) does have elements that most would take to be only culturally required (e.g., 9b). But verse 12 does not fit that pattern. It is not very specific but is indeed quite general: "I do not allow a woman to teach or exercise authority over a man." None of the terms have qualifiers; it is as general as a general principle can be. Also it is very doctrinal or theological in nature, as indicated by its connection with the creation and the Fall in verses 13-14. It is not an incidental remark, but is a vital part of the instruction Paul sets forth in verses 9-15. The proper spiritual adornment for women making a claim to godliness, he says in verse 10, is good works. One of these godly good works is to accept the role described in verse 12.

Galatians, on the other hand, is just as much an occasional letter as is 1 Timothy. Osborne has stated that "each of the epistles was written to meet a specific problem in the first-century Church,"[59] and Galatians is no exception. Paul is addressing the problem of the Judaizers and their perversion of the gospel of grace. He speaks specifically to the Galatians ("You foolish Galatians" – 3:1) in their historical situation. Tucker and Liefeld say that "the biblical teachings about women are not disembodied truths suspended, as it were, above the real world in some timeless abstract proposition."[60] *But this is exactly how all feminists tend to view Galatians 3:28* – as a disembodied truth suspended above the real world in a timeless abstract proposition. They ignore the context, the progression of Paul's argument, and the place of 3:28 in that argument. The point that ties this section together is the nature and conditions of the inheritance of the blessing promised to Abraham (3:14ff). One of Paul's points is that this blessing is not inherited according to the rules of inheritance in the Mosaic Law, where under normal circumstances Gentiles, slaves, and women could not inherit property. But these restrictions do not apply to the Abrahamic inheritance, which is available to Jews and Gentiles, slaves and free men, males and females. To affirm this universal availability of the Abrahamic inheritance is the sole intention of Galatians 3:28. This is the universal principle. The reference to Jews and Gentiles, slaves and free men, males and females is the cultural element in the verse, being occasioned by Jewish law and culture.

(Both of these passages will be discussed in more detail in the next chapter.)

Johnston has some very perceptive thoughts and questions about the hermeneutical procedure we have been discussing.

> ... What is dangerous in such a procedure, though it admittedly works in many cases, is the implied epistemological claim that objective, impersonal statements are of a somehow higher order of trustworthiness than the more personal and relational aspects of Scripture. Do we need systematic argument in order to be fully confident of the meaning of God's revelation? Is it not true that Paul's "purely" theological insights are, on closer inspection, responses to the cultural crises and life situations of young churches facing concrete problems, and that his "purely" practical advice has within it a theological dimension? Paul neither "did theology" in an abstract, academic manner nor "proffered advice" devoid of theological undergirding. Both his "systematic theology" and his "practical theology" are more accurately part of his one and the same "church theology."[61]

These thoughts are meant to be applied specifically to the way feminists make distinctions between Biblical texts. They sum up the problems involved in trying to use the guidelines commonly suggested for this purpose.

C. The Basic Cause of Disagreement

We are discussing what separates Biblical feminists from their conservative, Bible-believing colleagues who are non-feminists. We have seen that different understandings of the nature of Biblical authority are sometimes the problem. We have also seen that disagreements about Biblical interpretation are more often the culprit. It goes without saying that there is no agreement on how to interpret the relevant texts. But now the question must be squarely addressed, *Why* is there no agreement? Johnston likewise asks *"why* evangelicals cannot come to agreement on biblical interpretation, given their common commitment to the Bible's full authority. . . . What is behind our continuing inability as evangelicals to agree?"[62] He cites a number of suggested answers that boil down to creaturely finitude; but the basic issue of all, he says, is *"the role of the reader/interpreter in the hermeneutical process."* In other words, "The horizon of the reader is as crucial as the horizon of the author, if an adequate biblical interpretation is to be forthcoming." He seems to agree with the view that the "horizon of the reader" precludes objectivity in interpretation; thus the disagreement among evangelicals.[63]

We must acknowledge that there are indeed two horizons to be taken into account in hermeneutics. Everyone needs to be reminded always of how his own life context and presuppositions influence his interpretations. But it is simply not true that this influence is so strong that no one can approach the Bible with enough objectivity to discern the intended meanings of the Biblical writers in most cases. The problem arises when a person is unaware of his own predispositions or is unwilling to acknowledge them. The solution is to be critically aware of them and to be honest enough to transcend them. The very fact that we can talk about this problem shows that such a transcendence is possible. Also, if it were not, how can we account for the remarkable agreement Christians do have on scores, even hundreds of hermeneutical issues? And if it is not possible, then conservatives may as well adopt the hermeneutical methodology of liberal feminism, and allow human experience to be the final arbiter in determining Biblical meaning.

Though objectivity is possible, the fact is that the

"second horizon," that of the interpreter, often is the stumbling block to a correct interpretation of Biblical texts. In my judgment this is the real source of the disagreement between Biblical feminists and non-feminists: the Biblical feminists have never been able to escape the seductive power of women's experience. They are still unconsciously snared by the trap to which the liberal feminists have consciously capitulated. Hermeneutics is adapted to experience. The passages that must be labeled cultural or descriptive are selected first on the basis of *women's experience*, and then rules are sought to justify this selection. It is a case of "hermeneutical ventriloquism," in Pinnock's marvelous phrase.[64]

The appeal to the "two horizons" concept is often merely a way of justifying a preconceived idea. It is a concept fraught with confusion, especially as used by evangelicals. If the true key to meaning is the author's intention (the first horizon), as evangelicals generally agree, then the context of the reader (the second horizon) does not really contribute to the actual meaning of the text. In the final analysis it is irrelevant with reference to *meaning*; it relates only to the *application* of a text.

Ignorance of the presence and power of this second horizon may indeed be a hindrance to our *discovery* of the intended meaning of a text, but it does not affect it or alter it in the least. It only affects our ability to discern what that meaning is. But I repeat, if it is not possible for us to overcome this obstacle, then we should abandon our commitment to the priority of the author's intention and be satisfied with subjectivity and relativity in all our hermeneutics. Non-feminists should openly acknowledge the validity of women's experience as an interpretive principle for feminists, and feminists should quit complaining when their non-feminist colleagues cannot agree with them.

With regard to the continuing disagreement about women's roles as well as the continuing desire to resolve it, perhaps one simple suggestion would be in order: when all other rules have been applied and it is still difficult to decide between meanings, weight should be given to what a text *says* rather than to what it does *not* say. When we do this, we may be brought to agree with Pinnock's observation: "Unless the Bible is edited along feminist lines, it cannot be made to support feminism." Also, "the adjective *biblical* clashes with the noun *feminism* in the term *biblical feminism*. If it is the Bible you want, feminism is in trouble; if it is feminism you desire, the Bible stands in the way."[65]

III. PEOPLE AND PUBLICATIONS

Some conservative non-feminists have made the accusation that today's Biblical feminism is nothing more than a product of the secular feminist movement which began in the 1960s, and thus is just a cultural phenomenon of our time. It may well be the case that it received its impetus from the women's liberation movement; that question cannot be answered here. But it must be recognized that some Christian women have been arguing for a Biblically-based feminism since the seventeenth century. In 1667 a Quaker woman, Margaret Fell, later the wife of George Fox, published a sixteen-page booklet called *Womens Speaking Justified, Proved and Allowed of by the Scriptures*, which Robert Clouse calls "the first book in English defending the participation of women in Christian ministry."[66] Women preachers proliferated in the nineteenth and early twentieth centuries, especially in certain Brethren, Wesleyan, holiness, and Pentecostal churches. A major impetus for this was the revivalism of the nineteenth century, especially the second great awakening and the work of Charles G. Finney. But after about 1920 the Evangelical movement in general moved away from female leadership, only to await a renaissance of Biblical feminism around 1970.[67]

Biblical feminists today have done a lot of research on this subject of backgrounds specifically to show that the modern movement is *not* a product of secular feminism but has its own Christian roots. Tucker and Liefeld sum up this concern in these words:

> . . . While the feminist movement has had a significant impact on the more liberal churches that have in recent decades granted full equality to women in ministry, it has not necessarily been the motivating force behind the Evangelical women who have sought ordination and leadership positions. Women in Evangelical churches have a long heritage of seeking (and sometimes obtaining) meaningful positions in the church for the purpose of serving God more effectively.[68]

They conclude that "historically, women have had far more involvement in the church's mission and other ministries than has generally been realized."[69]

In this book we are focusing on the modern wave of Biblical feminism as it has developed since about 1970. The purpose of this section is to provide the reader with the names and major publications of some of the main representatives of this movement, as well as some of those who have written from the other side of the issue. Entries are ordered chronologically rather than alphabetically. In a sense this is a modest bibliographical history of modern Biblical feminism.

A. Modern Biblical Feminists

Feminist writings from a Biblical perspective began to appear around 1970. The first such articles in my files, all from *Christianity Today*, are Rolf E. Aaseng, "Male and Female Created He Them" (11/20/70), pp. 5-6; Ruth A.

Schmidt, "Second-Class Citizenship in the Kingdom of God" (1/1/71), pp. 13-14; and Letha Scanzoni, "The Feminists and the Bible" (2/2/73), pp. 10-15. Others were appearing at this same time. The following is an occasionally annotated listing of more important writings, the dates being determined by the first major works by the authors.

1972

RICHARD and JOYCE BOLDREY, "Women in Paul's Life," *Trinity Studies* (1972), 22:1-36. Reprinted as *Chauvinist or Feminist? Paul's View of Women* (Grand Rapids: Baker, 1976). They defend totally egalitarian marriage and equality in ministry.

1974

LETHA SCANZONI, co-author of *All We're Meant To Be: A Biblical Approach to Women's Liberation* (Waco: Word Books, 1974); second edition, *All We're Meant To Be: Biblical Feminism for Today* (Nashville: Abingdon, 1986). Thoroughly egalitarian, this was the early "bible" of Biblical feminism. Called "ground-breaking" and "epoch-making," it was early pronounced to be "one of the finest books to come out on the controversial subject of women's liberation,"[70] at least from the feminist point of view. In the opinion of Tucker and Liefeld, "For more traditional Christians, it posed a threat to what they considered biblical values. It still remains one of the most controversial books on the subject, but it has had considerable influence."[71]

NANCY HARDESTY, co-author of *All We're Meant To Be*. She has also written *Great Women of the Christian Faith* (Grand Rapids: Baker, 1980), and *Women Called To Witness: Evangelical Feminism in the Nineteenth Century* (Nashville: Abingdon, 1984).

1975

PAUL K. JEWETT, *Man as Male and Female: A Study in Sexual Relationships from a Theological Point of View*

(Grand Rapids: Eerdmans, 1975). This was another early feminist "bible." It was controversial more for its questioning of Biblical infallibility than for its feminism as such. Jewett also wrote *The Ordination of Women: New Testament Perspectives* (Grand Rapids: Eerdmans, 1980).

DAUGHTERS OF SARAH is a bimonthly Christian feminist magazine that began publication in 1975 as the outgrowth of a six-woman study group centered at North Park Seminary (Evangelical Covenant Church). Active in its founding were Nancy Hardesty and Lucille Sider Dayton.[72] Its promotional literature declares it to be "rooted in feminism, rooted in faith." It also says, "We are Christians; we are also feminists. Some say we cannot be both, but for us Christianity and feminism are inseparable." The name "Daughters of Sarah" is meant to parallel "sons of Abraham." For a description of its origin and ministry by its editor see Reta Halteman Finger, "The Bible and Christian Feminism," *Daughters of Sarah* (May/June 1987), 13:5-12. It seems to favor the more radical side of Biblical feminism.

1976

DOROTHY R. PAPE, *In Search of God's Ideal Woman: A Personal Examination of the New Testament* (Downers Grove: InterVarsity, 1976). She defends the ministry of women on the basis of her experience as a missionary.

1977

VIRGINIA RAMEY MOLLENKOTT, *Women, Men, and the Bible* (Nashville: Abingdon Press, 1977; revised ed., New York: Crossroad, 1988). She is considered to be one of the strongest voices in the early stages of Biblical feminism. She had already been speaking and writing considerably before the publication of this book. One significant article was "A Challenge to Male Interpretation: Women and the Bible," *Sojourners* (February 1976), 5:20-25. This was reprinted in *Mission Trends No. 4: Liberation Theolo-*

gies in North America and Europe, ed. Gerald H. Anderson and Thomas F. Stransky (Grand Rapids: Eerdmans, 1979). Later she wrote *The Divine Feminine: The Biblical Imagery of God as Female* (New York: Crossroad, 1983), and *Godding: Human Responsibility and the Bible* (New York: Crossroad, 1987). Her work is suspect to many Evangelicals because of what appears to be a weak view of Biblical authority.

PATRICIA GUNDRY, *Woman Be Free! The Clear Message of Scripture* (Grand Rapids: Zondervan, 1977). She later wrote *Heirs Together: Mutual Submission in Marriage* (Grand Rapids: Zondervan, 1980); *The Complete Woman* (Garden City, NY: Doubleday, 1981); and *Neither Slave nor Free: Helping Women Answer the Call to Church Leadership* (San Francisco: Harper and Row, 1987).

DON WILLIAMS, *The Apostle Paul and Women in the Church* (Ventura, CA: Regal Books, 1977).

1978

SCOTT BARTCHY, "Power, Submission, and Sexual Identity Among the Early Christians," in *Essays on New Testament Christianity*, ed. C. Robert Wetzel (Cincinnati: Standard Publishing, 1978), pp. 50-80. Further articles on these subjects include "Jesus, Power, and Gender Roles," *TSF Bulletin* (January-February 1984), 7:2-4; "Human Sexuality and Our Identity," *Mission Journal* (November 1983), 17:10-14; and "Issues of Power and a Theology of the Family," in three parts, *Mission Journal* (July-August 1987), 21:3-15; (September 1987), 21:3-11; and (October 1987), 21:8-11.

1979

PETER DeJONG, co-author of *Husband and Wife: The Sexes in Scripture and Society* (Grand Rapids: Zondervan, 1979). An egalitarian view of sex roles in general.

DONALD R. WILSON, co-author of *Husband and Wife*.

ROBERTA HESTENES, co-editor with Lois Curley,

Women and the Ministries of Christ (Pasadena: Fuller Theological Seminary, 1979). She also edited *Women and Men in Ministry: Collected Readings* (Pasadena: Fuller Theological Seminary, 1980; and Philadelphia: Westminster Press, 1984). Her article, "Women in Leadership: Finding Ways To Serve the Church," appeared in *Christianity Today* (10/3/86), pp. 4-10, CTI supplement. See her book, *The Ministry of Women* (Waco: Word Books, 1989). Tim Stafford profiles her in "Roberta Hestenes: Taking Charge," *Christianity Today* (3/3/89), pp. 17-22.

1981
PHILIP B. PAYNE, "Libertarian Women in Ephesus: A Response to Douglas J. Moo's Article," *Trinity Journal*, n.s. (Fall 1981), 2:169-197. Moo's article is listed in the next section. Payne also participated in the 1984 Evangelical Colloquium on Women and the Bible, giving a lengthy response to a paper on the meaning of *kephale* in the New Testament. It is printed in *Women, Authority and the Bible*, ed. Alvera Mickelsen (Downers Grove: InterVarsity Press, 1986), pp. 118-132. It has been announced that in 1992 Zondervan will publish a book by Payne called *Man and Woman, One in Christ*.

1982
E. MARGARET HOWE, *Women and Church Leadership* (Grand Rapids: Zondervan, 1982). See also "The Positive Case for the Ordination of Women," in *Perspectives on Evangelical Theology: Papers from the Thirtieth Annual Meeting of the Evangelical Theological Society*, ed. Kenneth Kantzer and Stanley Gundry (Grand Rapids: Baker, 1979).

KARI TORJESEN MALCOLM, *Women at the Crossroads: A Path Beyond Feminism and Traditionalism* (Downers Grove: InterVarsity Press, 1982).

DONALD BLOESCH, *Is the Bible Sexist?* (Westchester, IL: Crossway Books, 1982); and *The Battle for the Trinity* (Ann Arbor: Servant Books, 1985). Actually Bloesch is not completely at home in either camp. He argues for women in all forms of ministry, yet defends male headship. See the review essay by Randy Maddox, "The Necessity of Recognizing Distinctions: Lessons from Evangelical Critiques of Christian Feminist Theology," *Christian Scholar's Review* (1988), 17:307-323.

1983

MARY J. EVANS, *Woman in the Bible: An Overview of All the Crucial Passages on Women's Roles* (Downers Grove: InterVarsity Press, 1983), a thesis written under Donald Guthrie at London Bible College.

WILLARD M. SWARTLEY, *Slavery, Sabbath, War and Women: Case Issues in Biblical Interpretation* (Scottdale, PA: Herald Press, 1983). The section on women (pp. 150-191) is favorable toward egalitarianism.

1984

RICHARD N. LONGENECKER, *New Testament Social Ethics for Today* (Grand Rapids: Eerdmans, 1984). This study is based on Galatians 3:28 and is favorable toward egalitarianism. He also participated in the 1984 Evangelical Colloquium on Women and the Bible. See "Authority, Hierarchy and Leadership Patterns in the Bible," in *Women, Authority and the Bible,* ed. Alvera Mickelsen (Downers Grove: InterVarsity Press, 1986), pp. 66-85.

1985

AIDA BESANÇON SPENCER, *Beyond the Curse: Women Called To Ministry* (Nashville: Thomas Nelson, 1985). By an ordained minister in the PCUSA and a professor of New Testament at Gordon-Conwell Seminary, this book focuses on the relevant Biblical passages. Good bibliography. See the extensive review by Craig L. Blomberg, "Not Beyond What Is Written," *Criswell Theological Review* (1988), 2:403-421.

ELAINE STORKEY, *What's Right with Feminism*

(London: SPCK, 1985; and Grand Rapids: Eerdmans, 1986).
GILBERT BILEZIKIAN, *Beyond Sex Roles: What the Bible Says About a Woman's Place in Church and Family* (Grand Rapids: Baker, 1985; second ed., 1990). Tucker and Liefeld note that "some consider the clearly stated conclusions to be at times overdrawn,"[73] which is itself an understatement. Contains an excellent bibliography compiled by Alan F. Johnson. See also "Hierarchist and Egalitarian Inculturations," *Journal of the Evangelical Theological Society* (December 1987), 30:421-426.

1986

ALVERA MICKELSEN, ed., *Women, Authority and the Bible* (Downers Grove: InterVarsity Press, 1986). This is the volume that includes all the papers from the 1984 Evangelical Colloquium on Women and the Bible. It is a valuable resource for understanding the feminist view. Very few scholars from the opposite persuasion were invited to participate. Mickelsen and her husband, Berkeley Mickelsen, authored the article, "What Does *Kephale* Mean in the New Testament?" (pp. 97-111). Alvera Mickelsen also participated in the symposium, *Women in Ministry: Four Views,* ed. Bonnidell and Robert G. Clouse (Downers Grove: InterVarsity Press, 1989). Her main chapter is "An Egalitarian View: There Is Neither Male Nor Female in Christ" (pp. 173-206).

BERKELEY MICKELSEN is co-author of the article, "What Does Kephale Mean in the New Testament?", in *Women, Authority and the Bible.* This husband-and-wife team also authored "Does Male Dominance Tarnish Our Translations?", *Christianity Today* (October 5, 1979), 23:23-29; and "The 'Head' of the Epistles," *Christianity Today* (February 20, 1981), 25:20-23. Berkeley Mickelsen wrote a two-part article, "Who Are the Women in I Timothy 2:1-15?", for *Priscilla Papers* (Winter and Spring, 1988), 1:1-3 & 2:4-6.

DAVID M. SCHOLER has one of the main articles in *Women, Authority and the Bible,* namely, "1 Timothy 2:9-15 and the Place of Women in the Church's Ministry" (pp. 193-224). See also "Feminist Hermeneutics and Evangelical Biblical Interpretation," *Journal of the Evangelical Theological Society* (December 1987), 30:407-420.

CATHERINE CLARK KROEGER also had a main article in *Women, Authority and the Bible*: "1 Timothy 2:12 – A Classicist's View" (pp. 225-244). She has emerged as a leading voice among the more conservative Biblical feminists. Her articles began to appear in *The Reformed Journal* in the late 1970s. These include "Ancient Heresies and a Strange Greek Verb" (March 1979), 29:12-15; and three co-authored with her husband, Richard Kroeger: "Pandemonium and Silence at Corinth" (June 1978), 28:6-11; "Sexual Identity at Corinth: Paul Faces a Crisis" (December 1978), 28:11-15; and "May Women Teach? Heresy in the Pastoral Epistles" (October 1980), 30:14-18. She also wrote "The Apostle Paul and the Greco-Roman Cults of Women," *Journal of the Evangelical Theological Society* (March 1987), 30:25-38; and "The Classical Concept of *Head* as 'Source,'" included as Appendix III in Gretchen Gaebelein Hull, *Equal To Serve* (Old Tappan, NJ: Revell, 1987), pp. 267-283. Her latest work, also co-authored with her husband Richard, is a book entitled *I Suffer Not a Woman: Rethinking 1 Timothy 2:11-15 in Light of Ancient Evidence* (Grand Rapids: Baker, 1991).

KLYNE R. SNODGRASS has an article in *Women, Authority and the Bible* that deserves mention: "Galatians 3:28 – Conundrum or Solution?" (pp. 161-181).

1987

RUTH TUCKER is co-author of the comprehensive historical study, *Daughters of the Church: Women and Ministry from New Testament Times to the Present* (Grand Rapids: Zondervan, 1987). Chapter 11, "The Contemporary Church Faces the Issues," contains helpful notes on many of the individuals and their works listed here. Extensive bibliographies are included.

WALTER LIEFELD also co-authored *Daughters of the Church*. He has one of the main articles in *Women, Authority and the Bible:* "Women, Submission and Ministry in 1 Corinthians" (pp. 134-154). He has published "Women and the Nature of Ministry," *Journal of the Evangelical Theological Society* (March 1987), 30:49-61; and he was a participant in the symposium *Women in Ministry* with "A Plural Ministry View: Your Sons and Your Daughters Shall Prophesy" (pp. 127-153).

GRETCHEN GAEBELEIN HULL, *Equal To Serve: Women and Men in the Church and Home* (Old Tappan, NJ: Revell, 1987). She also edited *Serving Together: A Biblical Study of Human Relationships* (New York: Macmillan, 1987), and currently edits the feminist journal *Priscilla Papers*.

ANNE ATKINS, *Split Image: Male and Female After God's Likeness* (Grand Rapids: Eerdmans, 1987).

MARY HAYTER, *The New Eve in Christ: The Use and Abuse of the Bible in the Debate About Women in the Church* (Grand Rapids: Eerdmans, 1987).

1988

FAITH McBURNEY MARTIN, *Call Me Blessed: The Emerging Christian Woman* (Grand Rapids: Eerdmans, 1987).

1989

ROBERT G. AND BONNIDELL CLOUSE are editors of the volume already noted a couple of times above, namely, *Women in Ministry: Four Views* (Downers Grove: InterVarsity Press, 1989). Other participants will be mentioned in the next section. Good bibliography.

1990

JUNE STEFFENSEN HAGEN, ed. *Gender Matters:*

Women's Studies for the Christian Community (Grand Rapids: Zondervan, 1990). Discusses women's studies in the areas of religion, history, literature, and the social sciences.

MARY STEWART VAN LEEUWEN, *Gender and Grace: Love, Work and Parenting in a Changing World* (Downers Grove: InterVarsity Press, 1990). See her review article, "The Recertification of Women," *The Reformed Journal* (August 1986), pp. 17-24. Here she reviews and comments on Bilezikian, Evans, Mickelsen, and Spencer.

B. Modern Biblical Non-feminists

The works of Biblical feminists as listed above were written in response to the view of women that had predominated in Evangelical Christendom at least since the early twentieth century. Many if not most within Evangelicalism took for granted that the Biblical view of gender roles is hierarchical; this came to be called the "traditional" view. There was little need for polemical works on the subject.

But with the rise of modern Biblical feminism, and the appearance of increasing numbers of works supporting egalitarianism, many conservatives holding to the traditional hierarchical view felt it necessary to counter-respond to the feminist challenge. The following is a listing of some of the main individuals and their works from this perspective.

1958

CHARLES C. RYRIE, even before the current controversy began, wrote *The Place of Women in the Church* (New York: Macmillan, 1958). It has been reprinted as *The Role of Women in the Church* (Chicago: Moody, 1970). He defends a strict view of female subordination. "Ryrie's opinion became widely influential," say Tucker and Liefeld.[74]

1976

ELISABETH ELLIOT, an early critic of Mollenkott and other feminists, wrote *Let Me Be a Woman* (Wheaton: Tyndale House, 1976). A year earlier she had written "Why I Oppose the Ordination of Women," *Christianity Today* (June 6, 1975), 19:12-16.

1977

GEORGE W. KNIGHT III, *The New Testament Teaching on the Role Relationship of Men and Women* (Grand Rapids: Baker, 1977); reprinted as *The Role Relationship of Men and Women: New Testament Teaching* (Chicago: Moody Press, 1985). See also "Male and Female Related He Them," *Christianity Today* (April 9, 1976), 21:13-17; and "The Ordination of Women: No," *Christianity Today* (February 20, 1981), 25:16-19. An important study is *"Authenteo* in Reference to Women in I Timothy 2:12," *New Testament Studies* (1984), 30:143-157. Leland Wilshire carries this study further in "The TLG Computer and Further Reference to *Authenteo* in I Timothy 2:12," *New Testament Studies* (1988), 34:120-134.

1978

JOHN MARK HICKS, co-author of *Woman's Role in the Church* (Shreveport, LA: Lambert Book House, 1978).

BRUCE L. MORTON, co-author of *Woman's Role in the Church.*

1979

SUSAN T. FOH, *Women and the Word of God: A Response to Biblical Feminism* (Phillipsburg, NJ: Presbyterian and Reformed, 1979). This was the first comprehensive and widely-read critique of Biblical feminism. Bibliography. Foh has the chapter on "A Male Leadership View: The Head of the Woman Is the Man," in *Women in Ministry* (pp. 69-105).

1980

STEPHEN B. CLARK, *Man and Woman in Christ: An Examination of the Roles of Men and Women in Light of Scripture and the Social Sciences* (Ann Arbor: Servant Books, 1980). A massive and thorough work (753 pp.) by an Evangelical Roman Catholic.

DOUGLAS J. MOO, "1 Timothy 2:11-15: Meaning and Significance," *Trinity Journal*, n.s. (Spring 1980), 1:62-83. This article drew a response from Philip Payne (see above), to which Moo responded with "The Interpretation of 1 Timothy 2:11-15: A Rejoinder," *Trinity Journal*, n.s. (Fall 1981), 2:198-222.

1981

JAMES B. HURLEY, *Man and Woman in Biblical Perspective* (Grand Rapids: Zondervan, 1981). Another comprehensive and widely-used examination of Biblical feminism, considered by many still to be the best available. Bibliography. See the critical review by David M. Scholer, "Hermeneutical Gerrymandering: Hurley on Women and Authority," *TSF Bulletin* (May-June 1983), pp. 11-13.

1985

JOHN W. ROBBINS, *Scripture Twisting in the Seminaries, Part I: Feminism* (Jefferson, MD: The Trinity Foundation, 1985). This apostle of Gordon H. Clark's epistemology is so radically conservative that he thinks Foh, Knight, and Hurley have departed from Scripture and capitulated to feminism.

RONALD and BEVERLY ALLEN, *Liberated Traditionalism: Men and Women in Balance* (Portland, OR: Multnomah Press, 1985). A moderate view by a husband-and-wife team.

MARY PRIDE, *The Way Home* (Westchester, IL: Crossway Books, 1985). An active secular feminist until her 1977 conversion, now she is extremely conservative.

WAYNE GRUDEM, "Does *kephale* ('head') Mean 'Source'

or 'Authority Over' in Greek Literature? A Survey of 2,336 Examples," printed as Appendix 1 in George W. Knight III, *The Role Relationship of Men and Women* (Chicago: Moody Press, 1985), pp. 49-80. This important essay also appeared in *Trinity Journal*, n.s. (Spring 1985), 6:38-59. For a response to this article see Richard S. Cervin, "Does *kephale* Mean 'Source' or 'Authority Over' in Greek Literature? A Rebuttal," *Trinity Journal*, n.s. (Spring 1989), 10:85-112. Also by Grudem is "Prophecy – Yes, But Teaching – No: Paul's Consistent Advocacy of Women's Participation Without Governing Authority," *Journal of the Evangelical Theological Society* (March 1987), 30:11-23. This was a speech given at the 38th annual meeting of the Evangelical Theological Society (1986), the theme of which was "Male and Female in Biblical and Theological Perspective." Grudem was one of only a very few who spoke from the traditional perspective at this meeting. He argues his point on women and prophecy in more detail in *The Gift of Prophecy in 1 Corinthians* (Lanham, MD: University Press of America, 1982). Finally, Grudem is a co-editor and a co-author of one of the latest and best and most complete (566 pp.) non-feminist works, *Recovering Biblical Manhood and Womanhood: A Response to Evangelical Feminism* (Wheaton: Crossway Books, 1991). In this volume Grudem continues the discussion of *kephale* with a long appendix, "The Meaning of *Kephale* ('Head'): A Response to Recent Studies (pp. 425-468).

1986

CLARK H. PINNOCK, "Biblical Authority and the Issues in Question," in *Women, Authority and the Bible* (pp. 51-58). We mention this article not only because of its intrinsic merit but also because it is one of the very few non-feminist pieces in this volume.

1987

SAMUELE BACCHIOCCHI, *Women in the Church: A*

Biblical Study on the Role of Women in the Church (Berrien Springs, MI: Biblical Perspectives, 1987). A comprehensive study for all Evangelicals by a Seventh Day Adventist; endorsed enthusiastically by Grudem and Hurley in forewords (pp. 7-10). Good bibliography. See the review by Spencer in *Trinity Journal*, n.s. (Spring 1987), 8:98-101.

ROBERT D. CULVER, "Does Recent Scientific Research Overturn the Claims of Radical Feminism and Support the Biblical Norms of Human Sexuality?", *Journal of the Evangelical Theological Society* (March 1987), 30:39-47. This is one of the other scarce non-feminist papers from the 1986 Evangelical Theological Society meeting. Culver also presented "A Traditional View: Let Your Women Keep Silence" in the symposium *Women in Ministry* (pp. 25-52).

1989

F. LaGARD SMITH, *Men of Strength for Women of God* (Eugene, OR: Harvest House, 1989). Not without scholarship, but frustratingly without scholarly appendages such as footnotes and bibliography.

1990

H. WAYNE HOUSE, *The Role of Women in Ministry Today* (Nashville: Thomas Nelson, 1990). Incorporates much of the material from his five-part series in *Bibliotheca Sacra*, beginning with the January-March 1988 issue and ending with the January-March 1989 issue. He and Richard A. Fowler had already begun discussing this subject in *The Christian Confronts His Culture* (Chicago: Moody Press, 1983), pp. 1-58.

MARY A. KASSIAN, *Women, Creation, and the Fall* (Westchester, IL: Crossway Books, 1990).

1991

JOHN PIPER is the co-editor (with Wayne Grudem) of the significant work mentioned earlier, *Recovering Biblical*

Manhood and Womanhood, in which he also has authored or co-authored several chapters. This comprehensive study is not only a critique of Biblical feminism but also a positive statement of the non-feminist approach to role relations with many practical applications. It was published under the auspices of the Council on Biblical Manhood and Womanhood, which will be described below. This volume contains a total of 26 chapters, many of them written by scholars mentioned earlier in this section (e.g., Elliot, Knight, Moo, and House).

IV. ORGANIZED FEMINISM

The final section in this chapter is a brief survey of Evangelical efforts to promote Biblical feminism through formal organizations, plus a recent effort to promote the non-feminist alternative in a similar way.

A. Evangelical Women's Caucus

The formative meeting of the Evangelicals for Social Action took place in Chicago in 1973. Of those invited, seventy-five came; three of these were women. This group produced the Chicago Declaration, which included this statement: "We acknowledge that we have encouaged men to prideful domination and women to irresponsible passivity. So we call both men and women to mutual submission and active discipleship." The 1974 ESA Conference included a larger nucleus of women "all committed to feminism."[75] They formed the Evangelical Women's Caucus, which one observer describes as "an international organization of feminist Christian women and men who believe that the Bible, when properly understood, supports the fundamental equality of the sexes."[76]

The EWC held its own first national convention in Washington, D.C., in 1975. Over 360 (including a "handful" of men) attended, representing over twenty-three denominations. The theme was "Women in Transition: A Biblical Approach to Feminism." Main speakers included Virginia Ramey Mollenkott, Letha Scanzoni, and Lucille Sider Dayton. Mollenkott, the keynote speaker, called for a de-absolutizing of Biblical culture and repudiated the "idolatry of the male." She received a standing ovation. Two resolutions were passed, one supporting the Equal Rights Amendment (with eighteen opposing votes), and one supporting eleven Episcopal women priests whose ordination at that time was considered invalid. Galatians 3:28 "became the byword of the caucus."[77]

Not everyone who attended this meeting was impressed. Elisabeth Elliot complained that the *Christianity Today* report on the meeting skirted "the essential doctrines on which the feminist movement is founded – that the difference between men and women is a relatively unimportant physical matter with no metaphysical implications whatever, and that the notion of 'equality' is a valid alternative to hierarchy which is merely a hangover from Old Testament patriarchal prejudice." Concerning the meeting Elliot said,

> . . . For me the conference was a horrifying experience. Scripture was manipulated, language was drained of its meaning (e.g. the Ephesians 5 passage was said to illustrate egalitarian marriage in which a husband's submission to his wife is meant to differ not at all from a wife's to her husband). One workshop dealt with the logical conclusion of feminist thinking: homosexuality, which, it was stated, is not forbidden in Scripture except when it was adulterous – i.e. a lifelong commitment between adults of the same sex is not forbidden. . . .[78]

Elliot's was a minority opinion, however.

Other conferences followed, settling into a biennial pattern. The 1978 conference in Pasadena was jointly sponsored by Fuller Theological Seminary, which has become a leading center for Biblical feminism. It drew over eight hundred women and about fifty men from thirty-two denominations.[79] The 1980 meeting in Saratoga Springs, New York, with over four hundred in attendance, had Mollenkott as the keynote speaker and featured a communion service led entirely by women.[80] Seven hundred attended the 1982 meeting in Seattle.[81]

The 1984 meeting in Wellesley, Massachusetts, marked the beginning of a schismatic controversy over resolutions as such and the content of one resolution in particular. Six resolutions were presented. The one on reaffirming the Equal Rights Amendment passed. The other five – on peacemaking, political involvement for justice, racism, pornography, and homosexual oppression – were all referred to committees for the next two years. Meanwhile a poll of the full membership showed 48% favored EWC conferences taking stands on political issues via resolutions as such, while 46% opposed it. In a split decision the executive council decided to discontinue the resolution process in the interests of unity.[82]

This set the stage for the volatile and fateful meeting in Fresno in 1986, which resulted in a split within the EWC over the issue of lesbianism. Some came to the meeting upset about the way homosexuals are treated in churches and society in general, and also upset about the executive council's decision not to allow resolutions. At an informal, open meeting of "lesbians and friends" on the night before the business meeting, it was decided to try to introduce three resolutions anyway. Nancy Hardesty, a supporter of this decision, volunteered to chair the open-microphone portion of the meeting. She declared that the executive council's decision was not binding, and began to take the resolutions from the floor. The first was against racism; Catherine Kroeger tried to amend it to forbid any further resolutions. The amendment failed and the resolution passed, as did the second one against domestic violence.

Then Anne Eggebroten offered the third amendment: "I move that, whereas homosexual people are children of God, and because of the biblical mandate of Jesus Christ that we are all created equal in God's sight, and in recognition of the presence of the lesbian minority in Evangelical Women's Caucus International, EWCI takes a firm stand in favor of civil-rights protection for homosexual persons." After debate the resolution passed, with eighty in favor, sixteen opposed, and twenty-five abstaining.[83]

A strong minority of the EWC membership vigorously opposed this action. Though the proponents of the resolution had carefully formulated it in terms of civil rights, its opponents objected to the phrase "in recognition of the presence of the lesbian minority." (The lesbian membership of the EWC numbered about twenty to thirty, or about 5% of the membership of 650 at that time.) Opponents such as Alvera Mickelsen and Catherine Kroeger said that this wording implies official recognition of lesbianism and acceptance of homosexuality as a Biblically-sanctioned lifestyle. Though some members, including the influential Mollenkott[84] and Hardesty, indeed were teaching that monogamous homosexuality is not condemned by the Bible, they insisted that this was not the point of the resolution.[85] Nevertheless the objectors decided to withdraw from the EWC and form a new organization, which is discussed in the next section.

Supporters of the homosexuality resolution did not expect serious fallout from this episode. Even after the fact Eggebroten said that the risk factor had been calculated at "maybe ten percent," and that the EWC would probably continue "without too much damage."[86] The result was not quite this positive. At the 1988 conference in Chicago it was reported that membership in the EWC had dropped by 50%. Nancy Hardesty said that the original goals had been met anyway, and she called upon the group to seek new objectives and be more responsive to current issues. The remaining members were still divided over expanding the group's political involvement. A central item on the program was a plenary forum on sexuality, which was followed by "emotionally charged discussion . . . in which lesbianism appeared to be confirmed." The executive committee recommended that the organization's name be changed to Ecumenical Women's Coalition, since many members do not participate in Evangelical churches anymore. "Nevertheless, we want to retain our biblical feminism," said coordinator Kaye Cook.[87]

B. Christians for Biblical Equality

Opposition to the 1986 Fresno resolution centered in Minnesota and was led by Catherine Kroeger. She and others decided not only to withdraw from the EWC but also to start a new organization for Biblical feminists that would be firmly committed to a high view of Biblical authority and firmly opposed to homosexuality as an acceptable norm. A meeting of 103 people was held March 6-7 in St. Paul to explore the possibility of affiliating with a London group called Men, Women, and God (begun in 1985), which itself is affiliated with John Stott's London Institute for Contemporary Christianity. Elaine Storkey, a feminist associated with Stott's Institute, was the main speaker. The outcome of this meeting was a vote to affiliate with Men, Women, and God. A steering committee was formed, with Kroeger as temporary convener.[88]

As a result of the work of this committee, a new organization called Men, Women and God: Christians for Biblical Equality was officially organized on August 28, 1987, as an affiliate of the London group. This formal tie with the latter was soon severed for practical reasons, and the name was soon shortened to Christians for Biblical Equality.

Its latest promotional brochure (late 1991) describes it as "an organization of Christians who believe that the Bible, properly interpreted, teaches the fundamental equality of men and women of all racial and ethnic groups, all economic classes, and all age groups, based on the teachings of Galatians 3:28." The mission statement in the same brochure includes the following:

> Our focus is to make known the biblical basis for freedom in Christ. We seek to advance the cause of Christ and the work of the gospel by encouraging full development of the gifts and talents of all Christians in the service of God. We seek to educate Christians regarding the Bible's message about the equality of men and women of all races, ages, and economic classes in church, home, and society. . . .

Its statement of faith includes these significant affirmations: "We believe the Bible is the inspired Word of God, is reliable, and is the final authority for faith and practice. . . . We believe in the family, celibate singleness, and faithful heterosexual marriage as the patterns God designed for us."

A September 1989 promotional letter calls Catherine Kroeger the "founding mother" of CBE. She is a member of the board of directors, which at present (late 1991) also includes James Beck, Gretchen Gaebelein Hull, Deborah Olsoe Lunde, Faith McBurney Martin, Alvera Johnson Mickelsen, Robert Morris, Carolyn J. Olson, and Nancy Graf Peters. The board of reference includes Carl Armerding, Millard Erickson, W. Ward Gasque, Vernon Grounds, Roberta Hestenes, Rufus Jones, Kari Torjesen Malcolm, Lois McKinney, Roger Nicole, Virginia Patterson, Lewis Smedes, and Timothy Weber.

The first meeting of CBE was held on October 23-24, 1987, in St. Paul. It was sponsored by the Minnesota chapter and is not counted as a national conference. About seventy-five attended. The first national biennial conference was held on July 20-23, 1989, again in St. Paul, with 235 registered participants and over 300 conferees. The keynote speaker was Roger Nicole. A notable feature was the Priscilla and Aquila award, to be given at each meeting to those who have "risked their necks" (like Priscilla and Aquila, Rom. 16:3-4) for the sake of the feminist gospel. "The award will recognize a person who, in spite of risk to position or reputation, has stood for full freedom of women to use their God-given gifts in the service of Christ." The recipient in 1989 was David Clowney, who in 1988 resigned as assistant professor of apologetics at Westminster Theological Seminary "because he could no longer subscribe to that seminary's position that prohibited women from being ordained."[89]

Unveiled at the 1989 meeting was a brochure-length statement of egalitarian faith called "Men, Women and Biblical Equality." It contains twelve "Biblical Truths" on creation, redemption, community and family, each beginning with "The Bible teaches" or "The Bible defines," and including numerous Biblical references as proof texts. It also contains a statement of "Application" with reference to community and family. Listed as authors are Gilbert Bilezikian, W. Ward Gasque, Stanley N. Gundry, Gretchen Gaebelein Hull, Catherine Clark Kroeger, Jo Anne Lyon, and Roger Nicole. In early 1990 this statement was printed as an advertisement in several Christian magazines,[90] eliciting hundreds of responses.

Membership grew rapidly after this, and in 1991 exceeded 1500 (in at least 14 local chapters). Around 4000 more are on the mailing list.

CBE publishes a feminist magazine called *Priscilla Papers*. A six-page first issue appeared in early 1987; more recent issues (1991) have ranged from 12 to 24 pages. Gretchen Gaebelein Hull serves as editor.

The second national conference of CBE was held on August 15-18, 1991, at Winter Park, Colorado. The theme was "Your Sons and Daughters Shall Prophesy"; and the main speakers included Kenneth Kantzer, Ruth Tucker, and Mary Evans. Nearly three-score workshops were also scheduled.

The 1993 conference has been announced for July 29-August 1, 1993, at Wheaton College. Plenary speakers will include Gilbert Bilezikian and Mary Stewart Van Leeuwen.

C. *Council on Biblical Manhood and Womanhood*

One other general Evangelical organization must be mentioned, namely, the Council on Biblical Manhood and Womanhood. This is not a feminist organization, but was formed to promote the traditional non-feminist position among Evangelicals. Its first brochure states that in January 1987 nine Evangelical leaders met in Dallas, Texas, to talk and pray about manhood and womanhood in Biblical perspective. They decided to form the CBMW. They and others met again in December 1987 in Danvers, Massachusetts, and drew up a statement of hierarchical faith called "The Danvers Statement."

The formation of CBMW was announced at the annual meeting of the Evangelical Theological Society in Wheaton in 1988, with a brochure containing the final form of "The Danvers Statement" being distributed. The contents of this brochure, which included the statement along with information about CBMW, was published as an advertisement in *Christianity Today* (January 13, 1989, pp. 40-41).

"The Danvers Statement" has three parts: rationale for the formation of CBMW, purposes of the organization, and affirmations of belief. The following are some of the contemporary developments that form part of the rationale:

1. The widespread uncertainty and confusion in our culture regarding the complementary differences between masculinity and feminity; . . .
3. the increasing promotion given to feminist egalitarianism with accompanying distortions . . . ;
7. the emergence of roles for men and women in church leadership that do not conform to Biblical teaching but backfire in the crippling of Biblically faithful witness;

8. the increasing prevalence and acceptance of hermeneutical oddities devised to reinterpret apparently plain meanings of Biblical texts;

9. the consequent threat to Biblical authority as the clarity of Scripture is jeopardized and the accessibility of its meaning to ordinary people is withdrawn into the restricted realm of technical ingenuity;

10. and behind all this the apparent accommodation of some within the church to the spirit of the age at the expense of winsome, radical Biblical authenticity which in the power of the Holy Spirit may reform rather than reflect our ailing culture.

Among the affirmations are these statements: "Distinctions in masculine and feminine roles are ordained by God as part of the created order." "Both Old and New Testaments also affirm the principle of male headship in the family and in the covenant community." "Some governing and teaching roles within the church are restricted to men."

On CBMW's latest letterhead (from a letter dated September 1991) the council members are listed as Gary Almy, Gleason Archer, Donald Balasa, James Borland, Waldemar Degner, Lane T. Dennis, Thomas R. Edgar, John M. Frame, W. Robert Godfrey, Wayne A. Grudem, H. Wayne House, R. Kent Hughes, James B. Hurley, Elliott Johnson, S. Lewis Johnson, Mary Kassian, Rhonda Kelley, George W. Knight, Beverly LaHaye, Betty Jo Lewis, Connie Marshner, Richard L. Mayhue, Douglas J. Moo, Raymond C. Ortlund, Jr., Dorothy Patterson, John Piper, Joyce Rogers, Ken Sarles, James A. Stahr, Larry Walker, and William Weinrich. Names of those on the board of reference are Hudson T. Armerding, Harold O. J. Brown, D. A. Carson, Edmund Clowney, Jerry Falwell, Carl F. H. Henry, Paul Karleen, D. James Kennedy, Gordon R. Lewis, Erwin Lutzer, Marty Minton, John MacArthur, Thomas McComiskey, Stephen F. Olford, J. I. Packer, Paige and Dorothy Patterson, Pat Robertson, Adrian and Joyce

Rogers, Bob Slosser, R. C. Sproul, Siegfried Schatzmann, Joseph M. Stowell III, John F. Walvoord, Luder Whitlock, and Peter Williamson.

One of the stated purposes of CBMW is "to promote the publication of scholarly and popular materials representing" its view. This purpose has recently been fulfilled in the publication of a major book, *Recovering Biblical Manhood and Womanhood* (Crossway Books, 1991), with twenty-seven essays by twenty-two authors.

D. Christian Churches/Churches of Christ Alliance for Biblical Equality

In 1990 an organization was launched within the centrist fellowship of the Restoration Movement. It is called Christian Churches/Churches of Christ Alliance for Biblical Equality (CCCCABE), and has a mailing address in Oak Forest, IL. This group has the same goals as Christians for Biblical Equality, but seeks to target just this one specific fellowship of Christians and churches.

An early informational letter states that it supports the ideas that "the Bible sanctions women to operate in any and all areas of church life as they are gifted and desirous to serve," and that "within marriage the husband and wife are equal partners." The letter also states that the "group's goals are to educate the uneducated or misinformed about biblical equality through our quarterly newsletter and to offer discipleship to any women . . . who may be feeling isolated or alienated within their churches."

The newsletter, called *Neither Male Nor Female*, began publication in July 1990. Its masthead states that it is "dedicated to the restoration of biblical equality of the sexes in life, ministry, and leadership within the Christian Churches/Churches of Christ." Its first issue states, "We will be examining biblical equality and freedom for women from our own hermeneutic, restoration view of the Bible and the New Testament church and home. We will be dis-

287

cussing our style of church leadership and where women fit in. We will be looking at our traditions and comparing these to the living, breathing Word of God."

The names of the initial board of directors for CCC-CABE are Jacqueline S. Allen, Sky Allen, Cynthia A. Cornwell, Joseph M. Webb, and Jill L. Stanek (who also is listed as the editor of the newsletter).

V. CONCLUSION

In this chapter we have attempted to describe the movement called Biblical feminism, first by relating it to other forms of feminism and then by relating it to the non-feminists within Evangelicalism, of which it is a part. Then we have attempted a brief phenomenological survey of people, publications, and organizations on both sides of the issue.

Though we have engaged in some evaluation in the section dealing with the hermeneutical differences between Biblical feminists and non-feminists, this chapter has been mostly descriptive. The next chapter will be devoted to evaluation, as we turn our attention to the heart of Biblical feminism's stated Biblical basis for egalitarianism.

Endnotes

1. An example of this is seen in an article by Reta Halteman Finger, the editor of *Daughters of Sarah*, a magazine that falls within the broad scope of Biblical feminism. The title of the article is "The Bible or Women's Experience – Which Is Authoritative?" Her answer is that *both* are. She says, "This question has been the watershed dividing 'biblical' feminists from other feminists. No more. Feminist philosophy has taught us that sharp dichotomies tend to confuse rather than clarify issues. In reality, no one can choose either of these options in pure form" *(Daughters of Sarah,* [May/June 1987], 13:6).

2. Scott E. McClelland, "The New Reality in Christ: Perspectives from Biblical Studies," in *Gender Matters: Women's Studies for the Christian Community,* ed. June Steffensen Hagen (Grand

Rapids: Zondervan, 1990), p. 53.

3. Gordon D. Fee and Douglas Stuart, *How To Read the Bible for All Its Worth: A Guide to Understanding the Bible* (Grand Rapids: Zondervan, 1982), p. 26.

4. Ibid., p. 27.

5. Ruth A. Tucker and Walter L. Liefeld, *Daughters of the Church: Women and Ministry from New Testament Times to the Present* (Grand Rapids: Zondervan, 1987), p. 446.

6. Finger, "The Bible or Women's Experience," p. 7.

7. Terry C. Muck, "Can We Talk?", *Christianity Today* (July 16, 1990), 34:12.

8. Jack and Judith Balswick, "Adam and Eve in America," *Christianity Today* (July 16, 1990), 34:16-17. The responses of females differed very little from that of males in this poll.

9. Grant R. Osborne, "Hermeneutics and Women in the Church," *Journal of the Evangelical Theological Society* (December 1977), 20:351-352.

10. John Stott, *Involvement, Volume II: Social and Sexual Relationships in the Modern World* (Old Tappan, NJ: Revell, 1984), pp. 153-155.

11. See Bloesch's book, *Is the Bible Sexist?* (Westchester, IL: Crossway, 1982). See the summary of Bloesch's view in David W. Diehl, "Theology and Feminism," in *Gender Matters*, p. 38: "He suggests the alternative of 'covenantalism' in which man and woman freely submit to the service of God as Lord, and do not lord it over each other. Nevertheless, there still remains a kind of subordination of wife to husband and a precedence of male leadership in the church, even though both men and women can be ministers."

12. Diehl, "Theology and Feminism," pp. 37-38.

13. Paul K. Jewett, *Man as Male and Female: A Study in Sexual Relationships from a Theological Point of View* (Grand Rapids: Eerdmans, 1975), pp. 112-113.

14. Ibid., p. 119.

15. Ibid., p. 136. See pp. 134-135.

16. Though she does not identify the meeting, this description fits the first national conference of the Evangelical Women's Caucus on Thanksgiving weekend, 1975, at Washington, D.C.

17. Virginia Ramey Mollenkott, "A Conversation with Virginia Mollenkott," *The Other Side* (May-June 1976), pp. 22, 24-28.

18. Mollenkott, *Women, Men, and the Bible*, revised ed. (New York: Crossroad, 1988), pp. 78-79.

19. Ibid., p. 83.

20. Ibid.; "Conversation," p. 28. See also her letter to the editor,

Christianity Today (June 4, 1976), 20:24-25. In another place she says, "It is of course possible to harmonize Genesis 1 and 2 by seeing the second chapter as a symbolic and poetic expansion of the first, while viewing the first account as authoritative concerning the simultaneous creation of Adam and Eve – but if we do that, then Paul's argument falls flat" ("A Challenge to Male Interpretation: Women and the Bible," *Sojourners* [February 1976], 5:22). The weakest part of her argument, of course, is the unsupported assumption that Genesis 1 affirms a simultaneous creation of male and female.

21. Harold Lindsell, "Egalitarianism and Scriptural Infallibility," *Christianity Today* (March 26, 1976), 20:45.

22. Mollenkott, letter to the editor, *Christianity Today* (June 4, 1976), 20:24-25.

23. Mollenkott, "Conversation," p. 28.

24. Mollenkott, *Women*, pp. 86-87.

25. Susan T. Foh, *Women and the Word of God: A Response to Biblical Feminism* (Phillipsburg, NJ: Presbyterian and Reformed, 1980), p. 6. See Letha Scanzoni and Nancy Hardesty, *All We're Meant To Be: A Biblical Approach to Women's Liberation* (Waco: Word Books, 1974).

26. Scanzoni and Hardesty, *All We're Meant To Be: Biblical Feminism for Today* (Nashville: Abingdon Press, 1986), pp. 18, 21.

27. Ibid., pp. 26-27.

28. Ibid., p. 37.

29. Ibid., pp. 40-41.

30. Clark H. Pinnock, "Biblical Authority and the Issues in Question," in *Women, Authority and the Bible,* ed. Alvera Mickelsen (Downers Grove: InterVarsity Press, 1986), p. 55.

31. Foh, *Women*, pp. 6-7.

32. Tucker and Liefeld, *Daughters*, p. 449.

33. Robert K. Johnston, *Evangelicals at an Impasse* (Atlanta: John Knox Press, 1979), p. 50.

34. Pinnock, "Biblical Authority," p. 56.

35. Osborne, "Hermeneutics," p. 337.

36. Diehl, "Theology and Feminism," p. 44.

37. This is not the intended meaning of Paul's statements in these passages. Here the contrast is between commands of Jesus already given during his earthly ministry, and inspired instructions being given now for the first time through Paul. The latter are just as binding as the former (I Cor. 7:40; 14:37).

38. Mollenkott, "Conversation," pp. 27-28.

39. Ibid., p. 30.

40. Finger, "The Bible or Women's Experience," p. 7.

41. Tucker and Liefeld, *Daughters*, p. 444.

42. Diehl, "Theology and Feminism," p. 44.

43. Osborne, "Hermeneutics," pp. 338-339.

44. Willard M. Swartley, *Slavery, Sabbath, War, and Women: Case Issues in Biblical Interpretation* (Scottdale, PA: Herald Press, 1983), p. 230.

45. Johnston, *Evangelicals*, p. 49.

46. Scanzoni and Hardesty, *All We're Meant To Be* (1974), p. 18.

47. Osborne, "Hermeneutics," p. 338.

48. Ibid.

49. Scanzoni and Hardesty, *All We're Meant To Be* (1974), p. 18.

50. Mollenkott, "Conversation," p. 73.

51. Scanzoni and Hardesty, *All We're Meant To Be* (1986), p. 89.

52. Osborne, "Hermeneutics," p. 338.

53. Fee and Stuart, *How To Read the Bible*, pp. 65-66.

54. Osborne, "Hermeneutics," p. 338.

55. Ibid., pp. 338-339.

56. Ibid., pp. 339-340.

57. Tucker and Liefeld, *Daughters*, p. 444.

58. Fee and Stuart, *How To Read the Bible*, p. 66.

59. Osborne, "Hermeneutics," p. 338.

60. Tucker and Liefeld, *Daughters*, p. 444.

61. Johnston, *Evangelicals*, p. 65.

62. Robert K. Johnston, "Biblical Authority and Interpretation: The Test Case of Women's Role in the Church and Home Updated," in *Women, Authority and the Bible*, p. 34.

63. Ibid., pp. 35-36.

64. Pinnock, "Biblical Authority," p. 57.

65. Ibid., pp. 52, 58.

66. Robert G. Clouse, "Introduction," in *Women in Ministry: Four Views*, ed. Bonnidell Clouse and Robert G. Clouse (Downers Grove: InterVarsity Press, 1989), p. 12. See also Tucker and Liefeld, *Daughters*, pp. 229-232.

67. Historical details of this pre-modern Biblical feminism can be found especially in the book by Tucker and Liefeld, *Daughters of the Church*. Nancy Hardesty examines one era of women leadership in *Women Called To Witness: Evangelical Feminism in the Nineteenth Century* (Nashville: Abingdon Press, 1984). Robert Clouse's introduction to *Women in Ministry* is a good brief survey of the data. See also Donald W. Dayton and Lucille Sider Dayton, "Women as Preachers: Evangelical Precedents," *Christianity Today* (May 23, 1975), 19:4-7.

68. Tucker and Liefeld, *Daughters*, p. 17.

69. Ibid., p. 435.

70. Cheryl Forbes, "Books in Review: God and Women," *Christianity Today* (December 6, 1974), 19:36.

71. Tucker and Liefeld, *Daughters,* p. 411.

72. Hardesty, *Women,* p. 160.

73. Tucker and Liefeld, *Daughters,* p. 429.

74. Ibid., p. 405.

75. Hardesty, *Women,* p. 160.

76. Patrice Wynne, *The Womanspirit Sourcebook* (San Francisco: Harper and Row, 1988), p. 177.

77. Most of this data is from a news report by Carol Prester McFadden, "Christian Feminists: 'We're on Our Way, Lord,'" *Christianity Today* (December 19, 1975), 20:36-37.

78. Elisabeth Elliot, letter to the editor, *Christianity Today* (February 13, 1976), 20:28.

79. See the news report by Phyllis E. Alsdurf, "Evangelical Feminists: Ministry Is the Issue," *Christianity Today* (July 21, 1978), 22:46-47.

80. See the news report by Suzy Kane, "Feminists of a Feather Affirm Each Other," *Christianity Today* (August 8, 1980), 24:40-41.

81. See the news report by Julia Duin, "Evangelical Women Criticize the Church's 'Medieval Theology,'" *Christianity Today* (September 3, 1982), 26:72, 75.

82. Anne Eggebroten, "Handling Power: Unchristian, Unfeminine, Unkind?", *The Other Side* (December 1986), p. 21.

83. Ibid., pp. 21-22.

84. Mollenkott and Letha Scanzoni had already argued this position in *Is the Homosexual My Neighbor?* (San Francisco: Harper and Row, 1978).

85. See the news report by Beth Spring, "Gay Rights Resolution Divides Membership of Evangelical Women's Caucus," *Christianity Today* (October 3, 1986), 30:40-43. See also William O'Brien, "Handling Conflict: The Fallout from Fresno," *The Other Side* (December 1986), pp. 25, 41.

86. Eggebroten, "Handling Power," p. 23.

87. See the news report by David Neff, "Christian Feminists Regroup to Debate Future," *Christianity Today* (September 2, 1988), 32:43, 45.

88. See the news report by David Neff, "Women Explore Formation of Alternative Feminist Group," *Christianity Today* (April 17, 1987), 31:45-46. For these and other data see also "Happy Birthday: Now We Are Four! A Brief History of Christians for Biblical Equality," *Priscilla Papers* (Summer 1991), 5:14-15.

89. See "Christians for Biblical Equality To Offer Priscilla and Aquila Award," *Priscilla Papers* (Winter 1989), 3:16; and "Priscilla and Aquila Award," *Priscilla Papers* (Fall 1989), 3:11.

90. *Priscilla Papers* (Summer 1990, p. 9) says it appeared in *Leadership, Today's Christian Woman, The Reformed Journal, World Christian,* and *Christianity Today* (April 9, 1990, 34:36-37).

8 BIBLICAL FEMINISM: EVALUATION

Of the four types of feminism, the only one that is a serious option to someone who holds to a high view of Scripture is the fourth one, Biblical feminism. Though the first three types must be taken seriously because of their impact on modern society and the influential role they play in contemporary culture, the Evangelical faith will reject them from the outset because they do not accept the Bible's absolute and final authority in all things, including gender roles. Biblical feminism, though, is a quite different matter. It does operate with an expressed acceptance of the full authority of the Bible. It declares that its egalitarian faith and practice represent the Bible's true teaching; thus these are considered to be the revealed will of God.

Applying all the tools of Biblical scholarship with great zeal, they immerse themselves in the task of exegesis in order to demonstrate the Biblical basis for feminism. Their efforts cannot be lightly dismissed by their fellow Bible-believers.

This is the perspective from which I personally have approached the claims of Biblical feminism. I accept the final authority of the Bible, as do these feminists. We stand upon the same solid ground, the inspired Scripture whose nature is described in John 10:35 and 2 Timothy 3:16. This is our common starting point.

Also, I believe I understand the basic egalitarian ethic which these feminists believe is taught in the Bible: 1) In the home, husband and wife have a mutual partnership, with neither being the leader or the one in authority. 2) In the church, gender has nothing to do with who fills any particular role; there should be NO role distinctions between men and women. Whatever qualified men can do, qualified women can do also. This includes preaching, teaching men, and holding the office of elder in the local church.

Also, I have tried to understand not just the general position of the feminists but also the intricacies of the exegesis with which they attempt to support their view. Admittedly this is not an easy task, since the feminist literature is replete with what the Danvers statement aptly calls "hermeneutical oddities" and "technical ingenuity." So many new exegetical trails are being blazed that it is difficult to keep up with them all.

Also, I have tried to keep uppermost in my mind the seriousness and the sincerity with which Biblical feminists are doing their work. I try to make it my goal to be very sensitive to the sense of hurt and the sense of need and the sense of justice from which it springs. I will take their efforts seriously, and will do my best not to enter into any critique thereof lightly or superficially, nor with any malice or hostility.

This is simply to say that I have tried to evaluate the methods, arguments, and conclusions of Biblical feminism as objectively and as fairly as possible. I know that my "second horizon" is supposed to preclude this, and that as a part of the patriarchal establishment I am supposed to have vested interests that unconsciously influence my views and make me inescapably biased. But I will state unequivocally that I have no desire to defend a traditional view of this or any other subject just because it is the traditional view. I have never hesitated to abandon traditional ideas and practices if they cannot be justified by Scripture. My overarching concern in this or any other matter is the defense of truth as I understand it, the defense of sound doctrine as taught by the Word of God.

Some may judge these remarks to be overly personal, but I believe they are necessary. I want them to preface and to temper what I am about to say, so that none may think that I speak harshly or rashly or without sensitivity. My point is this: after studying the issues raised by Biblical feminism and evaluating them in the light of Scripture, my basic conclusion is that the non-feminist, hierarchical view is the true one, and that the feminist view is totally without foundation in the Word of God.

More specifically, my thesis is this: the feminist hermeneutic, i.e., the feminist attempt to find egalitarianism somewhere in the Bible, is a case of theology *ex nihilo*. This is an allusion, of course, to the Biblical doctrine of the creation of the world. In Scripture God is pictured as creating the universe *ex nihilo*, or "out of nothing." As such it was a pure act of His will. He wanted the universe, so He willed it into existence out of nothing. As Revelation 4:11 says, "Thou didst create all things, and because of Thy will they existed, and were created."

In an analogous way, it is my contention that the egalitarian view has been brought into existence *ex nihilo*, literally out of nothing. The alleged Biblical basis for it is non-existent. It is literally "created out of thin air." I am not saying that feminists are aware of this and are doing it deliberately or with an intent to deceive. On the contrary, they seem to be honestly convinced that their view is really taught in the Bible. My point is that their finding this view in the Bible is a sheer act of will: they WANT to find it so badly that they unconsciously call into existence that which does not exist (cf. Romans 4:17).

This is true of the small bits and pieces of feminist ore mined so laboriously from the Bible, of which I will give just two examples. First, to reinforce the feminist view that God's original creation plan for mankind included no role distinctions based on the priority of the creation of the man, it is asserted that Genesis 1:27 teaches that male and female were created simultaneously. This was the view promoted by Elizabeth Cady Stanton in her *Woman's Bible*, where she declared that the texts in Genesis 1 "plainly show the simultaneous creation of man and woman," and that "all those theories based on the assumption that man was prior in the creation, have no foundation in Scripture."[1] Scanzoni and Hardesty repeated this idea in their early work on Biblical feminism: "In Genesis 1 male and female are said to be created simultaneously by God."[2] Likewise Mollenkott says that we find "the statement in Genesis 1 that male and female were created simultaneously."[3] This assumption is crucial to her attack on the validity of Paul's arguments in 1 Corinthians 11 and 1 Timothy 2.

What does Genesis 1:27 say? "And God created man in His own image, in the image of God He created him; male and female He created them." This is the statement that is supposed to teach "simultaneous creation." Stanton says it *plainly shows* simultaneous creation; Scanzoni and Hardesty assert that in this verse male and female *are said to be* created simultaneously; Mollenkott labels it *the statement* that they were created simultaneously. But as anyone can plainly see, this text is absolutely silent about the order of the creation of male and female. It is a summary statement that asserts the bare fact that God created both the male and the female. Neither simultaneity nor priority is asserted or even implied in the verse. The idea

of simultaneous creation is literally drawn out of nothing –
created *ex nihilo* – as far as the text is concerned.[4]

The second relatively minor example of the *ex nihilo*
character of feminist theology has to do with Jesus. In
order to avoid unwanted implications of the fact that God
became incarnate in a MALE, some feminists assert that
the New Testament writers always refer to Jesus with the
generic term "human being" (*anthropos*) rather than either
of the specific terms for "male" (*aner* and *arsen*).

For example, Mollenkott says "there can be no doubt of
the significance of another fact: when New Testament writers refer to the incarnation of Jesus, they do not speak of
his becoming *aner*, 'male,' but rather of his being *anthropos*, 'human.' "[5] Spencer asserts, "The New Testament writers are always careful to describe Jesus with the generic
Greek term 'human' or *anthropos* rather than the term
'male' or *aner*."[6]

Although these statements are technically correct in the
sense that the New Testament *writers* do not refer to Jesus
as a "male" (*aner*), these feminists conveniently ignore two
relevant facts that make their argument completely base-
less. First, three *inspired speakers* quoted by New Testament writers DO in fact refer to Jesus as a "male," using
the specific word *aner*. In John 1:30 John the Baptist says,
"This is He on behalf of whom I said, 'After me comes a
Man [*aner*] who has a higher rank than I, for He existed
before me.' " In Acts 2:22-23 Peter says, "Men of Israel,
listen to these words: Jesus the Nazarene, a man [form of
aner] attested to you by God with miracles and wonders
and signs which God performed through Him in your
midst, just as you yourselves know – this Man, delivered
up by the predetermined plan and foreknowledge of God,
you nailed to a cross by the hands of godless men and put
Him to death." In Acts 17:31 Paul says, "He has fixed a day
in which He will judge the world in righteousness through
a Man [form of *aner*] whom He has appointed, having fur-
nished proof to all men by raising Him from the dead."

These statements describing Jesus as a male come from three of the most exalted apostles and prophets in the New Testament. Also, the content of their statements is not at all incidental or peripheral but is as profoundly theological as possible: eternal decree, preexistence, miracles, crucifixion, resurrection, final judgment. Jesus as male is the object of the eternal decree. Jesus as male is described as the preexistent one. Jesus as male was attested by divine miracles. Jesus as male was crucified. Jesus as male was raised from the dead. Jesus as male will judge the world.

The second relevant fact ignored by these feminists is that one New Testament *writer* DOES refer to Jesus with a Greek word for "male." In Revelation 12:5, in what can only be a symbolic reference to the birth of Jesus, the Apostle John says that the "woman clothed with the sun" (12:1) "gave birth to a son, a male child, who is to rule all the nations with a rod of iron." The word for "male" here is not *aner* but *arsen*, but the meaning is the same. The significance of this reference cannot be dismissed on the grounds that it appears in mere "apocalyptic symbolism." In fact, its significance is intensified by the symbolic context. It is also intensified by the double reference to Jesus' maleness. To say "she gave birth to a son" would have been quite sufficient to make the point of male gender, but the term *arsen* is added to this to emphasize it even further.

Thus these feminists' implication that Jesus is always called just a "human being" or *anthropos* and is never called "a male" simply contradicts the plain facts. It is created *ex nihilo*.[7]

These claims concerning the simultaneity of creation and the absence of any reference to Jesus as a male are just preliminary examples of my thesis that the alleged Biblical basis for egalitarianism is non-existent. This thesis applies not just to such smaller reinforcing elements of the feminist argument; it applies also to the main pillars of the argument. Specifically, my contention is that the five main supports of the feminist view, supposedly found in

300

Scripture, are totally without foundation in the Bible or anywhere else. They are created ex nihilo. These five main supports are as follows:

1) "The concept of mutual submission is taught in Ephesians 5:21 and negates the idea of a subordinate role for the wife in relation to her husband." (I am convinced that the idea of mutual submission is a myth.)

2) "The word *head* as it is used to describe the husband's or man's role means 'origin' or 'source'; it never means 'leader' or 'one in authority.' " (The fact is that there is not one shred of solid evidence that the Greek word for "head" ever means "origin" or "source." At the same time there is sufficient evidence for its being used to mean "a leader" or "one in authority.")

3) "Paul's prohibition of women as teachers of men in 1 Timothy 2:12 was intended to be limited to the church at Ephesus and intended even there to be temporary." (The alleged facts used to support this crucial feminist argument are literally manufactured out of thin air.)

4) "The kind of authority that Paul does not allow women to exercise in 1 Timothy 2:12 is not ordinary authority but a sinful, domineering authority." (Again, the evidence for this key idea is non-existent.)

5) "Paul's statement in Galatians 3:28 was intended to erase ALL role distinctions between men and women for all time." (This basic feminist contention ignores the context of Paul's statement as the determiner of its meaning.)

The rest of this chapter is a further explanation of these five points.

I. THE FEMINIST MYTH OF "MUTUAL SUBMISSION"

In six New Testament passages God's word clearly

teaches (at least) that wives are to be in submission to their husbands, with some of these passages suggesting that this applies to women in general in relation to men in general. These are the passages: "Let the women . . . subject themselves, just as the Law also says" (1 Cor. 14:34). "Be subject to one another in the fear of Christ. Wives, be subject to your own husbands, as to the Lord. . . . But as the church is subject to Christ, so also the wives ought to be to their husbands in everything" (Eph. 5:21-24). "Wives, be subject to your husbands, as is fitting in the Lord" (Col. 3:18). "Let a woman quietly receive instruction with entire submissiveness" (1 Tim. 2:11). The young women are to be "subject to their own husbands, that the word of God may not be dishonored" (Titus 2:5). "In the same way, you wives, be submissive to your own husbands" as the holy women of old were "submissive to their own husbands" (1 Peter 3:1, 5).

The Greek word used in each case is a form of *hupotasso*. In the Greek world this word meant "to place under, to subordinate" (active voice); "to be subject" (passive voice); or "to subject oneself, to submit voluntarily, to lose or surrender one's own rights or will" (middle voice). "Originally it is a hierarchical term which stresses the relation to superiors." In the New Testament its meanings range "from subjection to authority on the one side to considerate submission to others on the other." The submission is usually voluntary.[8] (We should be careful not to equate "voluntary" with "optional," though, when such submission is commanded by God.) As Donald Nash sums it up, the word "means to place under, in authoritative rank, as a private under a centurion, a centurion under a captain, or a captain under a general."[9] This general meaning of the word is unambiguous and is not disputed.

It should be noted that neither this term nor any like it is ever used to describe the husband's role in relation to his wife, or the role of men in general in relation to women in general.

302

How do feminists avoid what seems to be the clear implication of this teaching on female subordination? The general response is to make the whole concept hinge on one particular verse, Ephesians 5:21, which says, "Be subject to one another in the fear of Christ." From this verse is deduced the idea of *mutual submission,* which is then used to nullify or cancel out the force of the exhortations in the six passages listed above. Using the principle of mutual submission as the warrant, in any pair where the first member is required to submit to the second, it is *assumed* that the second member is required to submit to the first in the same or a similar way, even if this is not specifically stated. Thus "Wives, be subject to your husbands" automatically implies "Husbands, be subject to your wives also."

This is especially how Ephesians 5:22ff. is handled. Verse 22 specifically applies the command in verse 21 ("be subject to one another") to wives: "Wives, be subject to your own husbands, as to the Lord."[10] By using the principle of mutual submission, feminists then assume that this same command must apply equally to husbands: "Husbands, be subject to your own wives." This is not specifically stated in the text, but is assumed. What the text specifically says about husbands is in verse 25: "Husbands, love your wives." This is understood by feminists to be the WAY in which husbands submit to their wives; it is their own METHOD of submission.

The problem with this approach, and the fatal weakness of the whole concept of mutual submission, is that in this passage beginning with Ephesians 5:21 and ending with Ephesians 6:9, Paul talks about a relationship of submission not just between wives and husbands, but between three other pairs as well. If we are going to be consistent, we must apply the concept of *mutual* submission to these other three pairs also. Most feminists usually recognize this and, steeling up their nerves, plunge ahead and make these applications also. What are these other three pairs?

The first is children and parents (Eph. 6:1-4). The submission of children to parents is clearly required: "Children, obey your parents" (6:1). But the consistent feminist is forced by his commitment to the principle of mutual submission to say that parents must also submit to their children. Ephesians 6:4 is then taken as the MEANS or MANNER of submission as it applies to the father: "Bring them up in the discipline and instruction of the Lord." For example, in discussing how the principle applies to the second pair in this passage, James Beck says that in Ephesians 6:1-4 mutual submission "looks like obedience and nurture."[11]

The second of the other pairs in the passage is slaves and masters (Eph. 6:5-9). Slaves are specifically taught to "be obedient to those who are your masters according to the flesh" (6:5), along with explicit instruction about the proper *attitude* that should accompany such obedience (6:5b-8). The instruction to masters in verse 9 (to "do the same things to them, and give up threatening") refers to the same attitude or spirit required of slaves (sincerity, good will, acting as a slave of Christ). But the consistent feminist must take this verse as requiring masters to *submit* to their slaves. "In this text," says Bilezikian, "Paul enjoins masters to reciprocate submission in obedience and service to their slaves."[12]

The third of the other pairs in this context is the church and Jesus Christ (Eph. 5:22-33). This is the most significant of all, because it is Paul's model for the relationship between husband and wife. The wife is told to submit to her husband "as the church is subject to Christ" (verse 24). That the church should be subject to Christ her Lord is a requirement whose validity most would take for granted. But the concept of mutual submission requires feminists to say that *Christ must also be subject to the church.* Just as the church submits to Christ, Christ also submits to the church. This is never stated in this passage or in any other, but is simply asserted because the concept of mutual submission requires it. What the text does say is that Christ *loves* the church; and because he loves the church he gave Himself as a *sacrifice* for her, and *sanctifies* her, and *cleanses* her, and *nourishes and cherishes* her (5:25-29). But according to feminist thinking, all these expressions of love, including the love itself, are simply the means by which Christ *submits* to the church. They are meant to explain the main idea, which is that Christ submits to the church just as the church submits to Christ.

The more consistent feminists carry the idea of mutual submission to its logical extremes and apply it to ALL pairs where one is said to submit to the other. Just as the church submits to its elders (as in Hebrews 13:17), so the elders submit to the congregation.[13] It applies even within the Trinity: when Christ subordinated Himself to the Father in the incarnation (as in 1 Cor. 11:3), the Father reciprocated by serving and glorifying the Son.[14]

Though it is probably obvious to most, I will now state why I believe the feminist concept of mutual submission has been created out of nothing. It is a fact that if mutual submission is the point of Ephesians 5:21, then it MUST be applied at least to the other three pairs in the passage (children/parents, slaves/masters, church/Christ). But when we attempt to apply the principle here, it clearly breaks down, showing that this is NOT what Paul is talking about in 5:21. It shows that the idea of mutual submission is an idea born only of desire and will, i.e., created *ex nihilo*.

Even when the idea of mutual submission is applied to the first two of these other pairs, it strains our reason to the breaking point. Can anyone really think that Paul is telling fathers to submit to their children in Ephesians 6:4? or that he is telling masters to obey their slaves in Ephesians 6:9?

But when we attempt to apply it to Christ and the church, the idea of mutual submission truly shatters back into the nothingness whence it came. There is absolutely *nothing* in the term or the context that justifies saying that Christ in any sense of the term *submits* to the church. Saying that Christ's self-sacrifice for the church or His sanctifying and nourishing of the church is a form of submission stretches the meaning of the term beyond all reason and recognition. These are indeed things Christ does on behalf of the church. But just doing something on behalf of someone else, for that person's benefit, does not constitute subordinating oneself to that person.

Thus the failure of the analogy when applied to the other pairs shows that the point of Ephesians 5:21 is *not* mutual submission as this is understood by feminists. It is *not* a reference to two-way, reciprocal subordination of each to each. What, then, DOES it mean? The examples Paul uses clearly show that he means *submit yourselves to one another where your circumstances call for it.* Submit to one another wherever your position in life requires such submission, as it does for wives, children, and slaves. If you are a wife, submit to your husband. If you are a child, submit to your parents. If you are a slave, submit to your master. We are told to "be subject to one another" because the various authority-submission relationships often may overlap. The wife submits to her husband, but the husband in turn owes submission to the elders of the church. It is conceivable that the same person could have been both a slave in the home and an elder in the church, both yielding and receiving submission, both perhaps in relation to his master. And even elders, along with husbands, wives, slaves, and masters, owe submission to governing authorities (Romans 13:1).

The roles of the two sides of each pair are NOT mutual or reciprocal, but complementary. Each side in each pair has its own peculiar requirement. The one side submits, but the other side must exercise its headship or authority in a loving, kind, considerate manner. Thus the submission must never to taken as a license for mean-spirited treatment or domineering exploitation. The wife submits to and respects her husband, while the husband in his role as head loves and cares for his wife. These are *two different roles*, though they complement each other.

This complementarity is clearly seen in the more concise statement in Colossians 3:18-19, "Wives, be subject to your husbands, as is fitting in the Lord. Husbands, love your wives, and do not be embittered against them." First Peter 3:1-7 has exactly the same pattern. Verses 1-6 tell wives how to "be submissive to your own husbands" after the pattern of Sarah, who "obeyed Abraham, calling him lord." But then verse 7 gives the complementary side of the coin: "You husbands likewise, live with your wives in an understanding way, as with a weaker vessel, since she is a woman; and grant her honor as a fellow-heir of the grace of life." There is no hint of "mutual submission" in these passages, just as there is none in Ephesians 5:21.

The analogy with Christ and His church makes this absolutely clear. The church is a model for wives when it comes to submission; Christ is a model for husbands, showing them not how to submit but how to exercise headship in a spirit of love and self-sacrifice. Christ is the Head of the church; but he is a Head who LOVES his church, and because He loves it He sacrifices Himself for it, and sanctifies it, and nourishes it. These are expressions of love, not submission.

The idea of mutual submission has caught on with amazing speed and tenacity; it is encountered almost everywhere in discussions of marriage, the family, and gender roles in general. But the fact remains that it is an exegetical myth; it is a true case of "eisegetical fabrication" (see footnote 14). The submission in Ephesians 5:21 is not mutual; in any relationship where it applies at all, it is one-directional. Thus the command for wives to be subject to their husbands is not neutralized or cancelled out, and the first main support for egalitarianism crumbles into dust.

307

II. THE FEMINIST MYTH THAT
HEAD MEANS "ORIGIN"

Ephesians 5:23 says that "the husband is the head of the wife." How has this idea of headship been traditionally understood? Usually, when used is this figurative sense, it has been taken to mean "leader" or "one in authority."[15] This understanding corresponds exactly to the term *submission*. A hierarchical relationship is thus described: the husband is the head or leader, and the wife submits herself to her head.

Such an understanding does not fit very well, however, into the feminist ideal of egalitarianism. So how do feminists avoid the impact of this Greek term *kephale,* or "head"? How can they keep on asserting the idea of mutual submission in a context that so clearly says that the husband is the HEAD of the wife? They do so by completely redefining the meaning of the term "head."

First they declare that the term, when used metaphorically in the Greek-speaking world, *never* meant "chief, leader, one in authority." For example, Philip Payne says that "the idea of 'authority' was not a recognized meaning of *kephale* in Greek."[16] Scott Bartchy asserts, "The fact is that, in ordinary Greek usage, ancient and modern, the word *kephale* never means 'head' in the sense of 'director, boss, decision-maker.' "[17]

At the same time, they assert that *kephale* was often used by Greeks to mean "source" or "origin." As Bartchy says, "In Greek usage this term bears the metaphorical meaning 'source, origin' rather than 'chief,' 'boss.' "[18] This is one of the "common Greek meanings of *kephale,*" according to Alvera and Berkeley Mickelsen.[19] Other writers refer to this meaning as "normal,"[20] "well documented,"[21] and "demonstrated."[22]

Although it is not clear exactly how it should be understood, this is said to be the meaning of *head* when it is applied to husbands and to Christ. That the husband is the head of the wife means he is the origin or source of his wife; that Christ is the Head of the church means he is its origin or source. Though the former concept is rather nebulous, at least with regard to Christ and the church there is a sense in which it is true. Christ *is* the source of the church (see Matthew 16:18). The only question is whether this is the idea conveyed by the term *head*. Feminists say that it is. But to be consistent, they must say that this or a similar idea is what the term means in other New Testament passages which call Christ the head, e.g., Ephesians 1:22, which says, "And He put all things in subjection under His feet, and gave Him as head over all things to the church." Bartchy does indeed try to be consistent here, for he translates this verse as saying that God "has appointed him source (*kephale*) for all things for the Church."[23]

How shall we respond to this? My conclusion is that this is another case of theology *ex nihilo*. There is a complete lack of evidence to support this view. This is shown by an examination of the uses of the term outside the New Testament itself. The definitive study here is still Wayne Grudem's "Does *kephale* ('head') Mean 'Source' or 'Authority Over' in Greek Literature? A Survey of 2,336 Examples."[24]

What did Grudem learn in his survey of these 2,336 uses of *kephale*, which range from the eighth century B.C. to the fourth century A.D.? First, despite the claims of feminists that it is a common and normal meaning, there are *no* clear uses of *kephale* as "source" or "origin" in ancient Greek. Even the most common and seemingly clear example from Herodotus, in which he is supposed to use the term for the *source* of a river, is shown to actually have the connotation of "extremity" or "end point," since the term is also used for the *mouth* of a river.[25] The few other examples cited by feminists as evidence of their view are shown to be misinterpreted or to be from the fourth century A.D. and later. Grudem concludes, "In fact no Greek-speaking reader would have thought of the sense 'source' when reading *kephale*."[26]

Second, Grudem found the term *kephale* used thirty-seven times in the metaphorical sense of "ruler" or "one of superior authority or rank" in writings outside the New Testament. This does not include many of the early Christian writers, who used it often in this sense.

I am aware of two major attempts to refute Grudem's work, but in my opinion neither is convincing. The first is Bilezikian's ETS address cited in footnote 14 above. I heard this presentation and considered it at the time to be exceedingly weak. He attempted to turn Grudem's thirty-seven cases of *kephale* as "ruler" around, and interpret them as meaning "source" for the most part, but never "ruler." Many in the audience agreed that he was guilty of committing the "function fallacy." For example, if someone called *kephale* was pictured as providing protection or safety or well-being for others, he said this shows *kephale* means "source" since this person is the source of such things. A parallel would be that since someone called *teacher* is the source of information, therefore the word *teacher* must mean "source." This is clearly fallacious.

The other attempt to refute Grudem is Richard S. Cervin's article, "Does *Kephale* Mean 'Source' or 'Authority Over' in Greek Literature? A Rebuttal."[27] He says that Grudem misreads his examples of *kephale* and that very few clearly mean "leader," and these are from the Septuagint. But the meaning "source" is also quite rare, he says. (He cites the Herodotus example, but does not deal with Grudem's reasonable explanation of it.[28]) He concludes that its most common metaphorical meaning is "preeminence," and that this is what it means in Paul's letters. But even if this were the case, this is much closer to the concept of "leader" than to "source," and provides little support for the feminist view. The main problem with Cervin's view is that in the New Testament *kephale* is sometimes paired with "submission." The connotation of "preeminence" does not do justice to this; only "leader" or "authority" does.

Grudem himself has responded to Bilezikian and Cervin and other critics in an essay included as an appendix in the volume mentioned earlier, *Recovering Biblical Manhood and Womanhood*.[29] Once again he shows that there are no unambiguous examples of Greek literature where *kephale* means "source," and numerous examples where it means "ruler, authority over."

Thus Grudem's conclusions remain intact. The evidence from Greek usage of *kephale* outside the New Testament is exactly the opposite of what is claimed by feminists. Their view rests on thin air.

The New Testament's own use of the term leads to the same conclusion. In Ephesians 5, the husband's *headship* is paired with the wife's *submission*. The wife is to submit to her husband BECAUSE (*hoti*, v. 23) the husband is her HEAD. Thus coupled with submission, the obvious meaning of *head* is "leader, one in authority." Nothing could be more straight-forward or commonsensible.

The most conclusive evidence for the traditional meaning of head is the New Testament's teaching about the headship of Christ: "Christ also is the head of the church" (Eph. 5:23). We must remember that feminists say that head does NOT mean "ruler" or "one in authority over"; thus they have to argue that it never means this when used of Christ in the New Testament. It must always mean something else.[30]

This attempt to exclude the concept of authority from *kephale* when it is used of Christ just simply will not survive a careful (or even a not-so-careful) reading of passages such as Ephesians 1:22, Colossians 1:18, or Colossians 2:10. In what sense is Christ "the head over all rule and authority" (Col. 2:10)? In that he RULES OVER them, having "disarmed" them and "having triumphed over them" (Col. 2:15). This is the clear contextual connection.

In what sense is Christ the "head of the body, the church"? In the sense that he has FIRST PLACE or

SUPREMACY in everything (Col. 1:18).

In what sense is He the "head over all things to the Church" (Eph. 1:22)? In this context it is impossible to see this headship as anything but rulership and authority. Verse 21 says the Father has placed Him "far above all rule and authority and power and dominion." Verse 22 says, "He put all things in subjection under His feet." This is the statement directly paired with the headship idea; thus again, subjection defines headship. Also, verse 22 says Christ is the "head OVER" all things. The preposition is *huper*, which with the accusative case (as here) means "over, above." (It will be remembered that Bartchy translates this phrase "SOURCE FOR all things for the church." Why does he translate *huper* as "FOR"? It *can* mean "for," but only with the genetive case, which is *not* used here. Hence Bartchy's "source for" is simply incorrect, and it leaves the distinct impression that he is tailoring his translation to fit his feminist doctrine.)

In these verses the most natural meaning of *kephale* when used of Christ is "one having authority over." When we go back to Ephesians 5:23, we find the same is true. It says, "Christ also is the head of the church." What elements in this context help us determine the meaning of *head*? Feminists use every concept in the context to define headship except the ones most closely associated with it. For example, Bilezikian says that "headship is clearly defined in terms of saviorhood, servanthood, and nurturance," and "there is nothing in the text to suggest that *head* might have implications of rulership or authority."[31]

Such statements as these by Bilezikian appear to be symptomatic of exegetical blindness caused by doctrinal calcification. The fact is that the reference to Christ's headship in verse 23 is *surrounded* by concepts of rulership and authority, namely, the references to *submission itself* (verses 22, 24) and to *Lordship* (verse 22). These are the ideas in the text which most naturally correspond to headship and which show us what it means. This is especially true of the reference of Christ's Lordship: "Wives, be subject to your own husbands, *as to the Lord.* For the husband is the head of the wife, as Christ also is the head of the church" (italics added). A person submits to one's head because headship is a kind of lordship. In 1 Peter 3:6, Sarah is cited as an example of wifely submission to her husband Abraham in that she called him *lord.* This is the equivalent of *head,* as Ephesians 5:22 shows.[32]

Our conclusion is that the meaning of "head" (*kephale*) as "one in authority" still stands. The feminist attempt to reinterpret *kephale* as "source" has no basis in the Greek world or in the New Testament. It is a case of theology *ex nihilo,* a view willed into existence in order to support egalitarianism.

III. THE FEMINIST MYTH ABOUT FEMALE HERETICS AT EPHESUS

First Timothy 2:12 has always been a primary reference for those who believe that women should neither teach nor have authority over men. This is probably because Paul says it in exactly this way: "I do not allow a woman to teach or exercise authority over a man."

This seems to be a very straight-forward prohibition. What do feminists do with it? How can they argue for the elimination of all role distinctions and for the acceptance of women preachers and elders, and at the same time accept this statement of Paul as authoritative apostolic teaching? The most common answer is that Paul was here referring ONLY to a very specific kind of situation that had cropped up in Ephesus (where Timothy preached), and therefore that his prohibition was intended to apply ONLY to that time and place. Since the problem was temporary and local, the command was never intended to apply to the church in general. (Of course, if any other church ever has the same problem that was present at Ephesus, then the command would apply.)

What is supposed to be the nature of this limited problem to which Paul's prohibition applies? Here I will list five main theses that have been advanced by feminists as a part of this view. (Since the first two theses are the backbone of this view and can be found in almost any feminist treatment of 1 Timothy 2:12, there is no need to document them here. A brief documentation will be given for the last three theses, though.)

First is the thesis around which all the others revolve, namely, that there were certain women in the church at Ephesus who were guilty of teaching *false doctrine*. This is the problem Paul is addressing: he is not concerned that they might be teaching men as such; he is only concerned with the *content* of their teaching, which was false and heretical.

Second, these women were teaching false doctrine because they were *not properly taught*, because they were uneducated. This is because the pagan and Jewish cultures of that time and place did not provide for the education of women.

Third, in his prohibition Paul used the particular Greek word for "teach" that refers to the *content* of teaching (not the *act* of teaching), namely, *didasko*. If he had wanted to prohibit the act of teaching as such, he would have used another Greek word, namely, *didaskalia*. This shows he was prohibiting the women only from teaching false doctrine, not from teaching as such. For example, Catherine Kroeger says that in the Pastorals *didasko* generally refers to the content of the message. Thus she says, "I propose that 1 Timothy 2:12 forbids false teaching by Paul's opponents," and that "*didasko* prohibits the erroneous teaching."[33] For another example, Joseph Webb says Paul's use of *didasko* shows he was referring to the content of the teaching; if he had wanted to refer to the simple act of teaching, he would have used *didaskalia*.[34]

Fourth, Paul uses the *present tense*, "I do not allow." The present tense of the verb indicates temporary or limited action only; thus Paul is saying, "I am not *presently* (now, at this time) allowing women to teach, because they have not yet been properly taught. However, when they HAVE been properly taught, this prohibition will not apply." Examples of this thesis include this statement by Aida Spencer: "Paul does not command the women not to teach. He employs the present active indicative for 'allow.' . . . Paul is saying: 'I am not presently allowing a woman to teach.'"[35] Gilbert Bilezikian agrees: "Scholars have already pointed out that the present tense of Paul's 'I do not permit . . .' has the force of 'I do not permit *now* a woman to teach.' "[36] In one other example Dorothy Keister says, "Paul found it necessary to state, 'I am not presently permitting women to teach', I Tim. 2:12 (*epitrepo* Pres. Ind. Active), thus, restraining the women at Ephesus from teaching until they themselves were well instructed – a good principle for all churches."[37]

The fifth thesis is that the example of Adam and Eve is given only to illustrate this sort of problem. The reason Eve was so easily deceived by Satan and taught Adam falsely was that she had not been properly educated. Walter Kaiser says that 1 Timothy 2:13 should be understood thus: "For it was Adam who was first taught, and then Eve," with the Greek word *plasso* being taken to mean "formed" in the sense of "educated." As he explains it,

But how could Eve so easily have been duped unless she previously had been untaught? Adam had walked and talked with God in the Garden during that sixth "day," thus he had had the education and spiritual advantage of being "formed first" (v. 13). The verb is *plasso*, "to form, mold, shape" (presumably in spiritual education) not, "created first" (which in Greek is *ktizo*). Paul's argument, then, is based on the "orders of education," not the "orders of creation."

Thus, when the women have been taught, the conditions raised in the "because," or "for" clauses (vv. 13-14) will have been met and the ban removed. . . .[38]

These five theses sum up the feminist contention that 1 Timothy 2:12 was addressing the problem of female heretics in Ephesus. Now, despite the fact that the main thrust of this view is widely taught and widely believed, the fact is this: *none of these ideas has any basis in fact whatsoever, and some are the exact opposite of known facts.* It is theology *ex nihilo.*

A. Women Heretics at Ephesus?

It is true that the Pastoral Epistles show that false doctrine was a major problem at Ephesus, but the idea that women were guilty of teaching this false doctrine is based on "evidence" that is a thin tissue of assumptions and inferences. It is flimsy at best, and in reality non-existent. It is a string of "probablies" (which are better described as "possiblies" or "maybes"). For example, after referring to passages about false doctrine, Don Williams asks, "Could some of those teaching falsely be women? Quite probably so."[39] Similarly Mark Roberts says, "Numbered among these teachers, quite probably, were women."[40]

The crucial question is this: do any passages in the Pastorals specifically mention women as false teachers? Some cite 1 Timothy 4:7; 5:11-15; and 2 Timothy 3:6-7 as proof texts. For example, Richard and Catherine Kroeger say, "2 Timothy 3:6-7 and 1 Timothy 5:11-15 indicate that women were involved in the errors which plagued the church at Ephesus, and both references seem to imply that wanton behavior was part of the problem with the female apostates." These passages show that "women heretics were known to be involved in sexual immorality."[41]

What do these passages actually say? First Timothy 4:7 says, "Have nothing to do with worldly fables fit only for old women" [old wives' tales]. First Timothy 5:11-15 refers to "younger widows" who "learn to be idle, as they go around from house to house; and not merely idle, but also gossips and busybodies, talking about things not proper to mention." Second Timothy 3:6-7 says, "For among them are those who enter into households and captivate weak women weighed down with sins, led on by various impulses, always learning and never able to come to the knowledge of the truth."

Our first thought after reading these verses is this: "Surely there are other passages in the Pastorals that link women with false teaching in more specific ways than these do. Surely the feminist view of women heretics at Ephesus has a stronger textual basis than this. Surely." But this is not the case. These are *the* passages that are supposed to show that there were women heretics at Ephesus. Exactly what do they say about the women in question? The most reasonable and common-sense understanding is that they are talking about *gossipers* and *victims* of false teaching. The labels "women heretics" and "female apostates" are unfounded exaggerations, to say the least; they go far beyond what is warranted by these texts. To say that these passages show that there was a problem with women teaching false doctrine at Ephesus can only be called hyperexegesis, or theology *ex nihilo*.

If there are no other passages in the Pastorals that specifically identify women as false teachers, what about 1 Timothy 2:12 itself? Here women are specifically mentioned, and they are mentioned with respect to teaching. But is there any indication that the teaching associated with women in this text is *false* teaching? Absolutely none. It is purely an assumption, with no basis whatsoever. There are no modifiers or other descriptive terms in this context that give the slightest hint that Paul is talking about *false* teaching.

It is a well-known fact that the Pastorals do have a lot to say about false teaching and false teachers. Richard and

Catherine Kroeger list "the main passages dealing with
unorthodox beliefs and practice" as the following: 1 Timothy 1:3-11, 19-20; 4:1-10; 6:3-4, 20f.; 2 Timothy 1:15; 2:14,
16-18, 23; 3:1-9, 13; 4:3-4; and Titus 1:10-16; 3:9-11.[42] But
anyone who takes the time to examine these passages will
find that *each without exception* makes abundant and clear
reference to the *false* character of the doctrine. We are not
left to wonder whether Paul is talking about false teaching
or not. Such expressions as these occur in abundance:
strange doctrines, myths, speculation, blaspheme, fall
away from the faith, doctrines of demons, liars, a different
doctrine, does not agree with sound words, worldly and
empty chatter, gone astray from the faith – and these are
only *some* of the descriptions from *First* Timothy only. Like
expressions appear copiously in 2 Timothy and Titus.

Thus it appears that in the Pastorals, whenever Paul
condemns false teaching, he *always* very clearly and specifically identifies it as *false* in one way or another. But in 1
Timothy 2:12 there is no indication at all that he is referring to teaching that is false.

Another exceedingly relevant observation, often made
but usually ignored by feminists, is this: if Paul is prohibiting only the teaching of *false* doctrine in this text, why
does he limit the prohibition just to women, since men
were explicitly identified as being guilty of this practice?
See, e.g., 1 Timothy 1:19-20; 2 Timothy 2:17; 4:14-15; and
Titus 1:10-11 (where the forms of the words are male).
Another telling observation, also usually ignored, is this: if
the problem is the teaching of *false* doctrine, why does
Paul limit the prohibition to women's teaching *men*? Would
it not also be wrong to teach false doctrine to other
women?

The conclusion that must be drawn from these data and
observations can only be that there is *not one solid reason*
to think that there were women teaching false doctrine at
Ephesus and that 1 Timothy 2:12 is referring only to this.
It is an assumption built on thin air.

B. Were the Ephesian Women Uneducated?

It is commonly assumed that the women at Ephesus were susceptible to false teaching because they were uneducated, and that they were uneducated because their culture did not promote education for women. For example, in discussing 1 Timothy 2:12, W. F. Lown says,

Maybe the missing link here is in the cultural situation in the Mediterranean world at that time. *Women in general* were not allowed to speak publicly, especially to men, because for the most part, they had not been educated, and so had nothing helpful to contribute to the corporate meeting. And the forward woman was viewed in that day as being coarse.[43]

Anne Atkins says, "Most women at the time were ignorant, illiterate and strangers to any form of education."[44]

Though such statements as these are quite common, the assumption that the pagan culture of that day was prejudiced against females and female education is really just an assumption; it is simply not in accordance with the facts. The truth is that the women in Asia Minor quite often were well educated and took active roles in teaching and leading. "In fact," says Oepke, "the capable woman, especially in Hellenistic Asia Minor but also in Greece, could occupy a surprisingly independent and influential role even in public life." In religious life, "priestesses are very common both in public cults . . . and in those of the Mysteries. . . . Outstanding ecstatic endowment assures women of prophetic rank as sybils [prophetesses]."[45]

Manfred Hauke, professor of dogmatic theology at the University of Augsburg, has written extensively on this subject. He says, "In the Hellenistic world, from which Saint Paul came, the activity of women in social and religious life was much more extensive than in Palestine."[46]

The restriction of women to the domestic sphere that was particularly widespread in ancient Greece was . . . transformed by a virtual emancipation that took hold in most of the Roman Empire. In the imperial age there were numerous philosophically and artistically educated women, who even wrote books, and a whole succession of well-known poetesses. Regarding the relationship of women to men, many philosophers advocated an emphatic equality ideal. For example, the Stoic Musonius Rufus, a contemporary of Saint Paul, called for sons and daughters to be given the same sort of education, with certain differences to apply only in the area of sports.

Among the Pythagoreans we find female teachers of philosophy, and in the Epicurean school women were even given preference as teachers. Exactly like their male colleagues, many of these female philosophers traveled from place to place and gave full-fledged public sermons. Paul, too, made appearances in a style similar to that of these traveling preachers. If he had chosen female colleagues in office, instead of Timothy, Silas or Barnabas, then that would have been cause for no great offense among the Greeks.[47]

Hauke notes "the participation of women in leading positions within the religious sphere." In the mystery cults, often the women "themselves performed the ceremonies and delivered the relevant preliminary instructions, even in respect of male participants."[48]

In his comments on 1 Timothy 2 specifically, Hauke makes the following statements:

. . . The First Letter to Timothy refers to the situation in Ephesus, the economic, political and religious center of Asia Minor. In that region the social position of women was especially well developed. Professional activity by women in the Roman Empire was probably most widespread there . . . and in politics, too, women were thoroughly involved in leadership . . . .

Ephesus was also a center of philosophy. Particularly in the schools of the Stoics, Epicureans and

Pythagoreans, female philosophers were known to teach, probably appearing publicly in the same way as did Paul . . . .

In the religious sphere, female leadership was even more widespread: the Phrygian cult of Cybele, in which the god mother played the central role, had made its way to Ephesus, along with its priestesses and priests. . . .

Thus, the sociocultural environment in Ephesus was anything but hostile to priesthood for women; instead, this question was very much in the air.[49]

These data cited by Hauke show that we can hardly assume that the women of Ephesus were uneducated, or that their culture opposed their being educated. Thus the feminist idea that the Ephesian women were uneducated and thus uncritically imbibed false doctrine has no foundation in fact; it is built upon unwarranted assumptions.[50]

C. Does Didasko *Refer to the Content of Teaching?*

As noted above, it has been affirmed that Paul's prohibition in 1 Timothy 2:12 must be referring to teaching of a certain *content*, rather than teaching as such, because the word he uses has that connotation. Thus we must ask, is it true that the use of *didasko* in this verse shows that Paul is referring to the content of what the Ephesian women were teaching, i.e., heresy, rather than the act of teaching itself?

The answer is, absolutely not. The alleged distinction between *didasko* and *didaskalia* – that the former refers to content and the latter to the act – is absolutely without foundation. It is simply not true. In fact, if there is any such distinction, it is exactly the opposite of this. Although both words can refer to the *act* of teaching, *didaskalia* is the one that is also used to refer to content, or what is taught. The reason why Paul used *didasko* in 1 Timothy 2:12, instead of *didaskalia*, is because the former unambiguously refers to the ACT of teaching. The word itself gives no implication at all that Paul is concerned with the content of the women's teaching; it refers only to the act itself. If he had wanted to single out the content of their teaching for censure, he would have used *didaskalia,* or even *didache.*[51]

D. Does the Present Tense Mean Temporary Action?

The fourth point in support of the idea that 1 Timothy 2:12 is addressed to female heretics at Ephesus is the contention that the present tense of "allow" indicates temporary action; thus Paul's prohibition was only meant to be temporary. Is this an accurate understanding of the Greek present tense? The answer is no; in fact, again the very opposite is the case. The present tense of a verb, rather than indicating temporary action, most often represents *continuing* action. Thus it actually has a timeless force, and shows that Paul's prohibition is meant to be perpetual.

This is exactly how most Evangelicals explain the difficult statements in Hebrews 10:26 and 1 John 3:9. In the former, *just because* it is a present tense, we justify translating it, "If we *go on* or *keep on* sinning," as the NASB and NIV put it. In the latter we say, one who *"practices* sin" or "will *continue* to sin," again appealing to the present tense to justify the concept of continuing action. And this is quite proper, being consistent with the nature of the present tense.

Where, then, is the justification for claiming that the present tense in 1 Timothy 2:12 implies temporary or limited action? There is none. If it were Paul's intention to speak of temporary action, this connotation could have been included only by the addition of some qualifying word or phrase; it is not inherent in the present tense as such.

E. Was Eve Lacking in Education?

The idea that 1 Timothy 2:13 refers to Adam's priority

in *education* rather than creation is filled with fallacies. That the verb *plasso* "presumably" refers to shaping via education, as Kaiser says, is indeed a presumption without warrant. The word refers to the work of a potter making something of clay. "It means 'to form or fashion out of a soft mass.' "[52] It is the word used in the Septuagint in Genesis 2:7-8 to describe how God formed Adam from the dust, which is the obvious background of Paul's statement in 1 Timothy 2:13. Its usual parallel is *poieo*, "to make, to do." The word did have the figurative meaning of "to fashion by education and training" in the Greek world and in Philo, "though hardly in the LXX and not at all in the NT."[53]

Even if Kaiser's view of *plasso* were correct (which it is not), it should be noted that verse 13 says nothing about Eve's being *un*formed in the sense of *un*taught; it speaks only of the order in which she and Adam were "formed." In fact, contrary to the assumption that she was *un*formed, verse 13 specifically affirms (in the words "then Eve") that she WAS "formed." So even if *plasso* did mean "educated" here, it is affirmed that Eve WAS educated.

F. Conclusion

In this section we have seen how another main pillar of the egalitarian thesis lacks any kind of foundation. There is no evidence that Paul's prohibition against women teaching men in 1 Timothy 2:12 refers only to women teaching false doctrine and not to their teaching as such. Thus the heart and soul of the feminist exegesis of this crucial passage is constructed literally out of nothing and is supported by errors. It is theology *ex nihilo*.

IV. THE FEMINIST MYTH OF SINFUL AUTHORITY

In 1 Timothy 2:12 Paul also says, "I do not allow a woman to . . . exercise authority over a man." What does this mean? The non-feminist view is that this permanently prohibits women from holding positions or offices of authority over men in the church. The Greek word for "exercise authority" is *authenteo*. As non-feminists understand it, this refers to ordinary and proper authority, such as that exercised by elders in the church. Thus women are prohibited from holding the office of elder.

Feminists, however, usually take this term to refer not to ordinary and proper authority, but to a negative, domineering exercise of authority or an illegitimate usurping of authority. Why do they say this? Because, they say, the word *authenteo* as used by the Greeks had the meaning "to murder" or "to commit a crime." The noun form, *authentes*, meant "murderer." Thus the word had a harsh, negative connotation and referred to a harsh, domineering, autocratic exercise of authority. Thus it is no wonder that Paul prohibited women from having this kind of authority over men. But since the prohibition thus does not refer to ordinary, properly-exercised authority at all, there is no reason why women cannot hold offices of authority such as elder.

An example of this view is Spencer. Speaking of *authenteo* she says, "In contemporary Greek society it signified 'to commit a murder' " and thus referred to "destructive domination." Thus it "signifies 'to domineer' or 'to have absolute power over' persons in such a way as to destroy them."[54] Austin Stouffer agrees: "The word is translated by such terms as murder, perpetrate, author, master, domineer, or hold absolute sway over. The word was considered vulgar and almost invariably was used in a bad sense."[55] Bartchy declares that "the verb *authentein* clearly bears the nuance of using such absolute power in a destructive manner."[56] Joseph Webb says, "It is now generally understood that the word means to 'domineer,' to seize dominance or autocratic control over another. It refers to one who acts without authorized or legitimate authority . . . . It is a dictatorial kind of control."[57] He says that the term "did not mean legitimate authority, conferred authority."[58]

What shall we say to this? How can we determine the true meaning of *authenteo*? Since it is not used elsewhere in the New Testament, we can only look to other Greek literature to see what meaning was given to it. When we do this, we can see that the feminists' understanding of *authenteo* is not in agreement with the way the Greeks themselves used this word.

It is true that the word at times meant "to murder" or "to commit a crime." The fallacy of the feminist argument is the assumption that because the word had a negative connotation in some of its meanings, it therefore must have had a negative connotation in all of its meanings. Since it sometimes meant "murder," which is a destructive act, therefore when it meant "authority," it must have meant a destructive and thus an improper kind of authority.

This is a *non sequitur*: it does not necessarily follow. It was possible for the same Greek word to have one meaning which was negative and another entirely different meaning which was quite positive. For example, the common word *luo* sometimes meant "to loose, to set free"; but sometimes it meant "to destroy, to break."

The only proper way to decide this point is to see what the Greeks themselves actually meant when they used the term *authenteo*, not in the sense of murder, but in the sense of authority itself. Feminists emphasize that the term sometimes meant "to murder." This is granted. But what connotation did the Greeks actually put into the word when it *did not* mean "murder" but meant "authority"? Did the Greeks themselves use it in the sense of "destructive, domineering authority"? Or did they use it in the sense of the ordinary exercise of authority? Most feminist writing never deals with this question and never cites any uses of the term when it refers to authority as such. It usually cites only the passages where it means "murder."

But the fact of the matter is this: when the Greeks used the term in the sense of "authority," they did *not* imply a destructive, negative kind of authority; rather, they used it in the sense of a positive or at least neutral kind of authority. For example, according to Lampe's *Patristic Greek Lexicon*, when the church fathers used the term to mean "authority," they gave it four nuances, all of them positive or neutral in meaning: hold sovereign authority, possess authority over, assume authority, authorize.[59]

But what about the more "secular" literature, closer to the time of the New Testament? George Knight has researched the dozen or so uses of *authenteo* listed in the Arndt and Gingrich Greek lexicon, uses occurring near the time of the New Testament and a bit later. Only *one* of the uses actually meant "to murder," while all the others meant "to have authority" in some sense, but *never* in a negative sense. Thus Knight concludes from his study of the actual uses of the word that "the 'authority' in view in the documents is understood to be a positive concept and is in no way regarded as having any overtone of misuse of position or power, i.e., to 'domineer.' " Overall, "the recognized meaning for the first century BC and AD . . . is 'to have authority over'. The nuance is positive, or at least neutral, but in any case there is no inherent negative overtone such as is suggested by the word 'domineer'. "[60]

Leland Wilshire has done an even more thorough study, examining 314 uses of the verb and the noun ranging from the sixth century B.C. to the sixth century A.D. He shows that in New Testament times the terms sometimes referred to negative acts such as murder or suicide, but sometimes they referred simply to the exercise of authority. The important point is that *when authenteo meant authority*, there is no indication that it meant any kind of harsh, destructive, domineering authority. That is, when the word did have the connotation of authority, it meant authority in a legitimate and positive (or at least neutral) sense.[61]

Thus we must ask very seriously, where is the evidence for the widely-held view that *authenteo* means "domineer" when it refers to authority? It is completely unacceptable to say that just because the word sometimes meant "to murder," it *must* have had a negative, destructive connotation when it referred to authority. This is an assumption without foundation in fact. Thus to say that 1 Timothy 2:12 refers to "domineering authority" since that is what the word *means* is simply not true. It ignores the facts of the actual use and meaning of the term. It is theology *ex nihilo*.

A final point deals with the logic of the "domineer" or "usurpation" theory. I.e., if *authenteo* means something negative like domineering or usurping authority and thus an illegitimate kind of authority, why does Paul limit the prohibition to women only, and then only with respect to authority over men? If Paul is talking about sinful authority, then it is wrong for both men AND women to have it; and it is wrong to domineer over both men AND women.

V. THE BASIC FEMINIST MYTH: GALATIANS 3:28

Galatians 3:28 says, "There is neither Jew nor Greek, there is neither slave nor free man, there is neither male nor female; for you are all one in Christ Jesus." In feminist thinking this is the "basic," "fundamental," "central," "foundational" theological affirmation on the roles of men and women. For feminists it is especially important NOT to limit the implications of this passage to spiritual salvation only. Its scope must be taken as universal, as encompassing the place of men and women in church, family, and society as a whole.

Some feminists see it as God's deliberate erasure of all role distinctions in the sense of "reversing the curse," since such distinctions are said to be the result of sin in some way, and Christ has redemptively nullified all the effects of sin. Others see it as the institution of a new order of creation itself. Even if role distinctions were a part of God's original creation in Genesis 1 and 2, Christ has replaced that order of creation with one in which no such distinctions occur. Either way, women are now said to be free in Christ to fill any position or office or role held by men. "There is neither male nor female; for you are all one in Christ Jesus."

What shall we say about this, the central foundational pillar of egalitarianism? Just this, that it is a case of hyperexegesis, i.e., of trying to draw more out of the text than is actually contained in it. To make this apply to all role distinctions in family, church, and society goes far beyond Paul's purpose for making this particular statement in this particular context. The context is the key.

First, what is the context of the letter itself? The usual feminist analysis is that Galatians 3:28 is a "clear statement of theological principle," whereas 1 Corinthians and 1 Timothy deal with "concrete local situations."[62] But this seems to ignore the obvious fact that Galatians itself *is* dealing with a concrete local situation. It is very much an "occasional" letter, being occasioned by a specific situation and a specific problem, namely, the Judaizers. Don Williams says, "Galatians is written in the white-heat of theological and personal controversy. Paul's apostleship and message are under attack. False teachers have invaded the young Galatian churches demanding that Gentile converts be circumcised and keep the Old Testament law if they are to be true Christians. . . ."[63] Perhaps this is indeed a "clear statement of theological principle," but the historical situation shows that this kind of statement can be made when dealing with a "concrete local situation."

But what is the content of this principle? This is the crucial question, and this can be determined only by examining the immediate context of the statement in Galatians 3:1-4:7. The guiding question is why Paul lumps together these three categories of contrasting pairs: Jews/Greeks, slaves/free men, and males/females. What makes these three pairs meaningful together? It cannot be a case of "reversing the curse," since it is not accurate to attribute the distinction between Jews and Greeks to the curse or to sin as such. It cannot be a case of "instituting a new creation order" for the same reason. Neither this distinction nor the one between slaves and free men was a part of the old creation order as such.

So what is the point of Galatians 3:28? Why does this verse group these three pairs together? The context shows that the point at issue *must* have something to do with the Mosaic Law. In Christ, something is true with reference to these three pairs that was not true under the Mosaic Law. What is it? Again using the context as the key, we see that it has to do with *inheritance*. The question being addressed in this context is, how does one come into possession of the inheritance promised to Abraham, namely, the salvation that comes through Christ? How does one receive the rights of ownership with reference to that promise?

The answer to this question, in opposition to the Judaizers, is this: *not by Law* (represented by circumcision), *but by Promise* (received in faith). Speaking generally, this is the whole point of Galatians 3:1-4:7. One does not inherit the promises through observance of the Mosaic Law (summed up in circumcision), but by faith. Therefore inheritance has nothing to do with whether one is a Jew or Gentile, whether one is circumcised or not.

In fact, the period when the Law (circumcision) was in force was NOT the time of full ownership or possession. During that age the Jews themselves were more like slaves, i.e., in the childhood stage and not given the inheritance yet (cf. 4:1-3). But in Christ, a person passes into *full sonship* and thus full ownership of the inheritance (cf. 3:26, 29; 4:7). And this again is by faith. It has nothing to do with whether one is actually a slave or a free man. This is contrary to the Old Testament system, under which slaves could not hold property in the full sense (cf. 4:1).

Also under the Mosaic Law, only men could inherit and own property as a rule; except for unusual circumstances daughters did not inherit and own property. But again, in Christ this exclusion does not apply. The right to the inheritance *has nothing to do* with whether one is male or female. In Christ everyone is the same. Faith, not gender, qualifies one to receive the inheritance.

This is the point of Galatians 3:28, and this is how Galatians 3:28 relates to the work of Christ. The listing of the three pairs has nothing to do with replacing the creation order, removing the curse, or even removing the distinctions between the members of these pairs. The only issue at stake in the context is inheritance. Under the Mosaic Law (except for unusual circumstances), only free Jewish males could inherit and own property. Inheritance was passed along to *sons*. Gentiles, slaves, and women ordinarily did not inherit property. But under the New Covenant, in Christ, the rules of the Law do not apply, It does not matter whether one is a Jew or a Gentile, a slave or a free man, a male or a female. *Anyone and everyone* who has faith in Jesus Christ is counted as a *son* and thus an *heir* to the promise. Gentiles, slaves and females have just as much right to the Abrahamic blessing as their counterparts; these distinctions no longer apply in reference to receiving salvation in Christ.

This is the only thing that really holds these three pairs together. All other attempts to find a common category for the three of them do violence to the context. How does one inherit the blessings which Christ made available? How does one inherit the promise? Is the inheritance based on the Law (3:18)? No! Does a person have to be a *Jew* to receive the inheritance? No! Does he have to be a *free man*? No! Does the person even have to be a *man*? No! The three categories that could not inherit under the Mosaic Law – Gentiles, slaves, and women – may inherit the Abrahamic promise. This is one inheritance available to *anyone* who has the proper faith in Christ. Women have full rights of inheritance and ownership of this "property."

Understanding Galatians 3:28 in terms of inheritance helps us to see, too, that the scope of the implications of our oneness with Christ is limited to our spiritual status before God. To try to apply it to the whole scope of social, economic, and ecclesiastical relationships simply goes beyond Paul's point in this context. This can be clearly seen by tracing the thought from Galatians 3:8 through 3:29. At stake is the blessing promised to Abraham in Genesis 12:3, repeated in Galatians 3:8, "All the nations shall be blessed in you." Who inherits this "blessing of Abraham" (3:14)? Technically, since the promise was given to Abraham's *seed* – singular – there are not *many* heirs, but only *one*, namely, Christ (3:16). Christ is the only true heir of the Abrahamic blessing.

But even if others in addition to Christ were eligible to inherit the blessing, no one would actually do so under the conditions of the Law. Under the Law only sons could inherit, but even a male child did not have the status of a son until he had come of age. Until then, he was regarded as no different from a slave as far as inheritance is concerned (4:1ff.). This is why the Jews as Jews never really inherited the promised blessing, because they never really progressed beyond the childhood stage and thus the level of slaves (3:19-24).

The Abrahamic inheritance, though, is not given according to the rules of the Law, but according to promise (3:16-18). And the very thing that makes it available to us in terms of promise is the same thing that enables *us* to bypass the technicality that there is only one true heir of the promise, namely Christ. That thing is *faith* (3:24-25). Faith in Christ not only gives us the status of *sons* rather than slaves (3:26); it also identifies us with the one seed, Jesus Christ, thus giving us a right to share the inheritance that technically belongs only to Him (3:27-29). In other words, if we could just somehow be *identified with Christ* (become one with Christ), then what belongs to him would also belong to us by virtue of that union. But how can we become identified with Christ? "Through faith"! "For all of you who were baptized into Christ have clothed yourselves with Christ" – you have taken on His identity. Thus for purposes of receiving the inheritance, "there is neither Jew nor Greek, there is neither slave nor free man, there is neither male nor female," and therefore none will be excluded from the inheritance as they would be under the Mosaic Law. Actually, there are no longer "many"; there is only "one," namely, Jesus, since you have merged your identity with his: "for you are all one in Christ Jesus. And if you belong to Christ" through faith and baptism, where you took on his identity, "then you are Abraham's offspring" – *you* are the *one seed,* and thus you are "heirs according to promise," but not according to the rules of the Law.

The content of this inheritance promised to Abraham's seed is clearly described in this chapter in terms of spiritual salvation, specifically, justification (3:8, 11, 24) and the gift of the Holy Spirit (3:2, 5, 14). To say that the oneness in Christ in 3:28 refers to egalitarian marriage, an egalitarian church, and an egalitarian society in general is trying to take more out of it than Paul has put into it. It is theology *ex nihilo.*

Here are two other pertinent points that help to confirm this conclusion. First, if Paul were really intending to erase all role distinctions between males and females in this text, it seems strange that he would continue to speak of all Christians as "*sons* of Abraham" or "*sons* of God" (3:7, 26; emphasis added). Why would he keep emphasizing the theme of sonship: "Because you are *sons* . . . . Therefore you are no longer a slave, but a *son*; and if a *son*, then an heir" (4:6-7; emphasis added)? Would an egalitarian text have used such language? Actually this shows that Paul's main concern is FAR from leveling out male-female relationships, otherwise Paul missed a golden opportunity. He could have emphasized this point (or at least not undermined it) by saying "you are all sons *and daughters* of God," or "*children* of God." But he did not do this, because this was not the point he was trying to make. He emphasizes sonship because sons (not slaves) have the right of inheritance and ownership (4:1-7). In Christ we ALL (Jews/Greeks, slaves/free men, males/females) have the status of SONS.

Another pertinent point is that this understanding of Galatians 3:28 is supported by 1 Peter 3:1-7. This latter passage emphasizes both headship/submission (3:1-6) and spiritual equality in the inheritance (3:7). Verse 7 especially supports the interpretation of Galatians 3:28 as referring to inheritance of spiritual salvation: "Grant her honor as a fellow heir of the grace of life." *This is the whole point of Galatians 3:28,* but it does not nullify the headship-submission relationship, as 1 Peter 3:1-6 shows.

VI. CONCLUSION

My thesis in this chapter has been that the Biblical feminists' interpretation of key Bible concepts and key Bible texts is a case of theology *ex nihilo,* because their egalitarian conclusions have no basis in fact, no foundation in reality. We can only hope that all those who are concerned for sound doctrine will examine the evidence as objectively as possible and be open to the truth as it presents itself to us from the Word of God and from other relevant sources. We cannot *will* truth into existence. It is either there, or it is not. Our duty as students of God's word is to find what is there, to accept it, and to live by it even if it goes against our most dearly-held beliefs and our deepest desires.[64]

Endnotes

1. Elizabeth Cady Stanton, in *The Woman's Bible*, Part I (New York: European Publishing Company, 1895), pp. 14-15.

2. Letha Scanzoni and Nancy Hardesty, *All We're Meant To Be: A Biblical Approach to Women's Liberation* (Waco: Word Books, 1974), p. 28.

3. Virginia Ramey Mollenkott, *Women, Men, and the Bible*, revised ed. (New York: Crossroad, 1988), p. 83.

4. This concept of simultaneous creation also directly contradicts Genesis 2:21-22, I Corinthians 11:8-12, and I Timothy 2:13. We should also point out that not all Biblical feminists agree with this concept.

5. Mollenkott, *Women*, p. 48.

6. Aida Besançon Spencer, *Beyond the Curse: Women Called to Ministry* (Nashville: Thomas Nelson, 1985), p. 22.

7. We can only wonder if Mollenkott and Spencer consciously limit their statements to New Testament WRITERS and to the Greek word *ANER*. We say this because anyone with their obvious scholarship would have access to a Greek concordance and would surely have used it in their study of this point.

We should also emphasize again that even though writers like Mollenkott, Spencer, Scanzoni, and Hardesty are mainstream representatives of Biblical feminism, not every Biblical feminist subscribes to these particular claims concerning simultaneous creation and gender-neutral incarnation. These cases are cited as *examples* of the *type* of exegesis that underlies the feminist case for egalitarianism.

8. Gerhard Delling, "*tasso* [etc.]," *Theological Dictionary of the New Testament*, ed. Gerhard Friedrich, tr. Geoffrey W. Bromiley (Grand Rapids: Eerdmans, 1972), 8:39-42, 45.

9. Donald A. Nash, "Submission? Who?", *Christian Standard* (November 14, 1976), 111:15.

10. The verb *hupotasso* is not repeated in verse 22; its application is carried over from verse 21.

11. James R. Beck, "Is There a Head of the House in the Home? Reflections on Ephesians 5," *Priscilla Papers* (Fall 1988), 2:2.

12. Gilbert Bilezikian, *Beyond Sex Roles: What the Bible Says About a Woman's Place in Church and Family*, 2 ed. (Grand Rapids: Baker, 1990), p. 290.

13. Ibid., p. 155.

14. Bilezikian, in an address at the 1986 annual meeting of the Evangelical Theological Society, entitled "Case Study of an Eisegetical Fabrication: Wayne Grudem's Treatment of *Kephale* in Ancient Texts."

15. The Greek word is *kephale*. Its literal meaning is the piece of anatomy that sits on top of one's shoulders, the "head." Here we are dealing with a metaphorical or figurative use of the term.

16. Philip Barton Payne, "Response to 'What does *Kephale* Mean in the New Testament?', " in *Women, Authority and the Bible,* ed. Alvera Mickelsen (Downers Grove: InterVarsity Press, 1986), p. 118.

17. S. Scott Bartchy, "Power, Submission, and Sexual Identity Among the Early Christians," in *Essays on New Testament Christianity,* ed. C. Robert Wetzel (Cincinnati: Standard Publishing, 1978), p. 78.

18. Ibid., p. 61.

19. Berkeley and Alvera Mickelsen, "What Does *Kephale* Mean in the New Testament?", in *Women, Authority and the Bible,* p. 105.

20. Payne, "Response," pp. 131-132.

21. Catherine Clark Kroeger, "The Classical Concept of *Head* as 'Source,' " Appendix III in Gretchen Gaebelein Hull, *Equal To Serve: Women and Men in the Church and Home* (Old Tappan, NJ: Revell, 1987), p. 267.

22. Bartchy, "Issues of Power and a Theology of the Family, Part II," *Mission Journal* (September 1987), 21:10.

23. Ibid.

24. Printed as Appendix 1 in George W. Knight III, *The Role Relationship of Men and Women: New Testament Teaching* (Chicago: Moody Press, 1985), pp. 49-80.

25. Ibid., p. 57.

26. Ibid., p. 78.

27. *Trinity Journal,* n.s. (Spring 1989), 10:85-112.

28. Ibid., pp. 89-90.

29. Wayne Grudem, "The Meaning of *Kephale* ("Head"): A Response to Recent Studies," *Recovering Biblical Manhood and Womanhood: A Response to Evangelical Feminism,* ed. John Piper and Wayne Grudem (Wheaton, IL: Crossway Books), pp. 425-468.

30. See B. and A. Mickelsen, "What Does *Kephale* Mean?", pp. 106-109; and Bilezikian, *Beyond Sex Roles,* pp. 157-162. The maneuvering here would sometimes be humorous if such folks were not so serious and if so much were not at stake.

31. Bilezikian, *Beyond Sex Roles,* p. 158.

32. In view of this connection between headship and lordship in Ephesians 5:22, Bilezikian's comments are quite remarkable: "In this development on the meaning of headship, there is nothing in the text to suggest that *head* might have implications of rulership or authority. Had this been the case, Paul would have more appropriately stated, 'Christ is the head of the church. He is himself the Lord of the body' instead of 'the Savior of the body.' However, *the terminology of authority is not used in reference to Christ and His headship"* (ibid., italics added). Nothing could be further from the obvious truth, in view of Paul's clear linking of subjection, lordship, and headship in this passage.

33. Catherine Clark Kroeger, "I Timothy 2:12 – A Classicist's View," in *Women, Authority and the Bible*, pp. 225-226. To support her view of *didasko*, Kroeger cites in footnote no. 1 three pages from the TDNT article on this word. I checked these pages; they say *nothing at all* about the idea. In fact there is nothing in the entire article that supports her view. My question is, why were these pages cited?

34. Joseph M. Webb, "Where Is the Command to Silence?" (part one), *Christian Standard* (May 21, 1989), 124:5-6.

35. Spencer, *Beyond the Curse*, pp. 84-85.

36. Bilezikian, *Beyond Sex Roles*, p. 180.

37. Dorothy Keister, "Women as Leaders in the New Testament," an unpublished manuscript for a speech at the North American Christian Convention on July 7, 1986, in Indianapolis; p. 9.

38. Walter Kaiser, "Shared Leadership or Male Headship?", *Christianity Today* (October 3, 1986), 30:12, CTI supplement.

39. Don Williams, *The Apostle Paul and Women in the Church* (Ventura, CA: Regal Books, 1977), p. 111.

40. Mark Roberts, "Woman Shall Be Saved: A Closer Look at I Timothy 2:15," *The Reformed Journal* (April 1983), 33:19.

41. Richard and Catherine Clark Kroeger, "May Women Teach? Heresy in the Pastoral Epistles," *The Reformed Journal* (October 1980), 30:14, 18.

42. Ibid., p. 14.

43. W.F. Lown, "Women in Roles of Leadership" (part two), *The Lookout* (September 14, 1980), 92:6.

44. Anne Atkins, *Split Image: Male and Female After God's Likeness* (Grand Rapids: Eerdmans, 1987), p. 121.

45. Albrecht Oepke, *"gune,"* Theological Dictionary of the New Testament, ed. Gerhard Kittel, tr. Geoffrey W. Bromiley (Grand Rapids: Eerdmans, 1964), 1:778, 786.

46. Manfred Hauke, *Women in the Priesthood? A Systematic Analysis in the Light of the Order of Creation and Redemption*, tr. David Kipp (San Francisco: Ignatius Press, 1988), p. 340. Hauke's main sources are listed in footnote no. 2 on page 340.

47. Ibid., pp. 341-342.

48. Ibid., p. 343.

49. Ibid., pp. 401-402. In light of these facts, one could argue that this presence of female teachers and priestesses in the pagan world was the very reason why Paul gave his specific instruction *against* such a practice in I Tim. 2:12. Pagans may allow these things, but God does not.

50. Though the content of the letter to the Ephesians suggests that most of the Christians there were converts from paganism, there probably were also a number of converts from Judaism, where education was less common for women. But even if the Jewish women converts were relatively less educated when compared with pagan women, they would be no less educated in *Christian* doctrine than Jewish *men* at the time of conversion. Also, there is no reason to doubt that the women as well as the men were instructed alike in the Christian faith when they became a part of the Christian community (see I Tim. 2:11).

51. See Walter L. Liefeld's comments on this in his "Response to 'I Timothy 2:12 – A Classicist's View,'" in *Women, Authority and the Bible*, p. 245.

52. Herbert Braun, *"plasso* [etc.]," *Theological Dictionary of the New Testament*, ed. Gerhard Friedrich, tr. Geoffrey W. Bromiley (Grand Rapids: Eerdmans, 1968), 6:254.

53. Ibid.

54. Spencer, *Beyond the Curse*, pp. 86-87.

55. Austin H. Stouffer, "The Ordination of Women: Yes," *Christianity Today* (February 20, 1981), 25:15.

56. Bartchy, "Power, Submission, and Sexual Identity," p. 71.

57. Webb, "Where Is the Command to Silence" (part two), *Christian Standard* (May 28, 1989), 124:7.

58. Webb, "Women as Christian Leaders, 1 – Searching for the Meaning of I Timothy 2," *The Open Letter on Christian Communication* (Vol. 4, undated), p. 3.

59. G.W.H. Lampe, ed., *A Patristic Greek Lexicon* (New York: Oxford University Press, 1961), p. 262.

60. George W. Knight III, *"Authenteo* in Reference to Women in I Timothy 2:12," *New Testament Studies* (1984), 30:150-152.

61. Leland Edward Wilshire, "The TLG Computer and Further Reference to *Authenteo* in I Timothy 2:12," *New Testament Studies* (1988), 34:120-134.

62. W. Ward Gasque, "Response to 'Galatians 3:28: Conundrum or Solution,'" in *Women, Authority and the Bible*, p. 189.

63. Williams, *The Apostle Paul*, p. 79.

64. In this chapter I have focused only on what I consider to be the five central pillars of Biblical feminism's case for egalitarianism. I do not pretend to have covered all the relevant Biblical data and all the feminists' Biblical arguments for their view. Such a comprehensive evaluation does not lie within the purpose of this book.

CONCLUSION

One of the main goals of this book has been to inform interested inquirers of the nature of modern feminism, especially as it relates to the Bible. The four major types of feminism have been concisely explained: secular, Goddess, liberal Christian, and Biblical. How each interprets the Bible and compares with Biblical teaching has also been discussed.

Another goal has been briefly to evaluate these forms of feminism. Since we are working from within the framework of orthodox, conservative Christian faith, we have found the first three forms to be unacceptable because they build upon the authority of experience rather than the authority of the Word of God. But we have also found it necessary to reject the fourth form, Biblical feminism, because it does not have what we perceive to be a correct understanding of the teaching of the Bible on this subject.

In other words we find it necessary to reject the feminist ideal of egalitarianism in all of its forms, and vigorously to promote hierarchicalism as the Biblically-revealed will of God.[1]

For any Bible-believer, though, Biblical feminism is certainly more acceptable than the other three forms, simply because it acknowledges the full and final authority of the Bible and thus works within the total context of the supernatural creation, providence, and redemption of the God of the Bible. Except possibly for its most extreme forms, Biblical feminism can remain solidly within this framework; and it does not in itself nullify the Gospel of Jesus Christ. Non-feminists need to keep this in mind, especially in the heat of controversy. Differing beliefs on this subject do not divide the body of Christ; they do not separate brethren from one another.

This does not mean that the issue is not a serious one, however; nor does it mean that controversy over it will or should end. Because the subject is a serious one, the position one takes on it will affect at the very least his or her own state of mind, and more significantly the character of one's marriage, and most significantly the way the work of the church of Jesus Christ is conducted in this world. Those who believe the Bible teaches egalitarianism will build marriages and churches one way; those who believe the Bible teaches hierarchicalism will build them another way. In each case the failure of the church as a whole to conform to one's own belief will be a cause of great personal distress, since it will be interpreted as a failure to conform to God's will for His church. The church as the bride of Christ will be viewed as flawed and in need of further purifying, for its own sake as well as for the sake of the glory of its Bridegroom, Jesus.

Thus we should not be surprised at the zeal and passion with which partisans of both egalitarianism and hierarchicalism plunge headlong into this controversy, for the will of God and the glory of Christ are at stake. To defend the integrity of both is a noble motive. Perhaps for some, other motives are involved as well; but it does not behoove either side to suggest that the only thing some have in mind is the "lust for power" or the "desire to defend patriarchalism at all costs." In the final analysis none of us is engaged in this debate for our own sakes, but for the sake of our Creator and Redeemer. We want to order our lives, our homes, our churches, and our society according to His will as we understand it, simply because He wants it that way. This alone must be our motivation, as well as the source of our passion for this or any other issue.

Endnotes

1. It has not fallen within the scope of this book to pursue the practical implications of hierarchicalism for home, church, and society. For material of this nature I recommend John Piper and Wayne Grudem, eds., *Recovering Biblical Manhood and Womanhood: A Response to Evangelical Feminism* (Wheaton: Crossway Books, 1991).

BIBLIOGRAPHY

SECULAR FEMINISM (Chapters 1 & 2)

Brine, Ruth. "Women's Lib: Beyond Sexual Politics," *Time* (July 26, 1971). Pp. 36-37.

Brown, Scott, et al. "Onward, Women!", *Time* (December 4, 1989). Pp. 80-89.

Chesler, Phyllis. *Women and Madness.* Garden City, NY: Doubleday, 1972.

Cohen, Marcia. *The Sisterhood: The True Story of the Women Who Changed the World.* New York: Simon and Schuster, 1988.

D'Souza, Dinesh. "The New Feminist Revolt: This Time It's Against Feminism," *Policy Review* (Winter 1986). Pp. 46-52.

de Beauvoir, Simone. *The Second Sex,* tr. H. M. Parshley. New York: Alfred A. Knopf, 1953.

Decter, Midge. *The New Chastity and Other Arguments Against Women's Liberation.* New York: Coward, McCann & Geoghegan, 1972.

"Do These Women Speak for You?" (pamphlet), Concerned Women for America; 370 L'Enfant Promenade, Suite 800; Washington, D.C. 20024.

Evans, Richard J. *The Feminists: Women's Emancipation Movements in Europe, America and Australasia 1840-1920,* revised ed. New York: Barnes and Noble, 1979.

Foote, Timothy. "Lib and Let Lib," *Time* (March 20, 1972). Pp. 99-100.

Fordham, Jim and Andrea. *The Assault on the Sexes.* New Rochelle, NY: Arlington House, 1977.

Friedan, Betty. *The Feminine Mystique.* New York: Norton, 1963.

Friedan, Betty. *The Second Stage.* New York: Summit, 1981.

Garlock, Ruthanne. "Feminist Power: The Battle of Houston," *Christianity Today* (December 30, 1977). 21:38-40.

Gaylor, Annie Laurie. "Feminist 'Salvation,'" *The Humanist* (July/August 1988), 48:33-34.

Gilder, George F. *Men and Marriage.* Gretna, LA: Pelican Publishing Company, 1986.

Gilder, George F. *Sexual Suicide.* New York: Quadrangle Books, 1973.

Greer, Germaine. *The Female Eunuch.* New York: McGraw-Hill, 1971.

Henry, Josephine K. Untitled appendix, *The Woman's Bible,* Part II.

New York: European Publishing Company, 1898. Pp. 203-208.

Hochschild, Arlie. *The Second Shift*. New York: Viking, 1989.

Hole, Judith, and Ellen Levine. *Rebirth of Feminism*. New York: Quadrangle Books, 1971.

Hymer, Esther W. "Woman Suffrage," *The Encyclopedia Americana*, International Edition. Danbury, CT: Grolier, 1983. 29:102-107.

"International Woman's Year, Houston: Behind the Scenes," *Cincinnati Right to Life Bulletin* (December 1977). Pp. 2-3.

Lear, Martha Weinman. "The Second Feminist Wave," *New York Times Magazine* (March 10, 1968).

Levin, Michael. *Feminism and Freedom*. New Brunswick, NJ: Transaction Books, 1987.

Maddocks, Melvin. "Unraised Consciousness," *Time* (October 16, 1972). P. 88.

Millett, Kate. *Sexual Politics*. Garden City, NY: Doubleday, 1970.

"The Myth of Male Housework," *Time* (August 7, 1989). P. 62.

"National Organization for Women (NOW) Bill of Rights," in Judith Hole and Ellen Levine, *Rebirth of Feminism*. New York: Quadrangle Books, 1971. Pp. 441-442.

"The New Feminists: Revolt Against 'Sexism,'" *Time* (November 21, 1969). Pp. 53-56.

Seneca Falls Declaration, in Judith Hole and Ellen Levine, *Rebirth of Feminism*. New York: Quadrangle Books, 1971. Pp. 431-435.

Sommers, Christina Hoff. "Feminism and the College Curriculum," *Imprimis* (June 1990), 19:1-4.

Stanton, Elizabeth Cady. *The Original Feminist Attack on the Bible (The Woman's Bible)*, reprint ed., 2 vols. in 1. New York: Arno Press, 1974.

Stanton, Elizabeth Cady, et. al. *The Woman's Bible*, Parts I and II. New York: European Publishing Company, 1895, 1898.

"Stanton, Elizabeth," *Encyclopaedia Britannica*, 15th ed., 1975. Micropaedia IX:525.

"Stanton, Elizabeth Cady," *The Encyclopedia Americana*, International Edition. Danbury, CT: Grolier, 1983. 25:592.

"We've Changed So Much," *Ms.* (June 1984). Pp. 86-87.

Welter, Barbara. "Something Remains To Dare: Introduction to *The Woman's Bible*," in the reprint of *The Woman's Bible* entitled *The Original Feminist Attack on the Bible*, 2 vols. in 1. New York: Arno Press, 1974. Pp. v-xlii.

"Where She Is and Where She's Going," *Time* (March 20, 1972). Pp. 26-28.

"Women's Liberation Revisited," *Time* (March 20, 1972). Pp. 29-31.

"Women's Lib: A Second Look," *Time* (December 14, 1970). P. 50.

GODDESS FEMINISM (Chapters 3 & 4)

Adler, Margot. *Drawing Down the Moon: Witches, Druids, God-dess-Worshippers, and Other Pagans in America Today*, revised ed. Boston: Beacon Press, 1986.

Budapest, Zsuzsanna E. *The Holy Book of Women's Mysteries*. Berkeley, CA: Wingbow Press, 1989.

Christ, Carol. *Laughter of Aphrodite: Reflections on a Journey to the Goddess*. San Francisco: Harper & Row, 1987.

Daly, Mary. *Beyond God the Father: Toward a Philosophy of Women's Liberation*, new paperback ed. Boston: Beacon Press, 1985.

Daly, Mary. *The Church and the Second Sex*, Colophon edition, "With a New Feminist Postchristian Introduction by the Author." New York: Harper, 1975.

Daly, Mary. *Gyn/Ecology: The Metaethics of Radical Feminism*. Boston: Beacon Press, 1978.

Eisler, Riane. *The Chalice and the Blade: Our History, Our Future*. San Francisco: Harper & Row, 1987.

Gearhart, Sally, and Susan Rennie. *A Feminist Tarot*, rev. ed. Boston: Alyson Publications, 1986.

"Goddess Spirituality Catalogue," 1990 ed. Iris Sacred Circle, P.O. Box 68, Burlington, VT 05402.

Goldenberg, Naomi R. *Changing of the Gods: Feminism and the End of Traditional Religions*. Boston: Beacon Press, 1979.

Inglehart, Hallie. *Womanspirit: A Guide to Women's Wisdom*. San Francisco: Harper & Row, 1983.

Jones, E. Michael. "What Lesbian Nuns Can Teach Us About Vatican II," *Fidelity* (December 1985). 5:16-26.

Jones, E. Michael. "Witchcraft at Indiana University," *Fidelity* (May 1987). 6:20-28.

"Kwan Yin Book of Changes," *Llewellyn New Times* (November/December 1985). Pp. 10-11.

Lentini, Alison. "Circle of Sisters: A Journey Through Elemental Feminism," *SCP Newsletter* (Fall 1985). Pp. 12-17.

Nicholson, Shirley, ed. *The Goddess Re-Awakening: The Feminine Principle Today*. Wheaton, IL: Theosophical Publishing House, 1989.

Rominsky, Fran. "goddess with a small g," *WomanSpirit*, I (Autumn Equinox, 1974).

Sjöö, Monica, and Barbara Mor. *The Great Cosmic Mother: Redis-*

covering the Religion of the Earth. San Francisco: Harper &
Row, 1987.
Spretnak, Charlene. "Gaia, Green Politics, and the Great Trans-
formation," *The Womanspirit Sourcebook*, ed. Patrice Wynne.
San Francisco: Harper & Row, 1988. Pp. 88-90.
Starhawk [Miriam Simos]. *Dreaming the Dark: Magic, Sex and
Politics*, new ed. Boston: Beacon Press, 1988.
Starhawk [Miriam Simos]. *The Spiral Dance: A Rebirth of the
Ancient Religion of the Great Goddess*. San Francisco: Harper
& Row, 1979.
Steichen, Donna. "From Convent to Coven: Catholic Neo-Pagans
at the Witches' Sabbath," *Fidelity* (December 1985). 5:27-37.
Steichen, Donna. "The Goddess Goes to Washington," *Fidelity*
(December 1986). 6:34-44.
Stein, Diane. *The Kwan Yin Book of Changes*. St. Paul: Llewellyn
Publications, 1985.
Stone, Merlin. "Introduction," *The Goddess Re-Awakening: The
Feminine Principle Today*, ed. Shirley Nicholson. Wheaton, IL:
Theosophical Publishing House, 1989. Pp. 1-23.
Stone, Merlin. *When God Was a Woman*. New York: Dial Press,
1976.
Thorsten, Geraldine. *The Goddess in Your Stars: The Original
Feminine Meaning of the Sun Signs*. S & S, 1989.
"To Manipulate a Woman" (pamphlet), Concerned Women for
America; 370 L'Enfant Promenade, Suite 800; Washington,
D.C. 20024.
Walker, Barbara G. *The I Ching of the Goddess*. San Francisco:
Harper & Row, 1986.
Wynne, Patrice, ed. *The Womanspirit Sourcebook*. San Francisco:
Harper & Row, 1988.

LIBERAL CHRISTIAN FEMINISM (Chapters 5 & 6)

Anderson, Gerald H., and Thomas F. Stransky, eds. *Mission
Trends No. 4: Liberation Theologies in North America and
Europe*. Grand Rapids: Eerdmans, 1979.
Bruce, F. F. "Interpretation of the Bible," *Evangelical Dictionary
of Theology*, ed. Walter A. Elwell. Grand Rapids: Baker Book
House, 1984. Pp. 565-568.
Collins, Raymond F. "Structuralism," *The Westminster Dictionary
of Christian Theology*, ed. Alan Richardson and John Bowden.
Philadelphia: Westminster Press, 1983. Pp. 551-552.
Cross, Nancy M. "What's Christian About Christian Feminism?",
Fidelity (December 1985). 5:9-11.

Emswiler, Sharon Neufer, and Thomas Neufer Emswiler. *Women and Worship: A Guide to Non-Sexist Hymns, Prayers, and Liturgies.* San Francisco: Harper & Row, 1974.

Farley, Margaret A. "Feminist Consciousness and the Interpretation of Scripture," *Feminist Interpretation of the Bible,* ed. Letty M. Russell. Philadelphia: Westminster Press, 1985. Pp. 41-51.

Fiorenza, Elisabeth Schüssler. *Bread Not Stone: The Challenge of Feminist Biblical Interpretation.* Boston: Beacon Press, 1984.

Fiorenza, Elisabeth Schüssler. *In Memory of Her: A Feminist Theological Reconstruction of Christian Origins.* New York: Crossroad, 1987.

Fiorenza, Elisabeth Schüssler. "Toward A Feminist Biblical Hermeneutics: Biblical Interpretation and Liberation Theology," *The Challenge of Liberation Theology: A First World Response,* ed. Brian Mahan and L. Dale Richesin. Maryknoll, NY: Orbis Books, 1981. Pp. 91-112.

Fiorenza, Elisabeth Schüssler. "The Will To Choose or To Reject: Continuing Our Critical Work," *Feminist Interpretation of the Bible,* ed. Letty M. Russell. Philadelphia: Westminster Press, 1985. Pp. 125-136.

González, Justo L., and Catherine Gunsalus González. *Liberation Preaching: The Pulpit and the Oppressed.* Nashville: Abingdon Press, 1980.

Mudge, Lewis S. "Hermeneutics," *The Westminster Dictionary of Christian Theology,* ed. Alan Richardson and John Bowden. Philadelphia: Westminster Press, 1983. Pp. 250-253.

Rini, Suzanne M. "Dancing Around the Abyss: The Bishops Prepare a Pastoral on Women," *Fidelity* (September 1987). 6:34-44.

Ruether, Rosemary Radford. "Feminist Interpretation: A Method of Correlation," *Feminist Interpretation of the Bible,* ed. Letty M. Russell. Philadelphia: Westminster Press, 1985. Pp. 111-124.

Ruether, Rosemary Radford. "Feminist Theology and Spirituality," *Christian Feminism: Visions of a New Humanity,* ed. Judith L. Weidman. San Francisco: Harper & Row, 1984. Pp. 9-32.

Ruether, Rosemary Radford. *Sexism and God-Talk: Toward a Feminist Theology.* Boston: Beacon Press, 1983.

Ruether, Rosemary Radford. *Womanguides: Readings Toward a Feminist Theology.* Boston: Beacon Press, 1985.

Ruether, Rosemary Radford. *Women-Church: Theology and Practice of Feminist Liturgical Communities.* San Francisco: Harper & Row, 1986.

Russell, Letty M. "Authority and the Challenge of Feminist Interpretation," *Feminist Interpretation of the Bible*, ed. Letty M. Russell. Philadelphia: Westminster Press, 1985. Pp. 137-146.

Russell, Letty M. "Feminist Critique: Opportunity for Cooperation," *Journal for the Study of the Old Testament* (February 1982). 22:67-71.

Russell, Letty M. *Household of Freedom: Authority in Feminist Theology*. Philadelphia: Westminster Press, 1987.

Russell, Letty M. *Human Liberation in a Feminist Perspective – A Theology*. Philadelphia: Westminster Press, 1974.

Russell, Letty M. "Introduction: Liberating the Word," *Feminist Interpretation of the Bible*, ed. Letty M. Russell. Philadelphia: Westminster Press, 1985. Pp. 11-18.

Russell, Letty M. "Women and Ministry: Problem or Possibility?", *Christian Feminism: Visions of a New Humanity*, ed. Judith L. Weidman. San Francisco: Harper & Row, 1984. Pp. 75-92.

Russell, Letty M., ed. *Feminist Interpretation of the Bible*. Philadelphia: Westminster Press, 1985.

Sakenfeld, Katharine Doob. "Feminist Uses of Biblical Materials," *Feminist Interpretation of the Bible*, ed. Letty M. Russell. Philadelphia: Westminster Press, 1985. Pp. 55-64.

Stendahl, Krister. *The Bible and the Role of Women: A Case Study in Hermeneutics*, tr. Emilie T. Sander. Philadelphia: Fortress Press, 1966.

Trible, Phyllis. "Postscript: Jottings on the Journey," *Feminist Interpretation of the Bible*, ed. Letty M. Russell. Philadelphia: Westminster Press, 1985. Pp. 147-149.

Wahlberg, Rachel Conrad. *Jesus According to a Woman*. New York: Paulist Press, 1975.

Weidman, Judith L., ed. *Christian Feminism: Visions of a New Humanity*. San Francisco: Harper & Row, 1984.

Zikmund, Barbara Brown. "Feminist Consciousness in Historical Perspective," *Feminist Interpretation of the Bible*, ed. Letty M. Russell. Philadelphia: Westminster Press, 1985. Pp. 21-29.

BIBLICAL FEMINISM (Chapters 7 & 8)

Aaseng, Rolf E., "Male and Female Created He Them," *Christianity Today* (November 20, 1970). 15:5-6.

Allen, Ronald and Beverly. *Liberated Traditionalism: Men and Women in Balance*. Portland, OR: Multnomah Press, 1985.

Alsdurf, Phyllis E. "Evangelical Feminists: Ministry Is the Issue," *Christianity Today* (July 21, 1978). 22:46-47.

Atkins, Anne. *Split Image: Male and Female After God's*

Likeness. Grand Rapids: Eerdmans, 1987.

Bacchiocchi, Samuele. *Women in the Church: A Biblical Study on the Role of Women in the Church.* Berrien Springs, MI: Biblical Perspectives, 1987.

Balswick, Jack and Judith. "Adam and Eve in America," *Christianity Today* (July 16, 1990). 34:15-18.

Bartchy, S. Scott. "Human Sexuality and Our Identity," *Mission Journal* (November 1983). 17:10-14.

Bartchy, S. Scott. "Issues of Power and a Theology of the Family" (3 parts), *Mission Journal* (July-August/September/October 1987). 21:3-15; 21:3-11; 21:8-11.

Bartchy, S. Scott. "Jesus, Power, and Gender Roles," *TSF Bulletin* (January-February 1984). 7:2-4.

Bartchy, S. Scott. "Power, Submission, and Sexual Identity Among the Early Christians," *Essays On New Testament Christianity*, ed. C. Robert Wetzel. Cincinnati: Standard Publishing, 1978. Pp. 50-80.

Beck, James R. "Is There a Head of the House in the Home? Reflections on Ephesians 5," *Priscilla Papers* (Fall 1988). 2:1-4.

Bilezikian, Gilbert. *Beyond Sex Roles: What the Bible Says About a Woman's Place in Church and Family,* 2 ed. Grand Rapids: Baker, 1990.

Bilezikian, Gilbert. "Case Study of an Eisegetical Fabrication: Wayne Grudem's Treatment of *Kephale* in Ancient Texts," an address at the 1986 Evangelical Theological Society Meeting in Atlanta, GA.

Bilezikian, Gilbert. "Hierarchist and Egalitarian Inculturations," *Journal of the Evangelical Theological Society* (December 1987). 30:421-426.

Bloesch, Donald. *The Battle for the Trinity.* Ann Arbor: Servant Books, 1985.

Bloesch, Donald. *Is The Bible Sexist?* Westchester, IL: Crossway, 1982.

Blomberg, Craig L. "Not Beyond What Is Written," *Criswell Theological Review* (1988). 2:403-421.

Boldrey, Richard and Joyce. *Chauvinist or Feminist? Paul's View of Women.* Grand Rapids: Baker, 1976. (Reprint of next title.)

Boldrey, Richard and Joyce. "Women in Paul's Life," *Trinity Studies* (1972). 22:1-36.

Braun, Herbert. "*plasso* [etc.]," *Theological Dictionary of the New Testament*, ed. Gerhard Friedrich, tr. Geoffrey W. Bromiley. Grand Rapids: Eerdmans, 1968. 6:254-262.

Cervin, Richard S. "Does *Kephale* Mean 'Source' or 'Authority Over' in Greek Literature? A Rebuttal," *Trinity Journal*, n.s. (Spring 1989). 10:85-112.

"Christians for Biblical Equality To Offer Priscilla and Aquila Award," *Priscilla Papers* (Winter 1989). 3:16.

Clark, Stephen B. *Man and Woman in Christ: An Examination of the Roles of Men and Women in Light of Scripture and the Social Sciences.* Ann Arbor: Servant Books, 1980.

Clouse, Bonnidell and Robert G., eds. *Women in Ministry: Four Views.* Downers Grove: InterVarsity Press, 1989.

Culver, Robert D. "Does Recent Scientific Research Overturn the Claims of Radical Feminism and Support the Biblical Norms of Human Sexuality?", *Journal of the Evangelical Theological Society* (March 1987). 30:39-47.

Culver, Robert D. "A Traditional View: Let Your Women Keep Silence," *Women in Ministry: Four Views,* ed. Bonnidell and Robert G. Clouse. Downers Grove: InterVarsity Press, 1989. Pp. 25-52.

Dayton, Donald W., and Lucille Sider Dayton. "Women as Preachers: Evangelical Precedents," *Christianity Today* (May 23, 1975). 19:4-7.

DeJong, Peter, and Donald R. Wilson. *Husband and Wife: The Sexes in Scripture and Society.* Grand Rapids: Zondervan, 1979.

Delling, Gerhard. "*tasso* [etc.]," *Theological Dictionary of the New Testament,* ed. Gerhard Friedrich, tr. Geoffrey W. Bromiley. Grand Rapids: Eerdmans, 1972. 8:27-48.

Diehl, David W. "Theology and Feminism," *Gender Matters: Women's Studies for the Christian Community,* ed. June Steffensen Hagen. Grand Rapids: Zondervan, 1990. Pp. 25-50.

Duin, Julia. "Evangelical Women Criticize the Church's 'Medieval Theology,'" *Christianity Today* (September 3, 1982). 26:72, 75.

Eggebroten, Anne. "Handling Power: Unchristian, Unfeminine, Unkind?", *The Other Side* (December 1986). Pp. 20-25.

Elliot, Elisabeth. *Let Me Be a Woman.* Wheaton: Tyndale House, 1976.

Elliot, Elisabeth. Letter to the Editor, *Christianity Today* (February 13, 1976). 20:28.

Elliot, Elisabeth. "Why I Oppose the Ordination of Women," *Christianity Today* (June 6, 1975). 19:12-16.

Evans, Mary J. *Woman in the Bible: An Overview of All the Crucial Passages on Women's Roles.* Downers Grove: InterVarsity Press, 1983.

Fee, Gordon D., and Douglas Stuart. *How To Read the Bible for All Its Worth: A Guide to Understanding the Bible.* Grand Rapids: Zondervan, 1982.

Fell, Margaret. *Womens Speaking Justified, Proved and Allowed of by the Scriptures.* London: 1666; reprint, Amherst, MA:

Mosher Book and Tract Committee, 1980.

Finger, Reta Halteman. "The Bible and Christian Feminism," *Daughters of Sarah* (May/June 1987). 13:5-12.

Finger, Reta Halteman. "The Bible or Women's Experience — Which Is Authoritative?", *Daughters of Sarah* (May/June 1987). 13:6-7.

Foh, Susan T. "A Male Leadership View: The Head of the Woman Is the Man," *Women in Ministry: Four Views*, ed. Bonnidell and Robert G. Clouse. Downers Grove: InterVarsity Press, 1989. Pp. 69-105.

Foh, Susan T. *Women and the Word of God: A Response to Biblical Feminism*. Phillipsburg, NJ: Presbyterian and Reformed, 1979.

Forbes, Cheryl. "Books in Review: God and Women," *Christianity Today* (December 6, 1974). 19:36-38.

Fowler, Richard A., and H. Wayne House. *The Christian Confronts His Culture*. Chicago: Moody Press, 1983.

Gasque, W. Ward. "Response to 'Galatians 3:28: Conundrum or Solution?'," *Women, Authority and the Bible*, ed. Alvera Mickelsen. Downers Grove: InterVarsity Press, 188-192.

Grudem, Wayne. "Does *kephale* ('head') Mean 'Source' or 'Authority Over' in Greek Literature? A Survey of 2,336 Examples," Appendix 1 in George W. Knight III, *The Role Relationship of Men and Women: New Testament Teaching*. Chicago; Moody Press, 1985. Pp. 49-80.

Grudem, Wayne. *The Gift of Prophecy in 1 Corinthians*. Lanham, MD: University Press of America, 1982.

Grudem, Wayne. "The Meaning of *Kephale* ("Head"): A Response to Recent Studies," *Recovering Biblical Manhood and Womanhood: A Response to Evangelical Feminism*, ed. John Piper and Wayne Grudem. Wheaton, IL: Crossway Books, 1991. Pp. 425-468.

Grudem, Wayne. "Prophecy — Yes, But Teaching — No: Paul's Consistent Advocacy of Women's Participation Without Governing Authority," *Journal of the Evangelical Theological Society* (March 1987). 30:11-23.

Gundry, Patricia. *The Complete Woman*. Garden City, NY: Doubleday, 1981.

Gundry, Patricia. *Heirs Together: Mutual Submission in Marriage*. Grand Rapids: Zondervan, 1980.

Gundry, Patricia. *Neither Slave nor Free: Helping Women Answer the Call to Church Leadership*. San Francisco: Harper and Row, 1987.

Gundry, Patricia. *Woman Be Free! The Clear Message of Scripture*. Grand Rapids: Zondervan, 1977.

Hagen, June Steffensen, ed. *Gender Matters: Women's Studies for the Christian Community*. Grand Rapids: Zondervan, 1990.

"Happy Birthday: Now We Are Four! A Brief History of Christians for Biblical Equality," *Priscilla Papers* (Summer 1991). 5:14-15.

Hardesty, Nancy. *Great Women of the Christian Faith*. Grand Rapids: Baker, 1980.

Hardesty, Nancy A. *Women Called To Witness: Evangelical Feminism in the 19th Century*. Nashville: Abingdon, 1984.

Hauke, Manfred. *Women in the Priesthood? A Systematic Analysis in the Light of the Order of Creation and Redemption*, tr. David Kipp. San Francisco: Ignatius Press, 1988.

Hayter, Mary. *The New Eve in Christ: The Use and Abuse of the Bible in the Debate About Women in the Church*. Grand Rapids: Eerdmans, 1987.

Hestenes, Roberta. *The Ministry of Women*. Waco: Word Books, 1989.

Hestenes, Roberta. "Women in Leadership: Finding Ways To Serve the Church," *Christianity Today* (October 3, 1986). 30:4-10, CTI supplement.

Hestenes, Roberta, ed. *Women and Men in Ministry: Collected Readings*. Philadelphia: Westminster Press, 1984.

Hestenes, Roberta, and Lois Curley, eds. *Women and the Ministries of Christ*. Pasadena: Fuller Theological Seminary, 1979.

Hicks, John Mark, and Bruce L. Morton. *Woman's Role in the Church*. Shreveport, LA: Lambert Book House, 1978.

House, H. Wayne. *The Role of Women in Ministry Today*. Nashville: Thomas Nelson, 1990.

Howe, E. Margaret. "The Positive Case for the Ordination of Women," *Perspectives on Evangelical Theology: Papers from the Thirtieth Annual Meeting of the Evangelical Theological Society*, ed. Kenneth Kantzer and Stanley Gundry. Grand Rapids: Baker, 1979.

Howe, E. Margaret. *Women and Church Leadership*. Grand Rapids: Zondervan, 1982.

Hull, Gretchen Gaebelein. *Equal To Serve: Women and Men in the Church and Home*. Old Tappan, NJ: Revell, 1987.

Hull, Gretchen Gaebelein, ed. *Serving Together: A Biblical Study of Human Relationships*. New York: Macmillan, 1987.

Hurley, James B. *Man and Woman in Biblical Perspective*. Grand Rapids: Zondervan, 1981.

Jewett, Paul K. *Man as Male and Female: A Study in Sexual Relationships from a Theological Point of View*. Grand Rapids: Eerdmans, 1975.

Jewett, Paul K. *The Ordination of Women: New Testament Per-

spectives. Grand Rapids: Eerdmans, 1980.

Johnston, Robert K. "Biblical Authority and Interpretation: The Test Case of Women's Role in the Church and Home Updated," *Women, Authority and the Bible,* ed. Alvera Mickelsen. Downers Grove: InterVarsity Press, 1986. Pp. 30-41.

Johnston, Robert K. *Evangelicals at an Impasse.* Atlanta: John Knox Press, 1979.

Kaiser, Walter. "Shared Leadership or Male Headship?", *Christianity Today* (October 3, 1986). 30:12, CTI supplement.

Kane, Suzy. "Feminists of a Feather Affirm Each Other," *Christianity Today* (August 8, 1980). 24:40-41.

Kassian, Mary A. *Women, Creation, and the Fall.* Westchester, IL: Crossway Books, 1990.

Keister, Dorothy. "Women as Leaders in the New Testament," unpublished manuscript of an address at the 1986 North American Christian Convention in Indianapolis, IN.

Knight, George W. III. "*Authento* in Reference to Women in 1 Timothy 2:12," *New Testament Studies* (1984). 30:143-157.

Knight, George W. III. "Male and Female Related He Them," *Christianity Today* (April 9, 1976). 20:13-17.

Knight, George W. III. *The New Testament Teaching on the Role Relationship of Men and Women.* Grand Rapids: Baker, 1977. (Reprinted as *The Role Relationship,* below.)

Knight, George W. III. "The Ordination of Women: No," *Christianity Today* (February 20, 1981). 25:16-19.

Knight, George W. III. *The Role Relationship of Men and Women: New Testament Teaching.* Chicago: Moody Press, 1985.

Kroeger, Catherine Clark. "Ancient Heresies and a Strange Greek Verb," *The Reformed Journal* (March 1979). 29:12-15.

Kroeger, Catherine Clark. "The Apostle Paul and the Greco-Roman Cults of Women," *Journal of the Evangelical Theological Society* (March 1987), 30:25-38.

Kroeger, Catherine Clark. "The Classical Concept of *Head* as 'Source,'" Appendix III in Gretchen Gaebelein Hull, *Equal To Serve: Women and Men in the Church and Home.* Old Tappan, NJ: Revell, 1987. Pp. 267-283.

Kroeger, Catherine Clark. "1 Timothy 2:12 – A Classicist's View," *Women, Authority and the Bible,* ed. Alvera Mickelsen. Downers Grove: InterVarsity Press, 1986. Pp. 225-244.

Kroeger, Richard, and Catherine Clark Kroeger. *I Suffer Not a Woman: Rethinking 1 Timothy 2:11-15 in Light of Ancient Evidence.* Grand Rapids: Baker, 1991.

Kroeger, Richard, and Catherine Clark Kroeger. "May Women Teach? Heresy in the Pastoral Epistles," *The Reformed Journal* (October 1980). 30:14-18.

Kroeger, Richard, and Catherine Clark Kroeger. "Pandemonium and Silence at Corinth," *The Reformed Journal* (June 1978). 28:6-11.

Kroeger, Richard, and Catherine Clark Kroeger. "Sexual Identity at Corinth: Paul Faces a Crisis," *The Reformed Journal* (December 1978). 28:11-15.

Lampe, G. W. H., ed. *A Patristic Greek Lexicon.* New York: Oxford University Press, 1961.

Liefeld, Walter. "A Plural Ministry View: Your Sons and Your Daughters Shall Prophesy," *Women in Ministry: Four Views,* ed. Bonnidell and Robert G. Clouse. Downers Grove: InterVarsity Press, 1989. Pp. 127-153.

Liefeld, Walter. "Response to '1 Timothy 2:12 – A Classicist's View,'" *Women, Authority and the Bible,* ed. Alvera Mickelsen. Downers Grove: InterVarsity Press, 1986. Pp. 244-248.

Liefeld, Walter. "Women and the Nature of Ministry," *Journal of the Evangelical Theological Society* (March 1987). 30:49-61.

Liefeld, Walter. "Women, Submission and Ministry in 1 Corinthians," *Women, Authority and the Bible,* ed. Alvera Mickelsen. Downers Grove: InterVarsity Press, 1986. Pp. 134-154.

Lindsell, Harold. "Egalitarianism and Scriptural Infallibility," *Christianity Today* (March 26, 1976). 20:45-46.

Longenecker, Richard N. "Authority, Hierarchy and Leadership Patterns in the Bible," *Women, Authority and the Bible,* ed. Alvera Mickelsen. Downers Grove: InterVarsity Press, 1986. Pp. 66-85.

Longenecker, Richard N. *New Testament Social Ethics for Today.* Grand Rapids: Eerdmans, 1984.

Lown, W. F. "Women in the Roles of Leadership" (2 parts), *The Lookout* (September 7/14, 1980). 92:2, 4; 92:5-6, 14.

Maddox, Randy. "The Necessity of Recognizing Distinctions: Lessons from Evangelical Critiques of Christian Feminist Theology," *Christian Scholar's Review* (1988). 17:307-323.

Malcolm, Kari Torjesen. *Women at the Crossroads: A Path Beyond Feminism and Traditionalism.* Downers Grove: Inter-Varsity Press, 1982.

Martin, Faith McBurney. *Call Me Blessed: The Emerging Christian Woman.* Grand Rapids: Eerdmans, 1987.

McClelland, Scott E. "The New Reality in Christ: Perspectives from Biblical Studies," *Gender Matters: Women's Studies for the Christian Community,* ed. June Steffensen Hagen. Grand Rapids: Zondervan, 1990. Pp. 51-78.

McFadden, Carol Prester. "Christian Feminists: 'We're on Our Way, Lord,'" *Christianity Today* (December 19, 1975). 20:36-37.

Mickelsen, Alvera. "An Egalitarian View: There Is Neither Male Nor Female in Christ," *Women in Ministry: Four Views,* ed. Bonnidell and Robert G. Clouse. Downers Grove: InterVarsity Press, 1989. Pp. 173-206.

Mickelsen, Alvera, ed. *Women, Authority and the Bible.* Downers Grove: InterVarsity Press, 1986.

Mickelsen, Berkeley. "Who Are the Women in I Timothy 2:1-15?" (2 parts), *Priscilla Papers* (Winter/Spring 1988). 1:1-3; 2:4-6.

Mickelsen, Berkeley and Alvera. "Does Male Dominance Tarnish Our Translations?", *Christianity Today* (October 5, 1979). 23:23-29.

Mickelsen, Berkeley and Alvera. "The 'Head' of the Epistles," *Christianity Today* (February 20, 1981). 25:20-23.

Mickelsen, Berkeley and Alvera, "What Does *Kephale* Mean in the New Testament?", *Women, Authority and the Bible,* ed. Alvera Mickelsen. Downers Grove: InterVarsity Press, 1976.

Mollenkott, Virginia Ramey. "A Challenge to Male Interpretation: Women and the Bible," *Sojourners* (February 1976). 5:20-25.

Mollenkott, Virginia Ramey. "A Conversation with Virginia Mollenkott," *The Other Side* (May-June 1976). Pp. 21-30, 73-75.

Mollenkott, Virginia Ramey. *The Divine Feminine: The Biblical Imagery of God as Female.* New York: Crossroad, 1983.

Mollenkott, Virginia Ramey. *Godding: Human Responsibility and the Bible.* New York: Crossroad, 1987.

Mollenkott, Virginia Ramey. Letter to the Editor, *Christianity Today* (June 4, 1976). 20:24-25.

Mollenkott, Virginia Ramey. *Women, Men, and the Bible,* revised ed. New York: Crossroad, 1988.

Moo, Douglas J. "1 Timothy 2:11-15: Meaning and Significance," *Trinity Journal,* n.s. (Spring 1980). 1:62-83.

Moo, Douglas J. "The Interpretation of 1 Timothy 2:11-15: A Rejoinder," *Trinity Journal,* n.s. (Fall 1981). 2:198-222.

Muck, Terry C. "Can We Talk?", *Christianity Today* (July 16, 1990). 34:12.

Nash, Donald A. "Submission? Who?", *Christian Standard* (November 14, 1976). 111:15-16.

Neff, David. "Christian Feminists Regroup to Debate Future," *Christianity Today* (September 2, 1988). 32:43, 45.

Neff, David. "Women Explore Formation of Alternative Feminist Group," *Christianity Today* (April 17, 1987). 31:45-46.

O'Brien, William. "Handling Conflict: The Fallout from Fresno," *The Other Side* (December 1986). Pp. 25, 41.

Oepke, Albrecht. "*gune,*" *Theological Dictionary of the New Testament,* ed. Gerhard Kittel, tr. Geoffrey W. Bromiley. Grand

Rapids: Eerdmans, 1964. 1:776-789.

Osborne, Grant R. "Hermeneutics and Women in the Church," *Journal of the Evangelical Theological Society* (December 1977). 20:337-352.

Pape, Dorothy R. *In Search of God's Ideal Woman: A Personal Examination of the New Testament.* Downers Grove: InterVarsity Press, 1976.

Payne, Philip Barton. "Libertarian Women in Ephesus: A Response to Douglas J. Moo's Article," *Trinity Journal,* n.s. (Fall 1981). 2:169-197.

Payne, Philip Barton. "Response to 'What Does *Kephale* Mean in the New Testament?'," *Women, Authority and the Bible,* ed. Alvera Mickelsen. Downers Grove: InterVarsity Press, 1986. Pp. 118-132.

Pinnock, Clark H. "Biblical Authority and the Issues in Question," *Women, Authority and the Bible,* ed. Alvera Mickelsen. Downers Grove: InterVarsity Press, 1986. Pp. 51-58.

Piper, John, and Wayne Grudem, eds. *Recovering Biblical Manhood and Womanhood: A Response to Evangelical Feminism.* Wheaton, IL: Crossway Books, 1991.

Pride, Mary. *The Way Home.* Westchester, IL: Crossway Books, 1985.

"Priscilla and Aquila Award," *Priscilla Papers* (Fall 1989). 3:11.

Robbins, John W. *Scripture Twisting in the Seminaries, Part I: Feminism.* Jefferson, MD: The Trinity Foundation, 1985.

Roberts, Mark. "Woman Shall Be Saved: A Closer Look at 1 Timothy 2:15," *The Reformed Journal* (April 1983). 33:18-22.

Ryrie, Charles C. *The Role of Women in the Church.* Chicago: Moody, 1970. (Reprint of 1958 title, *The Place of Women in the Church.*)

Scanzoni, Letha. "The Feminists and the Bible," *Christianity Today* (February 2, 1973). 17:10-15.

Scanzoni, Letha, and Nancy Hardesty. *All We're Meant To Be: A Biblical Approach to Women's Liberation.* Waco: Word Books, 1974.

Scanzoni, Letha Dawson, and Nancy Hardesty. *All We're Meant To Be: Biblical Feminism for Today.* Nashville: Abingdon Press, 1986. (Revised edition of the previous title.)

Scanzoni, Letha, and Virginia Ramey Mollenkott. *Is the Homosexual My Neighbor?* San Francisco: Harper and Row, 1978.

Schlafly, Phyllis. "What Is Women's Liberation All About?", *The Lookout* (August 23, 1981). 93:2-4.

Schmidt, Ruth A. "Second-Class Citizenship in the Kingdom of God," *Christianity Today* (January 1, 1971). 15:13-14.

Scholer, David M. "Feminist Hermeneutics and Evangelical Biblical Interpretation," *Journal of the Evangelical Theological Society* (December 1987). 30:407-420.

Scholer, David M. "1 Timothy 2:9-15 and the Place of Women in the Church's Ministry," *Women, Authority and the Bible,* ed. Alvera Mickelsen. Downers Grove: InterVarsity Press, 1986. Pp. 193-224.

Scholer, David M. "Hermeneutical Gerrymandering: Hurley on Women and Authority," *TSF Bulletin* (May-June 1983). 6:11-13.

Smith, F. LaGard. *Men of Strength for Women of God.* Eugene, OR: Harvest House, 1989.

Snodgrass, Klyne R. "Galatians 3:28 – Conundrum or Solution?", *Women, Authority and the Bible,* ed. Alvera Mickelsen. Downers Grove: InterVarsity Press, 1986. Pp. 161-181.

Spencer, Aida Besançon. *Beyond the Curse: Women Called to Ministry.* Nashville: Thomas Nelson, 1985.

Spring, Beth. "Gay Rights Resolution Divides Membership of Evangelical Women's Caucus," *Christianity Today* (October 3, 1986). 30:40-43.

Stafford, Tim. "Roberta Hestenes: Taking Charge," *Christianity Today* (March 3, 1989). 33:17-22.

Storkey, Elaine. *What's Right with Feminism.* Grand Rapids: Eerdmans, 1986.

Stott, John. *Involvement, Volume II: Social and Sexual Relationships in the Modern World.* Old Tappan, NJ: Revell, 1984.

Stouffer, Austin H. "The Ordination of Women: Yes," *Christianity Today* (February 20, 1981). 25:12-15.

Swartley, Willard M. *Slavery, Sabbath, War, and Women: Case Issues in Biblical Interpretation.* Scottdale, PA: Herald Press, 1983.

Tucker, Ruth A., and Walter L. Liefeld. *Daughters of the Church: Women and Ministry from New Testament Times to the Present.* Grand Rapids: Zondervan, 1987.

Van Leeuwen, Mary Stewart. *Gender and Grace: Love, Work and Parenting in a Changing World.* Downers Grove: InterVarsity Press, 1990.

Van Leeuwen, Mary Stewart. "Life After Eden," *Christianity Today* (July 16, 1990). 34:19-21.

Van Leeuwen, Mary Stewart. "The Recertification of Women," *The Reformed Journal* (August 1986). 36:17-24.

Webb, Joseph M. "Where Is the Command to Silence?" (2 parts), *Christian Standard* (May 21/28, 1989). 124:4-6; 124:7-8.

Webb, Joseph M. "Women as Christian Leaders, 1 – Searching for the Meaning of I Timothy 2," *The Open Letter on Christian Communication* (vol. 4, undated).

Williams, Don. *The Apostle Paul and Women in the Church.* Ventura, CA: Regal Books, 1977.

Wilshire, Leland Edward. "The TLG Computer and Further Reference to *Authenteo* in 1 Timothy 2:12," *New Testament Studies* (1988). 34:120-134.